Australian & New Zealand Edition

Kids' Food Allergies

FOR

DUMMIES®

Australian & New Zealand Edition

Kids' Food Allergies

FOR

DUMMIES®

**by Assoc. Prof. Mimi Tang
and Assoc. Prof. Katie Allen**

WILEY

Wiley Publishing Australia Pty Ltd

Kids' Food Allergies For Dummies®, Australian & New Zealand Edition

Published by
Wiley Publishing Australia Pty Ltd
42 McDougall Street
Milton, Qld 4064
www.dummies.com

Copyright © 2012 Wiley Publishing Australia Pty Ltd

The moral rights of the authors have been asserted.

National Library of Australia
Cataloguing-in-Publication data:

Author:	Tang, Mimi
Title:	Kids' Food Allergies For Dummies / Mimi Tang and Katie Allen
Edition:	Australian and New Zealand ed
ISBN:	978 1 74246 844 0 (pbk.)
Notes:	Includes index
Subjects:	Food allergy in children
Other authors/ contributors:	Allen, Katie
Dewey Number:	618.92975

Cover image: © RedHelga/iStockphoto.com

Typeset by diacriTech, Chennai, India

Printed in China by
Printplus Limited

10 9 8 7 6 5 4 3 2 1

About the Authors

Associate Professor Mimi Tang is a paediatric immunologist allergist at the Royal Children's Hospital in Melbourne, Victoria. She is Director of the Department of Allergy and Immunology at the Royal Children's Hospital, which sees more than 2,000 children with allergic disease each year. Mimi is also Head of the Allergy and Autoimmunity Affinity Group, and Group Leader of Allergy and Immune Disorders Research at the Murdoch Children's Research Institute; she is also an Associate Professor in the Department of Paediatrics at the University of Melbourne, lecturing within the undergraduate science and biomedical science degrees.

Her research continues to focus on investigating immune mechanisms leading to allergic disease, and on evaluating probiotics and prebiotics as novel treatment or prevention strategies. She has published widely in the area of food allergy and anaphylaxis, and is committed to developing the next generation of clinicians and researchers in allergy and immunology through teaching and training.

Mimi is passionate about translating research into clinical practice and policy both nationally and internationally. As Chair of the Paediatric Committee of ASCIA, she led the development of national guidelines on 'Prevention of Allergic Disease' and 'Infant Feeding Advice' which are now widely adopted across Australia. She played a key role in developing the Anaphylaxis Guidelines and Policy for Schools and Children's Services in Victoria, and contributed to the development of ASCIA national guidelines for Prevention of Anaphylaxis in Schools.

Mimi sits on several expert committees including the World Allergy Organisation (WAO) Communications Council, the American Academy of Allergy Asthma and Immunology (AAAAI) Adverse Reactions to Foods Committee, and the Australasian Society of Clinical Immunology and Allergy (ASCIA) Anaphylaxis Committee and Paediatric Committee. Mimi leads a busy life outside of work, with three children aged between 11 and 17 years.

Associate Professor Katie Allen is a paediatric gastroenterologist and allergist practising in the field of food allergy at the Royal Children's Hospital, Melbourne. After completing her medical degree at Monash University and undertaking a research year at Cambridge University, UK, Katie spent two years as a Clinical Gastroenterology Fellow at the University of Chicago and then received a PhD from The University of Melbourne.

Katie is Director of the Environment, Genes and Health Research Theme at the Murdoch Childrens Research Institute and is group leader of the Gastro and Food Allergy research group. She is chief investigator on 6 NHMRC-funded cohort studies, which all seek to answer parts of the jigsaw with regards to population health and evolution of the new allergy epidemic. Katie has published extensively within the area of food allergy, has a prestigious Viertel Senior Medical Research Fellowship and was awarded the MCRI rising star award in 2008 for the most successful researcher within ten years of PhD completion at the MCRI.

Katie is the principal investigator of the HealthNuts study at the Murdoch Childrens Research Institute, which is the largest single-centre population-based study of food allergy in children ever mounted. She is a member of the Eosinophilic Gastrointestinal Disorders committee and Adverse Reaction committee for the American Academy of Allergy, Asthma and Immunology (AAAAI), and a member of both the Paediatric and Education committees for Australasian Society of Clinical Immunology and Allergy (ASCIA). She also teaches in the University of Melbourne Department of Paediatrics and currently supervises 6 PhD students. Despite this, she remains an active clinician in both the Department of Allergy and the Department of Gastroenterology at the Royal Children's Hospital, Melbourne, and has four children.

Authors' Acknowledgements

From Mimi: Firstly, I would like to thank all at John Wiley & Sons Australia who had a part to play in inviting me to author this *For Dummies* book. I appreciate this valuable opportunity and experience. I would especially like to thank Hannah Bennett and Rebecca Crisp for having faith in my ability to complete this task, despite having no prior experience in writing a book. Your guidance, helpful advice and encouragement throughout the project helped me to stay positive when the work seemed overwhelming, and I appreciated your support in negotiating the *For Dummies* writing format (as well as the occasional reminders to keep on going!). Your editorial input was most welcome, and I valued your counsel on how to develop the *For Dummies* style. Thank you also to Charlotte Duff for your expert editing that put the shine on our final finished product.

I would like to say a special thank you to Katie for agreeing to co-author this book with me. I thoroughly enjoyed working with Katie and can honestly say that it would not have been possible to finish this project without her help in sharing the workload. Katie — your focus and encouragement was always timed perfectly to help keep the work moving forwards. I think we pulled together an outstanding team effort.

I would like to say an enormous thank you to my family — to my wonderful, loving children, Callum, Elise and James, who remained interested and encouraged me to keep going when my work piled up, and to my ever-reliable, caring parents who were always ready to lend a helping hand. Your support and belief in me has been invaluable and made the difference between finishing the book and not getting there. Finally, thank you also to my patient and thoughtful friends who have put up with my prolonged absence for the months I was engrossed in writing.

Writing this book was certainly more fun than I expected but also a bigger commitment than I had imagined. I'm extremely proud of what Katie and I have achieved together and hope that our readers enjoy this book as well as finding it a useful resource to share with family and friends.

From Katie: I would like to thank all staff at John Wiley & Sons Australia involved in getting this book to print for making the process so enjoyable. They knew how to break down the tasks into achievable bite-sized chunks so that we could continue to make progress, despite both of us holding down busy clinical and research jobs and juggling housefuls of children. They had a sixth sense about when to 'go easy' but also when to crack the whip to help us reach those never-ending deadlines. And all the while they remained upbeat and positive. Those words of encouragement kept me going at the computer late at night when the rest of the family had gone to bed. Thank you specifically to Hannah Bennett and Rebecca Crisp for seeing the process through from start to finish and to Charlotte Duff for your magnificent editing of our sometimes sleep-deprived writing. I would also like to acknowledge Lindy Hayward for your words of wisdom in looking over early drafts of the book.

Importantly, I would like to thank Mimi for inviting me to co-author this book and trusting that we could get the job done. It has been an honour to work with Mimi and I think we really had a great team approach.

Finally, I would like to thank my family for their patience in getting this book written — to my constant husband, Malcolm, and my enthusiastic children, Monty, Jemima, Arabella and Archie. Thanks for being my guinea pigs for helping me simplify complex ideas — and thanks for believing in me.

Publisher's Acknowledgements

We're proud of this book; please send us your comments through our online registration form located at www.dummies.com/register.

Some of the people who helped bring this book to market include the following:

Acquisitions, Editorial and Media Development

Project Editor: Charlotte Duff

Acquisitions Editor: Rebecca Crisp

Editorial Manager: Hannah Bennett

Production

Graphics: diacriTech

Cartoons: Glenn Lumsden

Proofreader: Jenny Scepanovic

Indexer: Don Jordan, Antipodes Indexing

The authors and publisher would like to thank the following copyright holders, organisations and individuals for their permission to reproduce copyright material in this book.

- Page 106, Figure 6-1a: Reproduced with permission, *Australian Family Physician*, 2008.

- Page 142: Reproduced with permission of Australian Food and Grocery Council.

- Pages 210–213, 219, 221: This information has been reproduced with permission from the Australasian Society of Clinical Immunology and Allergy (ASCIA), from the ASCIA website www.allergy.org.au.

Every effort has been made to trace the ownership of copyright material. Information that enables the publisher to rectify any error or omission in subsequent editions is welcome. In such cases, please contact the Permissions Section of John Wiley & Sons Australia, Ltd.

Contents at a Glance

Table of Contents

Introduction

. . . .

When we first started thinking about this book, we wondered whether we had enough information and practical advice to fill an entire book. Well, it turns out we have a lot of information that we think you're likely to find both useful and interesting. So we hope that you enjoy reading *Kids' Food Allergies For Dummies*, Australian and New Zealand Edition, as much as we enjoyed writing it. Most importantly, we hope that the information we provide here helps keep your child healthy and happy and enables your child to safely engage in all aspects of childhood.

About This Book

A rapid change in many aspects of food allergy has occurred over the last few years. Not only has food allergy become much more common in Westernised countries such as Australia and New Zealand, but the way that we as medical practitioners diagnose and manage food allergy has also changed dramatically — even in the last three to four years. So a book that examines all the issues, including the management and treatment of food allergy, is timely.

Although quite a bit of research in food allergy is still in progress worldwide, a lot of new evidence is available now that has helped allergists better understand how to manage and treat this condition — and ideas about how best to prevent kids from developing food allergy are also emerging. It's a very exciting time to be involved in the field of food allergy research and enormously satisfying to be able to bring new evidence into practice in the discipline in which we work. More importantly, the studies being conducted now are already helping thousands of children around the world and are likely to be highly influential in the care of children in many future generations to come.

Note: The information provided throughout this book is current at the time of writing. Because research into causes and treatments of food allergy is continuing, guidelines and recommendations outlined in this book may change in the future, in line with new research.

This book isn't intended as a replacement for your child's doctor but as a supplement to help you navigate medical care of your child and to provide the safest and most positive environment for your child with food allergy to grow up in.

We hope that the information in this book

- ✔ Provides you with the information you need to more effectively team up with your health-care providers to arrive at an accurate diagnosis and obtain the most effective medical treatments.

- ✔ Empowers you and your child to work together to take control of your child's food allergy by presenting practical, plain-English advice, tips and strategies for living well with food allergies at home, work and school, while dining out or on school camps or holidays.

- ✔ Helps make your child's life as safe as possible without excessive restrictions on your child's lifestyle by giving you information that allows you to make decisions that best suit you, your child and your family.

- ✔ Gives you information that helps you explain to your family and your child's friends how best to keep you child with food allergy safe.

What You're Not to Read

Some people love to read books from cover to cover and digest all of the facts in a sequential order. Certainly, we know plenty of our colleagues in medical school who swear this is a tried and tested way to pass exams. However, neither of us finds this an easy way to access information, and retain that information in a meaningful way — unless you have hours of study time to commit to the task.

Certainly, very few parents have hours of idle time to read a book sequentially — not with the chaos of kids to deal with. Also, even though we're fascinated by this topic — enough to spend our lives seeing patients, doing research in the field and even writing a book — we know that most people really just want to have their burning questions answered.

This book has been divided into bite-sized chunks that let you dip in and out of the subject as you please. The table of contents is your best guide to pointing you in the direction you need, while the index obviously helps with a more focused search.

To help to prioritise key information, we've put information that's less critical in grey shaded boxes called *sidebars*. So although these boxes contain interesting asides, facts and case studies they're not essential to understanding the basics. Perhaps look at them as the icing on the cake — they're not essential but they certainly make your reading of the topic more digestible.

Foolish Assumptions

The title of the book kind of gives it away. This book is for people relatively new to the subject — not for experts. Of course, the most informed people are often those prepared to ask the questions that may appear foolish. We know of some people who are particularly good at asking probing, important questions in an ingenious way. For example, they may say 'If blind Freddie were to have a question, he might ask . . .'. So, although we don't assume you have any prior technical knowledge, we do assume that you're an inquisitive reader wanting answers that will help make life easier for you and the child you know who has food allergy.

We also make a few other assumptions. We figure that your situation matches one of more of the following scenarios:

- ✔ Your child has symptoms that you think may be related to food allergy and you want to know what your next step could be.

- ✔ Your child has just been diagnosed with a possible food allergy and you want to know more about the tests being discussed as a next step.

- ✔ Your doctor has diagnosed your child as having a food allergy and you're avoiding the foods diagnosed as being a problem, but your child's still experiencing symptoms.

- ✔ You're a parent or caregiver of someone who has food allergies and you want to know what you could and should be doing to help with all aspects of living with a food allergy.

- ✔ You're a grandparent or close friend of a child with food allergy and you want to make sure you can provide a safe, secure and supportive environment when you care for that child.

- ✔ You're a teacher, childcare worker, or school or childcare administrator who wants some definitive answers about food allergies so that you can more effectively discern real risks from overblown claims and put an effective and reasonable food allergy policy into place.

- ✔ You own a restaurant or run a school camp or after school club and you want to know more about how to support children with food allergy who visit your facility.

- ✔ You're a medical professional who underwent training before food allergies were as common as they are now and you want to learn more about food allergies in order to diagnose, treat or refer your patients more effectively.

- ✔ Your child has a friend with food allergy and you both want to know how to better support that friend.

- ✔ You are just plain curious since an epidemic of food allergy seems to be occurring!

Conventions Used in This Book

We don't like to think of our book as conventional — hopefully you find it stimulating and full of interesting facts — but we've used a couple of standard ways of presenting material that you may need to know when reading this book.

Conventions used are as follows:

✔ We understand that not just parents and guardians look after children with food allergies — extended family, friends, and childcare and school staff are among those who may need to care for children with food allergies and ensure appropriate management and treatment plans are in place. Where we've used 'your child' throughout this book, you can take this to also mean 'the child in your care'.

✔ When we introduce a new concept — particularly if it's a technical term — we *italicise* the term. If you see an italicised word that you don't understand, you can turn to the glossary section to find a more detailed explanation of the medical jargon.

✔ Websites appear in a different font and are never hyphenated even if they run longer than a line of text — you can simply type the line into your web browser.

How This Book Is Organised

We wrote this book so that you can approach it in two ways. You can either read the book from cover to cover or you can pick up the book and flip to any chapter for quick, stand-alone information on a specific food allergy topic. To help you navigate the book, we've divided the 17 chapters into five parts. Here we provide a quick overview of what we cover in each part of the book.

Part I: Introducing Food Allergies

This part provides a nice and compact overview of the whole book. So if you're pressed for time, this part gives you the short version of what's in this book. It also provides some basic definitions of the main terms and jargon surrounding food allergy, and helps you understand what other parts of the book you might wish to explore more. We also look at the rising rates of food allergy in Westernised countries, and what may be behind these rises. We then provide some information on possible ways to prevent food allergies in children.

Part II: Defining Food Allergies

This part really covers what food allergy is and how best to diagnose it in its various guises. We explain the different types of food allergies, how they're different from food intolerances, how they usually present as well as how diagnosis is confirmed through different types of tests.

Part III: Living with Food Allergies

This part outlines the four key steps to helping your child with food allergies stay safe and healthy. We explain how to avoid the food your child is allergic to (including providing some tips on interpreting ingredient labels), how to identify and manage high risk situations, how to treat allergic reactions should they happen and how to best optimise asthma management. We also look at the various places your child may need to manage their food allergies outside the home, including school and child care, friends' houses, other carers' houses, camps and restaurants. This part is for anyone who cares for a kid with food allergy — it provides important information and special tips to make the whole process safer and easier.

Part IV: Looking To the Future with Allergies

In this part, we look at whether or not your child is likely to grow out of food allergy. We also look at therapeutic options that are on the horizon.

Part V: The Part of Tens

This part presents key information that you won't want to miss. Here you discover key lessons to teach your child with food allergy, common food replacements for children avoiding certain foods, myths, misperceptions and falsehoods that you may have heard about food allergy and top allergy websites that provide useful further information to help you care for your child with food allergy.

Icons Used in This Book

Throughout this book we've sprinkled icons in the margins to highlight different types of information that call out for your attention. Here are the icons included and a brief description of each.

We use this icon to highlight really important flags for when you should call your doctor for further help with your child. Food allergy is a very serious condition — particularly if a severe reaction such as anaphylaxis occurs. Although we hope this book helps make life much easier for you and your child, it's no substitute for correct medical advice — this book is simply a supplement to the advice that your doctor can give you.

If you remember nothing else in a particular chapter, remember anything that's marked with one of these icons.

When we drift off and start using more doctor jargon than usual or provide in-depth technical information about a particular food allergy topic, we warn you by marking the text with this icon. We do, however, try our best to present the more technical material in plain English. After all — if we can't explain to our patients and their parents how to care for themselves in easy to understand language we're not doing our job properly!

Tips provide insider insight from behind the scenes. When you're looking for a better way to do something, check out these tips.

In our opinion nothing is like a true story to really help people to understand something that we're trying to explain. After all, the things we're talking about happen to real people. We may have changed some of the details of the true stories to protect anonymity of our patients and friends but the facts are correct. Of course, anecdotes are not necessarily evidence-based facts, but these stories do reflect our experience as clinicians and researchers — and also as mothers!

In some cases, you should be very careful about the way that you deal with a situation. We try to highlight when this is the case using these icons.

Where to Go from Here

Kids' Food Allergies For Dummies is written in modular format — which is basically a fancy way of saying that this book is structured so that you can open it to whatever topic interests you at a particular time rather than having to read it from front to back. Having said that, you may find that reading it in just that way works best for you.

If you're looking for a quick overview of food allergies along with their diagnosis and management, go straight to Chapter 1. Chapters 4 and 5 are key to understanding how different food allergies present and how they can be distinguished from intolerances. If you want to know more about the best tests for food allergy, don't miss out on Chapter 6. Chapter 11 is vital for anyone at risk of anaphylaxis and, if your child is due to go on camp in the next school year, you're likely to find Chapter 9 essential reading.

When you need some quick tips to pass along to your kids or caregivers, Part V is the place to go. Here you can also find a list of dietary replacements and food allergy websites.

Of course, you can dip in at any time to pick up something you missed or to refresh your memory on a specific topic. Most of all, we hope you enjoy what we've written and find it useful in your everyday life while you help a child you know navigate a life with food allergy.

Part I
Introducing Food Allergies

Glenn Lumsden

'Our little boy just read his first food label!'

In this part ...

Australia and New Zealand have some of the highest rates of allergic diseases worldwide and food allergies are no exception. Food allergies affect up to one in ten children and rates are rising rapidly. Recent studies have discovered that allergy problems are more common in Westernised countries, and less common in developing countries.

In this part, we introduce the different allergic diseases (including food allergies), and look at the different rates of the allergic conditions around the world. We discuss some theories on why the allergic diseases are more common in some countries as compared to others, and explain how a person's genes and the environment can both contribute to allergy problems. We then look at some things you can do to prevent your child from developing an allergic problem such as food allergy.

Chapter 1

Finding Out How Food Can Make Kids Sick

*F*ood allergies are much more common now than they used to be. People often say to us 'You know, when I was growing up, I didn't know anybody who had a food allergy. Nowadays, it seems like everyone has one, or more!' And it's true. Just about everyone we meet knows someone with food allergies and almost every school or childcare centre has at least one enrolled child with food allergy.

In this chapter, we give you an overview of food allergies in Australia and New Zealand, including why rates of food allergy may be rising, and define some allergy jargon. We also cover prevention and management of food allergies, in the home and in settings such as schools and childcare centres, and teaching kids about food allergies. Finally, we look at what treatments are on the horizon.

Describing Food Allergies in Kids

The term *food allergy* is bandied about quite a lot, and is often used incorrectly to describe any bad reaction to a food. A lot of confusion also surrounds what a food allergy is and what a food intolerance is; many people use these labels interchangeably, but these are very different conditions. Because of this confusion, almost ten years ago the World Allergy Organization brought together a team of experts from around the globe to develop consensus definitions describing the different reactions to foods.

These experts decided that any reaction to a food that's reproducible would be called a *food hypersensitivity*, and that these food hypersensitivities could be divided into either *food allergies* or *food intolerances* depending on what was causing the reaction.

We discuss these categories in the following sections.

Reacting badly to food

The body can react badly to a food for many different reasons. For example, a reaction may occur because of chemicals in the food itself, because the body can't break down the food properly or because the person's immune system has recognised the food as harmful and so reacts to the food.

Your immune system is an enormously complex army of cells that has the express purpose of protecting you from foreign invaders. The immune system has many parts to its army, each with a specific job of defending your body against a specific invader. This helps to protect you from infections. However, sometimes the immune system gets it wrong and recognises something as harmful even when it's not. (This same type of error is responsible for causing autoimmune conditions such as diabetes and multiple sclerosis. In these conditions, the immune system's mistake is to recognise parts of the body as being harmful when they're not.)

When the immune system incorrectly interprets food as harmful, you get a food allergy. Now, each time people with egg or peanut allergy eat egg or peanut, their immune system reacts to the food and causes an allergic reaction. (See Chapter 4 for more on the immune system's role in food allergies.)

Defining the difference between food allergies and intolerances

Most people have experienced an episode where a certain food didn't agree with them. Indeed, more than 25 per cent of people are believed to have experienced an adverse reaction to a food on a regular occasion at least some time in their life.

Not all reactions to food are caused by an allergic mechanism. Adverse reactions to food can result from intolerances (such as lactose intolerance), food poisoning (from foods contaminated with bacteria or toxins), or from other illnesses, such as irritable bowel syndrome, reflux, inflammatory bowel disease or migraines.

The term *food intolerance* is used to describe all reproducible reactions to foods that aren't food allergies. While food allergies are caused by the immune system recognising the food as harmful (see the preceding section), food intolerances are caused by substances within the food itself that can cause a bad reaction (such as scromboid food poisoning, from eating bad fish, or histamine-releasing compounds in tomatoes and strawberries), or problems in the body that make it difficult to digest the food (such as lactose intolerance, when a person lacks the enzyme lactase that breaks down lactose in foods — see Chapter 5 for more information about lactose intolerance).

Distinguishing between food allergies and other forms of adverse reactions to food is important, because food allergies, and more particularly IgE mediated food allergies, are the only types of reaction that are associated with *anaphylaxis* (a severe allergic reaction affecting the breathing or circulation) — which can be life-threatening. We discuss IgE mediated food allergies and anaphylaxis in Chapter 4.

If your child has food allergies and is at risk of anaphylaxis, you need to take very stringent measures to avoid the food that causes the allergies. People with food intolerances may experience unpleasant symptoms if they accidentally ingest a certain food, but they aren't endangering their lives. Chapter 7 looks at how you can manage your child's food allergy.

Pointing the finger at common allergies in kids

The most common allergies in children are to egg, milk and peanut, followed by soy, wheat and tree nuts. Children can also develop allergies to fish and shellfish, although these more commonly develop in adults. These eight food groups cause more than 90 per cent of all food allergies (see Chapter 4 for more details on foods that cause allergy). Doctors don't fully understand why these particular foods are more likely to cause allergy while all the other foods in the diet don't; many researchers are investigating this.

Even though most food allergies are caused by just a small number of foods, a person can develop an allergy to any food provided the food contains protein or complex carbohydrate molecules that can be recognised by the immune system — the immune system can't bind to or recognise small molecules such as sugar or salt, so being allergic to these types of simple molecules isn't possible, even though some parents have come to see us because they thought their child was allergic to sugar!

Food allergies can be caused by unusual foods that are only eaten in some regions of the world. For example, in South-East Asian countries such as Singapore, bird's nest soup (made from the saliva nests of certain birds) is a delicacy and children can develop allergy to bird's nest.

Busting myths about anaphylaxis

Anaphylaxis is a severe allergic reaction that's life-threatening. This reaction is the most severe form of an immediate, or IgE mediated, food allergy reaction, and can only occur in children with IgE mediated food allergy.

Children with delayed food allergies such as the non-IgE mediated food allergies or the mixed IgE and non-IgE mediated food allergies don't develop anaphylaxis.

The term *anaphylaxis* is used when an IgE mediated food allergy reaction affects the airways (breathing) or the circulation. If the breathing system is affected, you can have difficulty breathing, a hoarse voice, persistent coughing, or noisy breathing (wheezing or stridor). If the circulation is affected, children (especially babies) become pale and floppy or they may even collapse (although this is rare). The situation is very serious if the circulation becomes involved, because this is considered to be the most severe type of anaphylaxis. (Chapter 4 discusses anaphylaxis in more detail, and Chapter 7 helps you prepare for allergic reactions.)

While food allergies are common in children, affecting up to 10 per cent of children in Western countries, most food allergy reactions aren't life-threatening and are mild to moderate in severity, causing hives, swelling, vomiting, tummy pain or diarrhoea. Severe reactions (anaphylaxis) are less common, and only about 1 per cent of children with food allergy will have anaphylaxis.

The important thing is to know how to recognise a severe reaction so that you can act quickly and confidently to initiate the correct care as quickly as possible.

Anaphylaxis to foods is most common in young children under the age of five years and less common in adolescents and adults. But anaphylaxis reactions in adolescents and young adults aged 10 to 35 years are more likely to result in death.

Mimi's own research found that in the nine years between 1997 and 2005, only seven deaths due to food anaphylaxis occurred in Australia, with six of these seven deaths occurring in children and young adults aged between 10 years and 35 years, and no deaths in children under five years of age. This means the end of primary school and the secondary school years are the times of increased risk for children with food allergies.

Help your child learn how to manage food allergies as she comes to the end of primary school so that she can take greater responsibility for managing her condition while not with you. Learning about food allergies, how to avoid food allergens, and how to manage allergic reactions should be part of your child's preparation for starting secondary school. (See Chapter 10 for more on educating kids about their food allergies.)

No reliable method of predicting who's likely to have anaphylaxis and who's not is yet available. No skin test or blood test can identify with certainty at-risk children. Fortunately, however, some clinical signs can help doctors identify children who might be at greater risk of anaphylaxis. Your child's doctor takes these and other factors into account when developing a management plan for your child. (See Chapters 7 and 11 for more on managing food allergies and medical emergency action plans.)

Understanding Why Some Kids Have Allergies and Others Don't

Parents we talk to are often dismayed that one of their children has a food allergy while their other children, raised in exactly the same environment, don't.

What this tells us is that genes aren't the only factor that determine whether or not a child gets a food allergy, and also that the environmental factors that influence the risk of developing allergic disease are complex. While all children may seem to have been provided with exactly the same environment while they were growing up, the environments for each child were likely to be different in many ways.

The environment that matters is not just the environment the child is exposed to but also the environment that a mother is exposed to while she's pregnant with her child. What the mother's exposed to can have long-lasting effects on the baby's gene expression and can be passed on through many generations, which highlights the complex roles of the genes and the environment in the development of allergic diseases.

Also, we know that the genes interact with the environment and this interaction is what ultimately regulates the immune system towards a healthy state of tolerance or towards the development of allergy.

Although some families have multiple children with food allergies, this situation is actually the exception rather than the rule. Although food allergy does tend to run in families, researchers can't find any direct inheritance links. In fact, food allergies appear to have lower family history risks than other allergic diseases such as eczema, asthma and hay fever. Why this may be is anyone's guess, but what we can take from this evidence is that genes play some part in the risk of developing food allergy but they're by no means the major driver of disease risk. Lifestyle factors are far more likely to cause food allergies than inheriting allergy genes from your parents.

See Chapter 2 for more on theories about genetic and lifestyle causes of food allergy.

Getting a Grip on Allergy Jargon

Here we clarify some of the different terms we use throughout the book. What do we mean when we say, 'Sophie has food allergy', 'Thomas has anaphylaxis', 'Jessica has asthma' or 'Your husband is allergic to the vacuum cleaner'? And what does it mean if someone is atopic or lactose intolerant?

Understanding allergies and allergic reactions

An *allergy* occurs when your immune system recognises a substance in your environment as harmful and so mounts an immune response to that substance, which can then lead to symptoms of an allergic reaction every time you're re-exposed to that substance.

Food allergy is a very good example of an allergy. If you have an IgE mediated allergy to peanut, your immune system has recognised various proteins in the peanut (peanut *allergens*) as harmful and generated allergy antibodies (*IgE antibodies*) against these peanut proteins. Now, each time you eat peanut, you develop an allergic reaction with symptoms such as hives, swelling of the face, vomiting or even anaphylaxis.

IgE antibodies are one type of antibody that the immune cells called lymphocytes can make. These antibodies are really designed to protect you from worm and parasite infections; however, when you develop an allergy, the immune system has instructed the lymphocytes to make IgE antibodies that recognise food or environmental allergens that you're allergic to, even though these allergens are harmless. These IgE antibodies circulate in the blood and also bind tightly to specialised allergy cells, called *mast cells*, which sit in the skin, airways and intestines. If the IgE antibodies on the surface of mast cells encounter the allergen that they recognise, they bind to the allergen (much like a lock and key) and this binding process activates the mast cell to release a range of allergy factors that cause the allergic reaction. See Chapter 4 for more on how the immune system causes immediate allergic reactions to food allergens.

The immune mechanisms that cause the non-IgE mediated and mixed IgE/non-IgE mediated food allergies (also known as delayed food allergies — see the section 'Knowing the Symptoms', later in this chapter, for more) are less well understood, but don't appear to involve the IgE antibody or binding of the IgE antibody with the allergen. Instead, other immune cells, such as eosinophils and lymphocytes, are likely to be responsible for these delayed types of food allergies.

People can have allergies to foods, drugs, insect venoms and even latex, and allergies to all of these substances are examples of an allergic disease.

Comprehending allergic diseases

Allergic diseases are a group of conditions that are all caused by unwanted immune responses that lead to inflammation in tissues, where that inflammation involves the presence of allergy cells and allergy promoting factors such as mast cells, IgE antibodies, T helper type 2 lymphocytes, or eosinophils.

The allergic diseases are

- ✔ Asthma
- ✔ Eczema (also known as atopic dermatitis)
- ✔ Hay fever (also known as allergic rhinitis)
- ✔ Food allergy
- ✔ Drug allergy

✔ Insect sting allergy

✔ Other specific allergies (for example, to latex or blood products)

So, food allergy is just one of the allergic diseases. And asthma and eczema are also allergic diseases but aren't allergies.

For the specific allergies, such as food allergy or bee sting allergy, the allergic inflammation only occurs when you're exposed to the thing (allergen) that you're allergic to. So, you can be symptom-free if you avoid the allergen that triggers your symptoms. This is an important difference between the specific allergies and the other allergic conditions.

Asthma, eczema and hay fever aren't caused by an allergy. In asthma, eczema and hay fever, the immune system generates an unwanted inflammatory response in a target tissue (airways, skin or nasal passages) for an unknown reason. Many people mistakenly believe that asthma, eczema and hay fever are caused by an allergy to something, and that if this 'something' can be avoided, the asthma, eczema or hay fever will go away and they will be cured. This isn't the case. However, people with asthma, eczema or hay fever often also have an allergy to something, and exposure to the allergen can make their asthma, eczema or hay fever symptoms worse by triggering and/or aggravating the allergic inflammation. For example, most people with asthma, eczema or hay fever have an allergy to house dust mite, and exposure to dust mite can worsen their condition. The dust mite allergy isn't the cause of their disease but it can make things worse.

All about asthma

Asthma is an allergic disease involving allergic inflammation of the airways. This condition is the most common of the allergic diseases, and affects one in five Australian children, one in seven teenagers and one in ten adults. The condition is more common in boys during childhood, but more common in women after the teenage years.

In asthma, the chronic inflammation in the airways results in the airways being over-reactive — the airways contract more often and to a greater degree when exposed to things (such as cold air, exercise or cigarette smoke) that may not bother people who don't have asthma. Most children with asthma also have allergies to airborne allergens (such as pollen, dust mite and pet danders) and exposure to these allergens can trigger inflammation in the airway and cause asthma symptoms.

People with asthma are more likely to have other allergic diseases such as hay fever, eczema and food allergy. Foods rarely cause asthma symptoms (fewer than 2 per cent of people with asthma get symptoms of asthma due to a food), but having both asthma and food allergy makes you more likely to have a severe reaction to the food you're allergic to and also more likely to have a severe asthma attack.

Asthma is also an important risk factor for death due to a food allergy reaction so if your child has a food allergy and also has asthma, making sure that the asthma is well controlled is really important. (See Chapter 7 for more on managing food allergies.)

Take your child to see your doctor if your child has an asthma attack more than once every few months or if your child's asthma symptoms are noticeable every week.

Everything eczema

Eczema is an allergic disease where allergic inflammation occurs in the skin. The condition most commonly develops in the first six months of life and affects about one in five infants. It usually improves after the first three to five years of life; however, while some children outgrow their eczema, many continue to have eczema as adults.

The allergic inflammation in the skin causes a rash that is red, scaly and itchy. If your child scratches at the rash, it is worsened and, if untreated, can cause the skin to thicken. Most children with eczema, like those with asthma, also have allergies to airborne allergens (particularly house dust mite) and exposure to these allergens can trigger or worsen eczema symptoms. Some children, especially young babies with severe eczema, can also have food allergies and exposure to those foods can trigger or worsen eczema symptoms.

As well as scratching the skin and specific allergies, many other factors can make the inflammation in the skin that occurs with eczema worse, such as stress, overheating, bacteria on the skin, having vaccinations and teething.

Eczema and bacteria

Everybody carries bacteria on the skin, and the most common skin bacterium is called staphylococcus. Children with eczema carry more staphylococci on their skin than children who don't have eczema, and staphylococcus is a very potent trigger of inflammation in children with eczema — much more potent than any airborne or food allergens. Reducing bacterial loads on your child's skin by bathing daily with non-soap cleansers is one of the most effective ways to improve their eczema. Infection of the eczema with staphylococcus is also very common and, if this happens, your child needs antibiotic treatment in order for the rash to heal.

Like asthma, many children with eczema have other allergic diseases, particularly asthma and food allergy. Recent research suggests that having eczema may increase your chances of developing the other allergic diseases — being exposed to allergens through broken skin is more likely to result in a person being sensitised to that allergen, rather than developing tolerance to that allergen, whereas being exposed to an allergen by eating the allergen is more likely to result in a person developing tolerance to that allergen. If this turns out to be correct, improving the skin barrier in children with eczema may offer one approach to preventing food allergy in these children.

Having a look at hay fever (allergic rhinitis)

Allergic rhinitis, also known as hay fever, is an allergic disease involving inflammation in the inner lining of the nose. This allergic inflammation causes symptoms of sneezing, itchy and runny nose, and blockage of the nose (congestion). Often symptoms affecting the eyes (allergic conjunctivitis) also occur, with itchy, red, watery eyes. Children usually develop allergic rhinitis a little later than eczema and asthma — usually at around three to five years of age.

Children with allergic rhinitis are often allergic to house dust mite, pollens and pet danders and inhaling these allergens can trigger inflammation in the nose. In addition, as with asthma and eczema, when inflammation in the lining of the nose is already apparent, many other factors can also trigger symptoms including irritants such as strong smells, cigarette smoke and dry air.

Many people believe that allergic rhinitis is a trivial condition and tend to ignore symptoms in themselves and their children. However, allergic rhinitis has the same impact on quality of life as asthma does, and has been shown to reduce concentration and learning at school, affect sleep and cause other health problems such as ear infections and sinus infections. If you have both allergic rhinitis and asthma, poorly managed allergic rhinitis can make your asthma worse, increasing the chances and severity of an asthma attack and admission to hospital for asthma. So controlling and managing allergic rhinitis is just as important as for asthma and eczema, and this involves controlling the inflammation with topical corticosteroids.

Defining atopy

Most people with allergic disease(s) have an underlying genetic tendency or predisposition to develop unwanted allergic responses to allergens, which is called *atopy*.

If you have this genetic predisposition, or atopy, you're more likely to develop an allergic disease and make allergy antibodies (IgE antibodies) to substances in the environment that are normally harmless (such as foods or pollen). When you make allergy antibodies to an allergen, you're said to be *sensitised* to that allergen. But not all people who are atopic develop an allergic disease — just as not all people who are sensitised develop an allergic disease.

Taking on the atopic march

If you're a parent, you've probably heard the terms *atopic march* or *allergic march* and wondered what they mean. No, they're not a marching band! These terms have been used to describe the progression of allergic disorders during childhood.

Food allergy and eczema are typically the first allergic conditions to develop and usually present in the first 3 to 12 months of life. The most common food allergies at this age are egg, milk and peanut allergy, and these peak at around one to two years. Most food allergies (including egg, milk, wheat and soy) resolve in later childhood so that the overall prevalence of food allergy reduces after five years of age and stabilises from adolescence onwards. Peanut and tree nut allergies tend to persist into adulthood, and allergy to shellfish and fish commonly present for the first time in young adults, so that the most common food allergies in adults are peanut, tree nut, shellfish and fish allergy.

Asthma and allergic rhinitis generally have a later onset, at around three to five years of age. Some children have wheezing illness in the first year of life, but most asthma starts around preschool age, and asthma prevalence increases steadily into the school years before plateauing. Allergic rhinitis continues to increase in prevalence through to adult life. This pattern of eczema and food allergy appearing in the early months of life, followed by later development of asthma and then allergic rhinitis is what's described as the allergic or atopic march.

Having one allergic disease increases the chances that you develop other allergic diseases, and many children who have eczema or food allergy go on to develop asthma and hay fever. This doesn't mean that one allergic disease is the cause of other allergic diseases. More likely, people develop more than one allergic disease because they have an underlying atopic predisposition, and so are at greater risk of developing any of the allergic problems.

Figure 1-1 illustrates the atopic march in young children.

Figure 1-1:
The atopic
march: Food
allergy and
eczema
affect young
infants and
children
and asthma
and allergic
rhinitis
develop
later.

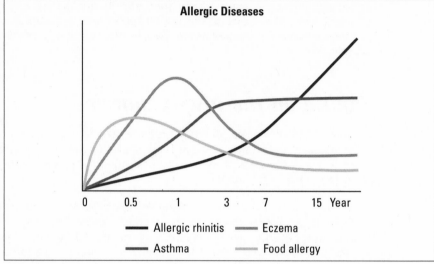

Allergic Diseases

0   0.5   1   3   7   15 Year

━━ Allergic rhinitis   ━━ Eczema
━━ Asthma   ━━ Food allergy

Source: World Allergy Organization

Watching Allergy Rates Rise

A rapid rise in all of the allergic conditions (asthma, eczema, hay fever, food allergy) has occurred in the last 30 to 50 years, mainly in countries with a Westernised lifestyle. Rates of asthma were the first to rise, increasing rapidly from 1980 onwards. More recently, asthma rates have stabilised or even fallen in some countries, while rates of eczema and allergic rhinitis are still increasing but at a slower rate. In contrast, food allergies and anaphylaxis started to increase somewhat later, in the 1990s, and are rising at an exponential rate.

Researchers know that both people's genes and their environment contribute to the regulation of their immune system and so can determine whether a person develops one of the allergic diseases. However, the rapid rise in allergy problems in the last half of a century tells experts that this increase must relate to changes in the environment rather than to changes in people's genes, because this time frame is too quick for genes to have shifted to any great degree. Because these increases have mainly affected developed countries, experts also believe the environmental factors driving the rise in allergic diseases are likely to relate to the Western lifestyle.

Several factors are thought to be especially important:

- **Improved living conditions with increased sanitation and reduced infections.** The association between improved living conditions and allergies is known as the *hygiene hypothesis* or *microbial hypothesis*. Researchers now believe that the overall reduction in exposure to microbes has influenced allergic disease rates, rather than just the lower rates of infection in Westernised countries. Diverse and abundant microbial exposures in early life play an important role in the development of a healthy immune system that averts allergic responses.

- **Reduced UV exposure and vitamin D.**

- **Delayed introduction of allergenic foods.**

- **Reduced exposure to other immunomodulatory diet factors, such as omega 3 fatty acids (fish oils).**

Chapter 2 looks at the rising rates of allergies in more detail.

Foiling Food Allergies: Prevention versus Cure

Unfortunately, at the moment, doctors can recommend very few things for the prevention of allergic diseases, including food allergy. This is partly because researchers are still trying to understand the factors that contribute to the development of allergic disease. If the important factors driving allergy problems can be identified, developing effective ways to prevent or reduce the risk of a child developing allergic diseases, including food allergy, may be possible.

The guidelines for prevention of allergic disease only apply to children at increased risk for developing allergy problems — that is, children who have a first-degree relative (mother, father or sibling) with one of the allergic diseases. However, because of the high rates of food allergy in Australia and New Zealand, more than 50 per cent of babies are at increased risk of allergic disease and so these guidelines apply to the majority of babies rather than the minority:

- Breastfeed for at least six months, or if the mother is unable to breastfeed during this time, introduce a hypoallergenic hydrolysed HA baby formula (such as Nan HA or Karicare Aptamil).

✔ Introduce complementary solid foods, from around four to six months — don't avoid the allergenic foods. This applies to all babies, not just those at increased risk of having an allergic disease.

✔ Avoid exposure to cigarette smoke during pregnancy and early childhood.

Note: The guidelines outlined in the preceding list are based upon ASCIA guidelines that are similar to those in the United Kingdom, European Union and United States. The Cochrane meta-analysis evaluating the effects of HA partially hydrolysed formulas on the prevention of allergic disease are being updated to include recent studies that have reported conflicting results. As expert guidelines are based upon the findings from Cochrane and other meta-analyses, these recommendations may change — see Chapter 3 for more.

No evidence exists that elimination diets in the mother during pregnancy or breastfeeding prevent allergic disease in the baby, and these aren't recommended.

See Chapter 3 for more detailed information on preventing food allergies.

Knowing the Symptoms

Food allergy reactions can be mild, moderate or severe. The symptoms of an IgE mediated food allergy reaction are much the same for allergies to all types of foods. Allergists usually divide food allergies into two categories:

✔ **IgE mediated food allergies (also known as immediate food allergies).** Symptoms include *hives* (itchy lumps that look like mosquito bites), swelling of the face, eyes or mouth, vomiting or anaphylaxis (when the breathing or circulation is affected). All of these symptoms usually occur within minutes of food ingestion, although some symptoms, such as vomiting, diarrhoea or an eczema flare, may occur up to a few hours later. The symptoms of an IgE mediated food allergy reaction are described in more detail in Chapter 4.

✔ **Non-IgE mediated and mixed IgE/non-IgE mediated food allergies (also known as delayed food allergies).** Symptoms associated with delayed reactions are usually gut problems, with the most common symptoms being vomiting, diarrhoea, abdominal pain and colic, usually occurring several hours after ingestion of the food. Non-IgE mediated food allergies and mixed IgE/non-IgE mediated food allergies are discussed further in Chapter 5.

An important difference between delayed (non-IgE mediated and mixed IgE/non-IgE mediated) and the immediate (IgE mediated) food allergies is that delayed food allergies don't cause anaphylaxis, or hives or swelling of the face, which are characteristic of the IgE mediated immune reactions.

Testing Times: Finding the Cause of Allergic Reactions

An allergy test that looks for allergen-specific IgE antibodies (allergy antibodies that recognise allergens) shows if your child has made an IgE antibody against a particular food. Allergen-specific IgE antibodies can be measured in the skin (skin prick test) or in the blood. The presence of this allergen-specific IgE antibody against a food only means that your child has become sensitised to that food — or, in other words, that your child's immune system has recognised that food and mounted an immune response to it. The presence of these antibodies doesn't always mean that your child is allergic to the food. (Indeed, in more than 50 per cent of positive allergy tests, the child doesn't have a clinical allergy to that food and can tolerate that food just fine without having any bad reaction.)

The reasons only some children who have made allergy antibodies to a food are allergic to the food aren't understood, and this is an important area of research that we are both involved with. In our research, we're trying to discover what protects some children from having a clinical allergy even when their immune systems have already recognised the food and made allergy antibodies to the food.

Nevertheless, if a child has experienced a reaction to a food that fits with an IgE mediated food allergy and the subsequent blood or skin allergy test is positive for that food, this confirms that the child has IgE mediated food allergy to that food. So these allergy tests are very helpful to doctors when diagnosing food allergies in children.

Researchers have shown that the higher the level of the specific IgE antibody to a food, and the larger the skin prick test size, the more likely it is that the child does in fact have a clinical allergy. Based on this information, researchers have developed 95 per cent thresholds for skin prick tests and the allergen-specific IgE blood tests to the common food allergens. These thresholds allow the tests to predict, with 95 per cent certainty, that the child has clinical food allergy rather than just being sensitised to the food, even if the child hasn't experienced a reaction to that food.

Checking for immediate food allergies

The most common food allergy tests for immediate or IgE mediated food allergies (listed in order of most common) are

- **Skin prick tests:** Allergen-specific IgE can be detected in the skin using a skin prick test (SPT), which introduces a small amount of allergen into the skin. When the allergen binds to allergen-specific IgE antibodies on the surface of mast cells, the mast cells are activated and release a host of immune factors that cause redness and a *wheal* (bump on the skin) at the site of the skin test. The result is obtained by measuring the size of the wheal. The higher the level of allergen-specific IgE in the body, the bigger the wheal caused by the SPT. A positive test is defined as a wheal that's at least 3 millimetres larger than the negative control (saline is used as a negative control and should not cause a wheal on the skin).

    Note: The SPT wheal reaction can vary depending on who does the test, which skin test device is used, the time of day and where on the body the test is done; these factors must be taken into account when interpreting the skin test result.

- **Blood tests:** The level of allergen-specific IgE in the blood can also be measured. These tests are very accurate and reproducible and aren't affected by the time of day or other factors that can affect the SPT. However, the test is more expensive and takes longer to provide a result, so the SPT is usually preferred by most allergists.

- **Food challenges:** Challenges are the gold standard tests for diagnosing all food allergies — both the IgE mediated and the delayed food allergies. The food challenge test involves giving a child the food in question, starting with small amounts and progressively increasing the amount every 15 to 20 minutes, while watching to see if a reaction develops. The food challenge test is positive if a reaction develops and negative if the child completes the challenge and takes a standard serving of the food without reacting.

Testing for delayed food allergies

In contrast to the IgE mediated food allergies, no blood or skin tests can diagnose non-IgE mediated and mixed IgE/non-IgE mediated food allergies, also known as the delayed food allergies. For these food allergies, doctors make a diagnosis based upon the history and examination findings, together with seeing what happens when the food in question is taken out of the diet and then put back (a *food elimination and reintroduction challenge*).

If symptoms improve with elimination of the food and recur when the food is reintroduced, this confirms the diagnosis of a non-IgE mediated food allergy or a mixed IgE/non-IgE mediated food allergy. If the doctor is certain that the food allergy doesn't involve an IgE mediated component (that is, the allergen-specific IgE blood test or the skin prick test are negative), reintroducing the food at home is safe.

In some cases, an endoscopy test may be used to help with diagnosing non-IgE and mixed IgE/non-IgE mediated food allergies. This test is performed by gastroenterologists (physicians specialising in gut conditions), allowing the specialist to look inside the gut and to take samples of the intestine wall for more detailed examination under the microscope. Non-IgE mediated and mixed IgE/non-IgE mediated food allergies can cause inflammation in the intestinal wall, so looking for these signs can help to confirm the diagnosis.

We provide a more detailed discussion of allergy testing for diagnosis of food allergy in Chapter 6, as well as a discussion of unproven tests.

Managing Allergies Day by Day

Looking after a child with food allergies can be a daunting task for parents, and for any school and childcare staff, family and friends also responsible for the child. How do I manage my child's allergies? What if Jack has an allergic reaction when he comes over to play with Harry? What will I do if Susie has anaphylaxis? How do I treat an allergic reaction? Should I let Ellie eat Sarah's birthday cake? All of these questions can flood into your head when you discover you have or you're going to be looking after a child with food allergy.

Four key elements are involved in managing food allergies:

- ✔ **Avoid food allergens.** Read ingredient labels looking for the allergen that your child is allergic to. (Chapter 8 discusses ingredient labels and how to interpret the statements.)

- ✔ **Manage situations that have an increased risk for your child accidentally eating their food allergen.** Develop specific strategies for these high-risk situations, which include going to a friend's home, eating out at a restaurant, or going to a party, the movies or other event. If your child is old enough, teach your child about taking extra care to ensure any food she eats doesn't contain the food allergen that she's allergic to.

✔ **Learn how to recognise an allergic reaction and how to treat an allergic reaction in an emergency.** You and other people caring for your child, as well as your child if he's old enough, must learn about how to recognise an allergic reaction and the emergency management of allergic reactions. All of this information is contained in the medical emergency action plan that your child's doctor should prepare for your child, and update each year. (See Chapter 11 for more detailed information on emergency action plans.)

✔ **Control medical problems such as asthma or heart conditions, which can increase the risks of anaphylaxis.** Many children with food allergies also have asthma, and asthma is known to be a risk factor for having a severe food allergy reaction (anaphylaxis), as well as for an anaphylaxis reaction causing death. Children with food allergies who have asthma should be reviewed regularly to ensure that their asthma is well controlled. Other medical problems that can increase the risk of anaphylaxis reactions, such as heart conditions, should similarly be reviewed regularly to ensure they're properly managed.

As part of the ongoing management of your child's food allergy, your child should be reviewed by a doctor (either your child's GP or paediatrician, or an allergist) every year. At this annual visit, the doctor can review your child's diet and ability to avoid the food allergen, confirm that your child's diet is nutritionally adequate (this may require referral to a dietitian), and remind you and your child about high-risk situations for accidental exposure to food allergens. The doctor can also update your child's emergency action plan, re-educate you on all aspects of this plan, and review whether your child needs an adrenaline auto-injector if not already prescribed with one.

Importantly, the doctor can review your child's asthma and any other medical conditions that can increase the risk of anaphylaxis to ensure that these are properly managed and well controlled.

In Chapter 7, we discuss managing food allergies in children in more detail.

Supporting Parents, Schools and Kids

The management of food allergies in children is a major task that involves parents, staff in schools or childcare centres, as well as other carers who look after your child with food allergies. As your child grows older, your child also needs to take some responsibility for managing their food allergy. The level of responsibility you give your child depends on your child's level of maturity and confidence.

For parents

Looking after children with food allergies is no easy task, we know! But you can access lots of support (especially online, as outlined in Chapter 17).

Managing your child's food allergies in your home and when you're out and about with your child involves shopping and preparing appropriate food, and paying special attention to avoiding cross-contamination of food allergens in your home.

Travelling or going on holidays can also be challenging for parents of children with food allergies, because your usual routine is disrupted and you're more likely to have to eat out at restaurants or eat foods prepared by friends or family (who may not be as aware about the importance of cross-contamination and excluding food allergens in cooking).

One of the most difficult situations for parents of kids with food allergies is getting relatives, especially grandparents, to take the same care in preparing food for your child. You may need to spend more time helping grandparents to understand the importance of managing your child's food allergy; food allergies were uncommon when they were growing up and they may not have encountered anyone with a food allergy during their lifetime until now.

In Chapter 8, we provide more information on managing your child's food allergies when your child's at home, with other family members and on holidays. We give you some tips on how to reduce the risks in these situations, including when you are flying in an airplane, and offer some suggestions on how to talk to family members and other carers about your child's food allergies.

For schools and childcare centres

When your child is at school or child care, staff have a duty of care to manage your child's food allergies. They must be aware of the things they can do to reduce the risks for your child with food allergies while your child's involved in school or childcare activities.

The most vital things that schools and childcare centres can do for kids with food allergy are the following:

- ✔ **Being aware of the children who have food allergies enrolled in their care.**

✔ **Preparing an individualised food allergy management plan for each child with food allergy.** This plan should contain

- Information about the **child and their specific allergies**

- **Emergency contact information**

- The child's **medical emergency action plan**

- A **risk minimisation plan** that outlines situations when your child with food allergies is at risk of having an accidental exposure to the food allergen, strategies on how to minimise these risks and who's responsible for implementing these strategies.

✔ **Developing a clear emergency response plan that outlines how staff should respond should your child have an allergic reaction while at school or child care.** A separate emergency response plan needs to be developed for each different setting at school.

✔ **Undertaking training in the recognition and emergency treatment of allergic reactions and anaphylaxis.** This includes training in the use of adrenaline auto-injectors, and in approaches to risk minimisation in the school or childcare setting. A number of courses are available that specifically cover these issues in relation to schools and childcare services.

In Chapter 9, we discuss in more detail how staff in schools and childcare services can help to manage your child's food allergies and provide a safe and supportive environment for your child — both in school or child care, and during special events, excursions and school camps.

For kids

As your child gets older, he can take more responsibility for managing his own food allergies. Older children and adolescents can start to learn about food allergies, how to avoid allergens, and high-risk situations for accidentally eating their food allergens. They can also understand the importance of telling people about their food allergies, how to recognise and treat allergic reactions, how their friends can help them manage their food allergies, and how to deal with children who try to bully them about their food allergies. Becoming familiar with this information can empower your child to take responsibility for his food allergies and manage his food allergies effectively.

Ways your older child or adolescent can become more responsible for her food allergy are covered in more detail in Chapter 10.

Looking to the Future

Management of food allergies in children now relies upon avoiding the food allergen and being prepared for situations when an allergic reaction occurs. This approach is fraught with difficulties, since avoiding their food allergens is difficult for children — many children have an allergic reaction as a result of accidentally eating their food allergen within a few years.

Although children usually grow out of their allergies to milk, egg, wheat and soy by the time they're teenagers, most children with peanut and tree nut allergies (as well as fish and shellfish allergies) have these allergies throughout their lives, and these food allergies are most likely to cause severe reactions (anaphylaxis).

Because of all these issues, the need for an effective treatment that can address the existing and rising burden of food allergy is pressing. Researchers are working hard to identify new treatments for food allergy, and although it's still too early to introduce any of the experimental treatments into standard clinical care, a number of approaches appear to be promising.

The therapies under research are the following:

- ✔ **Peptide immunotherapy:** Subcutaneous allergen-specific immuno-therapy has been used for the treatment of specific allergies to insect venom, such as bee venom allergy, for many decades. It involves the injection of the allergen into the fatty tissue in the arm, starting with very small amounts and building up to a high dose, continued as a monthly injection for up to five years. The immunotherapy can reprogram the immune response to the allergen and the patient is cured of their allergy to bee venom. This immunotherapy approach has also been used in patients with asthma and allergic rhinitis to induce tolerance to selected inhaled allergens; although the patients continue to have asthma and eczema, they no longer develop symptoms when they're exposed to the allergens that were included in the immunotherapy.

  This subcutaneous immunotherapy approach using crude peanut extract was attempted for food allergy; however, this was associated with a very high rate of anaphylaxis and the approach was abandoned. Now researchers are trying to develop modified peanut protein molecules that can be safely used for subcutaneous immunotherapy to treat peanut allergy (this is called *peptide immunotherapy*) and studies are ongoing, although no clinical trials have been commenced so far.

- ✔ **Oral immunotherapy:** Many clinical trials have evaluated oral immunotherapy in food allergy; however, most have only looked for the development of *desensitisation* (the ability to eat a food while you're still on immunotherapy), with only a few trials assessing for *tolerance* (the long-lasting ability to tolerate a food after immunotherapy is stopped — a cure).

  The oral immunotherapy trials so far show that most people treated with oral immunotherapy become desensitised, and experience immune changes in the direction of the immune responses typically associated with tolerance; however, oral immunotherapy doesn't appear to have induced tolerance in any of the trials. Nevertheless, the changes that have been detected suggest the possibility that oral immunotherapy can be used to induce tolerance. Researchers (including Mimi) are investigating possible ways to achieve this, and results of these studies should be available soon.

- ✔ **Chinese herbal formulas:** A herbal formula, called *Food Allergy Herbal Formula* (FAHF), was highly effective in both preventing and treating food allergy in mice and is being investigated in a first stage clinical trial in humans to show that the treatment is safe and can be studied further in larger clinical trials to assess its effectiveness.

- ✔ **Probiotics:** Live bacteria, which can promote a healthy gut and so confer health benefits, have been investigated for the treatment of food allergy and food allergy associated with eczema; however, results have been variable and the summary findings suggest that probiotics aren't effective for the treatment of established food allergy. Similarly, prebiotics, which favour the growth of the healthy gut bacteria, have been tested for the treatment of food allergy or food allergy associated with eczema, with variable results; further studies are underway. Neither probiotics nor prebiotics can as yet be recommended for the treatment of established food allergy. Their roles in preventing allergic conditions are more promising (see Chapter 3 for information about preventing food allergies).

Chapter 13 discusses future therapies for food allergy in more detail.

Chapter 2

Investigating the Rising Rates of Food Allergies

. . . .

. . . .

*B*ecause we work in the area of food allergy research, one of the first questions people often ask us, whether they're patients or someone we've just met over dinner, is 'Why is food allergy on the increase?' Often, before we've even opened our mouths to respond, we're bombarded with their beliefs on the matter. (Everyone seems to have an opinion!)

The real answer is that at the moment we just don't know the reason for the increased rates. But the good news is that research is in progress, and the results of these studies are likely to give us some answers to the question — very soon!

In this chapter, we discuss what we know about the rise in food allergies, and how researchers in Australia, New Zealand and around the world are studying the increasing rates of food allergy and other allergic diseases. We also look at the ways genes, the environment and lifestyle factors may explain the rising incidence of food allergy in young children.

Examining Recently Rising Rates of Food Allergies and Other Allergic Diseases

Over the last half a century, rates of food allergy and other allergic diseases, including asthma, eczema and hay fever, have increased quite dramatically. (Refer to Chapter 1 for more on the difference between food allergy and allergic disease.)

Rates of these conditions appear to rise in parallel with economic development and in populations that have a Western lifestyle. (See the section 'Being allergic to a Western lifestyle', later in this chapter for the factors that define this kind of lifestyle.) Australia and New Zealand, for example, have some of the highest rates of allergy problems, including food allergy, in the world. As the economic situation and lifestyle in developing countries approaches that of the developed world, the rates of food allergy and allergic diseases in those countries are also expected to increase.

So, although economic growth and improved living conditions are great for many reasons, side effects can also be seen.

Food allergy increases in Aussie and Kiwi kids

Australia and New Zealand are in the midst of an explosion of food allergy and anaphylaxis. If you're reading this book, you're probably doing so because you have a child (or know a child) with food allergy. And you're not alone. These days, most people at least know a child with an allergy problem. Almost every week, you can read or hear something in a newspaper or popular magazine or on the radio about allergy and anaphylaxis, and the topic is always a popular one!

Very few studies have investigated changing rates of food allergy over time, and most haven't used the gold standard approach of a food challenge to diagnose food allergy (see the sidebar 'Understanding food challenge tests' for more). Nevertheless, studies in Australia, the United Kingdom and the

United States that used repeated questionnaires or patient history combined with allergy testing to identify food allergy have shown dramatic increases in food allergy in the last decade.

Findings from studies such as the EuroPrevall study (see the sidebar 'Global studies on the varying rates of allergy') are also soon to be released and should tell us a lot more about how the rates of food allergy are changing in different parts of the world. In addition, findings from both our ongoing HealthNuts study in Australia and the EuroPrevall study may offer new information on the factors that contribute to the development of food allergy.

Understanding food challenge tests

A *food challenge* test is an allergy procedure carried out under careful observation by an allergist and/or an allergy nurse to determine whether or not a child's allergic to a food. Many people who report that they have bad effects from a food don't have a true food allergy, and the food challenge is the best way to clarify the existence of an allergy. The test takes at least four hours, sometimes longer, and involves feeding a child the food in question — starting at a low dose and increasing the dose every 15 to 20 minutes until a standard serve of the food is reached.

All the while, the allergy specialist and/or nurse monitor the child for signs of an allergic reaction. If the child has a food allergy, the child develops typical symptoms of hives, vomiting, tummy pain or anaphylaxis, which can be treated immediately by the allergy doctor and/or nurse supervising the challenge. If no food allergy is apparent, the child is able to tolerate all of the doses of the food without developing any symptoms of an allergic reaction.

A food challenge can be

- ✔ **Open:** When both the parents and child and the doctor and nurse know when the food is being offered.

- ✔ **Single blind:** When the doctor and nurse know when the food is being offered but the child and parents don't.

- ✔ **Double blind:** When both the parents and child and the doctor and nurse don't know whether the food or a placebo is being offered to the child.

The double blind food challenge takes more time, since the child is challenged to consume both a placebo food and the food in question; however, this is the type of challenge commonly used in research studies because it's the best way to do a challenge. In clinical practice, an open challenge is usually performed because this is simpler to do and can provide reliable results in most children.

Our own research into food allergy provides strong evidence for dramatic increases in rates of food allergy and food anaphylaxis in Australia. Mimi's research found that the number of children diagnosed with peanut allergy increased by 200 per cent between 2001 and 2004, and that admissions for food anaphylaxis across Australia increased by 300 per cent in the last decade. Remarkably, her research showed that these increases mainly affected young children under five years of age, and that allergies to peanut, tree nuts and shellfish have increased much more quickly than allergies to milk or egg. Admissions to hospital for peanut and shellfish anaphylaxis increased more than 300 per cent in the last ten years, whereas milk and egg anaphylaxis only increased by 50 per cent and under 200 per cent, respectively. That's why, ten years ago, you probably hadn't even heard the words 'peanut allergy', but now at least one child in every school has the condition so you're much more likely to have heard of it.

We recently performed a large population-based epidemiological study of food allergy in Melbourne using food challenges to confirm the diagnosis (the HealthNuts study). To our surprise, we found that more than 10 per cent of 12-month-old infants have a food allergy, which is the highest rate of food allergy reported globally. This supports our hunch that food allergy is a major health problem for Aussie kids. See the section 'Speculating about Why Allergies Are on the Rise' later in the chapter for some theories. No similar studies of food allergy have been performed in New Zealand, but rates are likely to be the same in this country.

Increasing rates of other allergic diseases in Aussie and Kiwi kids

Rates of all the allergic diseases have increased dramatically in Australia and New Zealand in the last few decades. However, the different allergic problems haven't increased concurrently. Rates of asthma, for example, were the first to increase but have now stabilised. Eczema and hay fever followed soon after the increase in the asthma rate and are still rising, although more slowly in the last ten years. Most recently, food allergy and anaphylaxis appear to be accelerating (see preceding section), and if these trends continue, rates of food allergy are likely to catch up to asthma. You may soon see just as many kids with food allergy as have asthma in your child's classroom.

Increases in the allergic diseases have occurred too quickly to be due to changes in our genes, and must instead be caused by changes in our environment and the way we live (see the section 'Judging genes and food allergies' later in this chapter).

Global studies on the varying rates of allergy

Doctors have known for a while that rates of food allergy and allergic disease vary widely in different countries around the world, but little information has been available on these differences or why they might be occurring.

In 2005, a large European collaborative study called EuroPrevall was set up to compare the global differences in rates of food allergy using standardised formal food challenges (the accepted gold standard for diagnosis of food allergy). The study involves 24 countries including 17 European member states, Ghana, Russia, India and China; more recently, Australia and New Zealand have also joined in.

Results from this exciting global study aren't available yet but are expected in the near future and should provide new and important information on rates of food allergy around the world as well as what factors contribute to development of food allergy.

To explore the increase of allergic disease, the International Study of Asthma and Allergies in Children (ISAAC) was established in 1991, and is the largest global epidemiological study of asthma and allergic disease in children.

ISAAC compared the rates of asthma, allergic rhinitis and eczema in children around the world, to better understand the factors leading to disease and to obtain baseline data that could be used to monitor future trends in prevalence. The study confirmed that the highest rates of allergic disease were found in developed countries such as the United Kingdom, Australia, New Zealand, and North, Central, and South America, while the lowest rates were seen in developing countries such as in Eastern Europe and Asia. This was the first evidence that differences in the environment are likely to play a critical role in determining the development of allergic disease.

The findings from these studies so far show that changes in the environment caused by a Western lifestyle and economic development are the most important factors causing the rise in allergic disease. Our own HealthNuts study has found that more than 10 per cent of Melbourne children aged 12 months have a food allergy confirmed by the gold standard food challenge test, which is the highest reported in the world. This fits with the findings from the ISAAC study, which found higher rates of allergic disease in countries with a Westernised lifestyle.

More research is needed to understand how these factors contribute to disease, and hopefully the continuing EuroPrevall, HealthNuts and ISAAC studies can help to unravel some of these unknowns.

Speculating about Why Allergies Are on the Rise

Both your genes and the environment you're exposed to are important factors behind allergic problems, and both can influence the immune system to direct whether or not an allergic problem develops. However, the speed at which rates of allergic disease have increased means that changes in genes are unlikely to play a big role in the increased rates. Changes to gene coding occur over thousands of years and yet food allergy is a very recent phenomenon, with most of the rise in prevalence occurring in the last 20 years. Genes just don't change that quickly; however, your genes do influence your disposition to allergy.

Studies such as the EuroPrevall, HealthNuts and the ISAAC (see the sidebar 'Global studies on the varying rates of allergy' for more) suggest various environmental and lifestyle factors are the most significant contributors to rates of food allergy and allergic diseases. In particular, improved hygiene, less exposure to microbial organisms, changes in diet (for example, eating fewer serves of fish and vegetables or changing the timing of introduction of allergenic solids) and reduced exposure to sunlight (meaning reduced exposure to UV and, therefore, reduced levels of vitamin D) are thought to be the main factors contributing to the rise in allergy.

The good news is that if researchers can discover more about which specific aspects of the modern environment and lifestyle contribute to the development of the allergic conditions, you can modify the way you live to prevent allergy problems from occurring — you can change the environment you put yourself in to reduce the chances of allergy problems developing in your children. (In Chapter 3, we cover ways you can help prevent allergic diseases developing in babies and children in more detail.)

Judging genes and food allergies

One of the big questions families ask is why one child has food allergies and the other children don't. Often parents outline how they provided exactly the same nurturing environment for all of their children and yet only one (or two) was unlucky enough to develop food allergies or other allergic diseases.

While researchers have shown that allergic diseases such as asthma, eczema and hay fever run in families (meaning inheritance of genes must play a role in developing these types of allergic conditions), the research available on food allergies shows genes to be less of a factor in these conditions.

The evidence for a genetic risk of food allergy comes from two types of studies. The first type, which looks at rates of the conditions in very close relatives such as twins, is the strongest and most convincing. These studies show that an identical twin is significantly more likely to share peanut allergy with the twin sibling than a non-identical twin. However, the chance of identical twins both having peanut allergy isn't 100 per cent, demonstrating that having the same set of genes isn't sufficient to develop food allergy and other factors are required.

The second type of study looks at family risk of food allergy more generally. Fewer of these studies are available, but those that have been performed show an increased rate of food allergies in families with allergic conditions although the contribution of genes appears less than for the other allergic diseases such as eczema, asthma and hay fever. The reasons for this are unknown but point to the fact that the rise in food allergy is most likely something to do with a recent factor that has emerged in our 'modern' lifestyle, rather than inheriting food allergy genes from your parents.

 Although some families have multiple children with food allergies, this situation is actually the exception rather than the rule. Although food allergy can run in families, researchers can't find any direct inheritance links.

Looking at the immune system's role in food allergies

The immune system ultimately controls whether or not a person develops an allergic condition, and the immune system can, in turn, be influenced by a person's genes and the environment that person is exposed to. So, the status of a person's immune system at the time of being exposed to the food may be important in determining whether a food allergy develops. For example, if a person's immune system is secreting factors that promote the development of allergy at the time it's first exposed to that food, it may be more likely to react to the food with an allergic response rather than seeing the food as harmless.

All babies' immune systems are in a pro-allergic state in the first years of life, which may be why food allergy is more common in young children than adults, and why most food allergies disappear as children grow older.

Most children with immediate food allergy have their first allergic reaction to the food when they eat that food for the first time. This puzzles many people, and when we see children with food allergy in our clinic, parents often ask how it is possible to have an allergic reaction to a food that you have never eaten before. That a person's immune system must have at least seen the food previously to be able to mount an allergic response to it certainly makes sense.

What researchers have shown is that after a person has eaten a food, small amounts of the food's protein components can be found circulating in the blood, and they can also be detected in the breast milk if the mother is breastfeeding. So all babies have already been exposed to the common foods that their mother eats while they're in the womb or while they're being breastfed.

Of course, this is the situation for all mothers and babies, yet most babies don't develop food allergy, so the simple situation of being exposed to the food isn't sufficient to cause food allergy. Researchers are still trying to work out why only some (and not all) babies become allergic to foods that they're exposed to when they are developing in the womb or during breastfeeding, because this can help us learn about the important factors that cause food allergy.

Just being exposed to a food protein isn't the reason babies become allergic, and taking a food out of the mother's diet during pregnancy or breastfeeding has been shown to be of no benefit in preventing the baby developing an allergy to that food. In fact, in order for you to develop tolerance to a food, which is the natural situation for most foods in most people, you must have been exposed to that food. Being tolerant to the foods you eat involves a very active process in which your immune system has to specifically instruct the body to tolerate the food and not react against it.

Being allergic to a Western lifestyle

The increasing rates of allergic disease have only occurred in some parts of the world, mainly those countries with a Western lifestyle — that is, a more sedentary lifestyle spent indoors, with reduced exposure to good bacteria and a reduced intake of fresh fruit, vegetables and fish. So, along with economic growth and improved mortality rates, the trade-off has been increased rates of allergic disease.

Here we discuss some of the changes to living conditions that might have contributed to the growth in allergy problems.

Missing out on good bacteria — the hygiene hypothesis

The *hygiene hypothesis* suggests that reduced exposure to a broad range of microbial species due to improved living conditions and sanitation has led to the recent increases in allergic disease — in other words, yes, we humans are too clean! This means we're missing out on bugs, both on the inside and the outside.

Children with allergic disease (especially eczema) have an altered profile of intestinal bugs, with reduced diversity compared to healthy children without allergic disease, and these abnormalities are present from the first weeks of life — well before the allergic problem develops — suggesting that these abnormalities may be one of the factors causing the problem. Researchers are looking into whether preventing the development of eczema and other allergic diseases (including food allergy) might be made possible by changing the intestinal *microbiota*, or the living organisms in the gut, of affected children towards what's seen in healthy children.

Using *probiotics* (so-called good bugs) and *prebiotics* (indigestible fibres in foods that selectively promote the growth of good bugs) are two approaches that can change the profile and diversity of intestinal bugs towards that of a healthy person. Research into whether probiotic supplements taken by the pregnant mother and/or newborn, or prebiotic supplements taken by the newborn, can prevent allergic disease in the baby are ongoing and, while confirming whether these approaches are effective isn't yet possible, early results look promising. Further studies are needed to work out which probiotic or prebiotic mix might work, the best timing for treatment (for example, whether to the mother or baby or both), and the dose that should be used. However, modifying the profile of bugs in the intestine offers an exciting potential approach for prevention of allergic disease, so watch this space!

Increasing use of antibacterial household cleaners may also be a problem. An increasing number of TV and magazine ads promote the use of these products — and no doubt you want to make sure the area your baby eats and plays in is clean. However, the overuse of antibacterial cleaners, wipes and gels may not be the best thing for preventing allergy problems.

See Chapter 3 for how to introduce some good old-fashioned bugs into your children's lives.

Eating a Western diet

A reduced intake of fruits and vegetables and omega-3 fatty acids (found in fish oils) is common in a Western diet and has been linked to allergic sensitisation and allergic diseases. Reduced levels of antioxidant nutrients such as vitamin D and E and selenium also correlate with increased allergy problems. So, basically, you really are what you eat! Researchers are now looking at whether increasing the intake of these foods and nutrients can protect against the development of allergic diseases.

Food in developed or Western countries is also handled in special ways to reduce microorganisms and increase shelf-life. For example, milk is pasteurised so it can be kept longer without going off. This has probably contributed to reduced exposure to good bugs. The problem is that reducing microorganisms in food has led to reduced rates of illness and disease — so producers can't just stop doing it. Instead, researchers are exploring other ways of increasing people's exposure to good bugs.

Delaying giving foods to babies

Recent studies suggest that earlier introduction of foods (including the foods that commonly cause allergy) to children may reduce the chances of developing allergy to that food. Some studies also show that the chances of developing allergy to a food are particularly reduced if the food is introduced while a baby is still being breastfed — although our own HealthNuts study didn't confirm this.

The optimal timing for introducing foods is not really known, but studies suggest that an optimal 'window' for induction of tolerance might be between four and six months of age. See Chapter 3 for details on how and when to introduce food to your baby.

Avoiding the sun too much

Research has shown that some allergic diseases (although this has not been studied for food allergy) correlate inversely with the level of vitamin D in the blood — that is, people with lower levels of vitamin D have higher rates of allergic disease. Humans need UV light from sunlight to convert vitamin D to its active form, because vitamin D can't be made by cells in the body. The only evidence regarding its association with food allergy is that rates of food allergy and allergic disease do increase the further away you live from the equator, which is thought to be due in part to reduced exposure to UV light.

Kids generally are spending much less time outside in the sun these days compared to several decades ago. On top of that, parents have been told to 'slip, slop, slap' whenever their child goes in the sun, so kids get even less UV exposure. Because of the relationship between sunlight, vitamin D and allergy, researchers believe these trends are contributing to increased allergy.

Researchers still don't fully understand how UV light and vitamin D help to prevent disease, however, and research in this area is ongoing.

Taking too many antibiotics

Does a dark side exist to the public health benefits of the last 50 years? Are we overusing or misusing antibiotics for viral infections in children? Should we be banning antibiotics from cattle feed? Actually, we don't know for certain that antibiotics are contributing to allergy problems, but the widespread use of antibiotics for treating infections in children and also in the food chain could be contributing to reduced microbial exposure. Based on what we understand about the importance of being exposed to a broad range of microbial species, this reduction may not be a good thing.

The common antibiotics prescribed for infections kill many good bacteria in the gut, destroying the healthy microbiota profile. In older children and adults, this effect is only transient and, over time, the healthy microbiota profile returns. But in the first two years of life, especially in the early newborn period, antibiotics can lead to more prolonged changes in the microbiota.

Use antibiotics only when a bacterial infection that needs treatment is present, and avoid unnecessary use for viral infections. The first bacteria to colonise your baby's intestine are extremely important in determining whether or not your baby acquires a healthy microbiota profile.

Cooking foods can change allergens

Researchers are studying the various proteins in foods that cause allergic reactions, and whether changing the proteins so that people with allergies are less likely to react to them is possible. Studies have shown that heating or cooking proteins can degrade them — for example, cooking an egg rapidly destroys the protein present in the egg white that people with egg allergy react to. This may mean that some people who are allergic to egg can tolerate well-cooked egg but still react to raw or less well cooked forms of egg such as in cake mix or scrambled egg. This doesn't mean that all people with egg allergy can safely eat well-cooked egg, so you shouldn't try this at home. But the finding explains why someone with egg allergy may not react to all forms of egg.

The way we prepare foods can also have the opposite effect on some food allergens. For example, roasting peanuts increases the binding of allergy antibodies to the proteins in peanut that people are allergic to.

Chapter 3

Preventing Food Allergy in Kids

*W*hat steps can you take to prevent food allergy in your child? You may be pregnant and want to know whether you should avoid peanuts or not. Or perhaps your infant is fully breastfed and you don't know when you should start feeding solids. Perhaps you have an older child with allergies and want to know if you can prevent the condition occurring in your baby, or maybe you have a family history of allergic disease and are worried your children are at high risk. No doubt you're confused by all the conflicting advice from medical professionals, the internet and well-meaning friends and family.

As a parent, you want to know whether you should act now to change factors in your life to prevent your children from developing food allergy. But we only have theories about why food allergies are now more prevalent (refer to Chapter 2), so the advice we offer to our patients, and to you, to prevent food allergy in your children are only recommendations based on the latest and best data available.

In this chapter, we talk about the age food allergies usually rear their ugly heads in children, and discuss the research into preventative measures and the findings so far. We cover why you can't eliminate the risk of allergies entirely, but offer some insight into the current recommendations for how you can help prevent food allergies in your children. We also offer tips on introducing foods to your baby.

Establishing When Food Allergies Develop in Kids

Food allergies are most likely to first show up in infants and young children, with the majority appearing before the first birthday. In healthy babies, a critical window of opportunity exists (probably around the age of four to six months; see the section 'Introducing Foods into Baby's Diet', later in this chapter) when the body's immune system is ideally prepared to tolerate new foods. (The immune system and its involvement in food allergies is discussed further in Chapter 4). In some babies, the immune system doesn't develop properly — instead of developing tolerance to a food, the immune system decides to mount an immune response to the food and reject that food when it's eaten again. The body's inappropriate immune defence reaction to a food normally tolerated by most people is called an allergic reaction (refer to Chapter 1), and we still don't really understand why some children develop an allergy to a food and others don't.

Although food allergies are most likely to occur in early infancy or when first introduced into a diet, they can occur at any stage of a person's life. Curiously, adults appear more prone to nut (tree nut and peanut) and seafood (fish and shellfish) allergies than to the other common food allergies of early childhood, which include allergies to cow's milk, egg, soy and wheat. Children tend to outgrow most of the common allergies of early childhood (to egg, cow's milk, wheat and soy), while nut and seafood allergies are more likely to be lifelong. Allergies to other foods such as fruit and vegetables are less common in children but can occur in adolescence and adulthood, especially in association with hay fever.

Researching Ways to Prevent Food Allergies

Doctors and scientists would love to be able to prevent food allergies — not just in your child but in the whole generation of children now being born. Researchers are confident that this might be possible because the rise in food allergies is recent — so the cause must be within researchers' reach. Research has focused on trying to identify risk factors that are easy to change and safe for families to implement. (See the section 'Reducing the Chances of Food Allergy Developing in Kids' for guidelines available.)

Conducting a quality research trial

Research studies need to collect as much data about a situation as possible to make sure that researchers aren't missing out on any important information about contributory factors. Of course, when you're looking at something like food allergies, where many theories but very few facts exist for the rise in prevalence, studies have to try to be as all-inclusive about potential causes as possible.

Researchers mainly use two types of research studies to gather information:

- **Observational studies:** These are simply a gathering of observed data. However, different levels of quality for observational studies exist. For example, if a researcher is trying to determine how much food allergy is in the community, a properly conducted study that involves a large random sample of participants from the general population (a *population-based study*) is of much higher quality than one where a researcher goes to an allergy clinic and only recruits a small group of study participants. The latter study is likely to be biased and won't reflect a true population estimate of food allergy prevalence.

- **Clinical trials:** These are more like an experiment where a patient or animal is given an intervention to prevent or treat a food allergy. The best trials are those that are controlled (one group of participants don't receive the treatment and are called a control group) and those that are randomised (subjects are randomly allocated to receive either the active treatment being tested or a control (dummy)

treatment). Studies that are controlled and randomised are called randomised controlled trials (RCT). The researchers in these studies can then compare whether those who have had the intervention have fared better than those who didn't. In trials, a well-known phenomenon called the placebo effect can occur — where even patients who don't receive active treatment (and instead received the dummy control treatment) feel better. This effect is one of the important reasons why controlled trials are better in quality than uncontrolled trials.

A controlled trial can be undertaken in one of three ways:

- **Open trial:** Both the researchers and the patients know who is receiving the treatment and who isn't. If patients know they're receiving an intervention, they may think they're better even if the treatment hasn't worked — the placebo effect — which can undermine the veracity of the study findings.

- **Single blind trial:** Study participants are unaware of whether they're receiving the intervention or the placebo, but the researchers aren't blinded. Unfortunately, this knowledge can be unintentionally transmitted to study participants and again elicit a placebo effect.

- **Double blind trial:** Neither the researcher nor the participants know who's receiving the treatment and who's not until after the study is completed. Results of a double blind trial are the most reliable.

(continued)

(continued)

If the factor under consideration is something related to lifestyle, such as sunshine exposure or clean living, controlled trials become more difficult. What makes these studies even more difficult again is that study participants often seek information themselves (from sources like the internet) and may start the factor in their lives without declaring their actions to the researcher — which can make things very confusing if the participant is meant to be in the control arm of the study.

As covered in the preceding list, the very best sort of study is when both the participant and the researcher are ignorant of who has been allocated to the factor (the double blind study) but, again, blinding something like exposure to pets, farms or sunshine can be very hard!

Another major issue for allergy researchers is the concept of *reverse causation*. This is when the lifestyle factor is found to be associated with the outcome (that is, the food allergy) but in the reverse direction. Simply put, being at risk of food allergy is the reason someone has chosen a lifestyle factor — the lifestyle factor isn't the cause of the food allergy.

Breastfeeding can be used as an example. Many allergy guidelines have recommended that breastfeeding should be encouraged in order to prevent food allergies. Unfortunately, these guidelines are based on weak evidence that may be compromised by reverse causation. For example, people may choose to breastfeed for a whole host of reasons, including having read that breastfeeding may protect against allergic disease. But it is difficult to avoid this reverse causation, because an RCT would be unethical. Some research studies have found that prolonged breastfeeding was associated with a paradoxical increase in risk of developing allergies. However, this doesn't necessarily mean that prolonged breastfeeding causes allergies and its much more likely that those families at increased risk of allergy chose to breastfeed longer. This is a classic example of a confounding factor and every study in allergy needs to make sure this effect has been correctly adjusted for in its analysis. This may go some way to explain why sometimes researchers appear to describe opposite findings; one study may have correctly adjusted for this effect and the other may not have.

At the population level, work is being done to investigate the various factors that might contribute to the development of food allergies — for example, studies examining the protective effect of TB vaccination, and the role of food processing and the widespread use of antibiotics in increasing the risk of developing food allergies are all proceeding. The results of these studies are keenly awaited.

In order to prove whether a specific factor is a critical factor in developing a disease, controlled trials need to be undertaken; however, these are often difficult to implement. The most common way scientists initially assess whether a lifestyle factor or event might be associated with developing a disease is through observing the differences between groups who develop a disease and those who don't. However, observational trials don't necessarily control all of the other factors that might have an effect, and a controlled intervention trial is usually required to confirm whether or not a specific factor is important. (See the sidebar 'Conducting a quality research trial' for explanations of the different types of trials.)

The quality of information provided by observational studies can be improved by studying a large population, and the findings from these bigger studies tend to be more robust. However, large population studies take a long time — so the results can take a few years to finally make their way to the public domain. Smaller studies take less time to complete (and so results can be released more quickly), but the evidence released may be less reliable due to the smaller scale. So, even though some early findings seem to be very promising, doctors and expert committees may not change guidelines to reflect these new findings until confirmatory studies of a better quality are completed.

Finding Out If Your Child Is at High Risk of Food Allergy

Until recently, guidelines for the prevention of food allergy were only recommended for those infants with a family history of allergic disorders, because these children were perceived to be at high risk and because most studies looking at prevention strategies had focused on such babies. This group was previously thought to be a small proportion of the population; however, in recent times, a very high rate of family history of allergic disease has been reported in the community, with 50 to 70 per cent of all families reporting that at least one member has a history of one of the allergic conditions, such as eczema, food allergy, asthma or allergic rhinitis. So those with a family history of allergic disease don't represent a small, high-risk population — rather, they represent the majority of the population! Because of this, more recent recommendations regarding introduction of foods apply to everyone, not just high-risk families.

You can reduce but not eliminate the risk of your child developing a food allergy. When it comes to reducing versus eliminating risk, everyone views risk differently. While one family may believe that a one in a million chance of an allergic reaction is totally unacceptable, another may be comfortable with a very occasional, mild reaction from an accidental ingestion of a food, provided that the reaction is not severe and life-threatening. (That's not to say that we recommend this latter attitude — rather, we've just made this observation in our clinics.)

Understanding your own comfort level for risk is important when you're deciding which lifestyle choices you're prepared to make for preventing the development of food allergy in your kids, and also for preventing an allergic reaction to food if your child has already been diagnosed with food allergy. (We discuss how to minimise risk of allergic reactions in Chapter 7.)

What doesn't protect against food allergy

You may have heard of a variety of ways to help reduce the chances of your child developing food allergy. Here, we list the most common theories, and look at whether any of these ideas are supported by evidence:

✔ **A restricted diet:** No evidence is available to suggest that a restricted diet (that excludes the allergenic foods) prevents your child from developing food allergies.

✔ **An organic diet:** No evidence has proven that eating an organic diet provides protection against the development of food allergy.

✔ **Delayed introduction of certain foods:** Some older guidelines recommended

(incorrectly) delaying the introduction of certain allergenic foods (such as peanut, tree nuts, eggs and seafood) in the belief that avoidance would prevent the development of food allergy. Little evidence supports the theory that delaying the introduction of complementary solid foods beyond six months reduces the risk of allergy. In fact, delaying introduction of foods may actually increase (rather than decrease) allergy — although this is unproven at this stage. Almost all of the allergy guidelines from around the world have been changed to reflect the most up-to-date evidence about this.

Reducing the Chances of Food Allergy Developing in Kids

In our clinic, our advice for parents when it comes to food allergy is to 'do no harm' — we don't provide recommendations for prevention measures that could either endanger a child's life or have unexpected adverse consequences for children.

In the following sections, we cover some simple measures you can take to help reduce the risk of your child developing a food allergy.

The evidence supporting the recommendations we provide in the following sections isn't yet proven but expert groups have considered the evidence and agree that these recommendations can be made, based upon what's known and unlikely to cause harm.

Breastfeed for at least six months

If you can breastfeed (and we understand that not all mothers are able to), we advise that you do so until your baby is at least six months old, because some evidence suggests that breastfeeding for the first four months of life and also introducing a food while your baby is still breastfeeding may prevent food allergy.

Breastfeeding has been shown to have many health benefits for both you and your child, including strengthening the mother–infant bond, your baby having lower rates of infection in early life, and a lower rate of obesity, cardiovascular disease and diabetes for your baby later in life.

In general, infants can start trying solid food between the ages of four and six months, and breastfeeding during the period that foods are first introduced may help prevent the development of allergy to those foods.

If infant formula is required in the first months of life before solid foods are introduced, the evidence available about which formula to use is conflicting. The Australasian Society of Clinical Immunology and Allergy (ASCIA), the American Association of Paediatrics (AAP) and the European Society of Pediatric Gastroenterology, Hepatology and Nutrition (ESPGHAN) guidelines for the prevention of allergic disease all recommend introducing a hydrolysed formula in infants with a family history of allergic disease if breastfeeding isn't possible in the first four to six months of life.

However, these guidelines don't specifically address the development of food allergy and are mainly directed at reducing the development of eczema (because most studies have only found an effect on reducing eczema). As well, recent studies continue to report conflicting findings with the most recently published study showing no benefit from hydrolysed formulas in preventing food allergy.

A *meta-analysis* (which combines the results from all available high-quality studies) is often relied upon to provide the best level of evidence on which to base expert guidelines, and the Cochrane meta-analysis is generally considered to offer the highest quality analysis of all of data. The international guidelines for the prevention of allergic disease, as described above, are based in part upon the 2006 and 2009 Cochrane meta-analyses of hydrolysed formulas for the prevention of allergic disease. However, in light of recent findings from new studies, the Cochrane meta-analysis is being updated and, after the newer studies are included, the meta-analysis may change. Guidelines are likely to be revised in the light of these more recent findings, with the potential that hydrolysed formula may no longer be recommended for allergy prevention.

In Australia and New Zealand, only partially hydrolysed (HA) formulas are available to be used for the prevention of allergic disease — extensively hydrolysed formulas (eHF) are only available with a doctor's prescription for the treatment of cow's milk and soy allergy. (See Chapter 7 for more on hydrolysed formulas for the treatment of food allergy.)

If you're breastfeeding, go ahead and eat a wide range of foods; no evidence suggests that avoiding foods like peanut or egg if you're pregnant or breastfeeding prevents an allergy. And no evidence suggests that eating those foods during pregnancy or lactation protects a child from developing allergy either.

Introduce solids at around six months

We recommend that you expose your baby to a wide and varied diet early on — at around four to six months of age (see the sidebar 'Working out the ideal time to start solids'). If your child hasn't experienced an allergic reaction to a food, no reason exists to avoid any particular food with the hope of preventing an allergy. See the section 'Introducing Foods into Baby's Diet', later in this chapter, for more.

At last count, Australia has at least eight infant feeding guidelines from various organisations including the State Department of Human Services, the National Health and Medical Research Council (whose guidelines are effectively compliant with the World Health Organization's) and the Australasian Society of Clinical Immunology and Allergy. Unfortunately, these guidelines each say something slightly different about the ideal time to introduce solids into your baby's diet.

More research is needed to determine the optimal time to start complementary solid foods. But based on the evidence available, many experts across Europe, Australia, New Zealand and North America recommend introducing complementary solid foods from around four to six months.

Working out the ideal time to start solids

Recommendations about when to introduce solids have dramatically changed over the last 40 years. In the 1960s and early 1970s, babies who were bottle-fed often had cereal added to the bottle. (Presumably in order to 'fatten them up' — a more common objective in the post-war era, when food deprivation was a recent memory and before the obesity epidemic had become the problem it is today.)

However, in the mid-1970s this practice was thought by some experts to have contributed to the rise in *coeliac disease* (a form of wheat intolerance) that seemed to be happening around that time. So the recommendation was changed to delay the introduction of solids until four to six months of age. This recommendation remained until about 15 years ago, when the World Health Organization (WHO) started recommending exclusive breastfeeding of all infants for at least six months, and delaying the introduction of solids until after six months.

The main reason for this latest change was the fact that infant mortality rates in developing countries are reduced if mothers breastfeed for longer. This is partly because of the good nutritional qualities of breast milk and its ability to protect against infant infections through its immune properties, but also because formula feeds require a clean water supply in order to be safely consumed and this is not reliably available in some developing countries. Adequate sterilisation of bottles and teats is also required for bottle feeding and isn't readily available in some developing countries. So the WHO recommendation to avoid the introduction of solids until after six months was at least partly made to improve infant mortality in the developing world.

Recently, however, allergy experts have wondered whether a critical window of opportunity may exist when the immune system is best prepared to learn to tolerate foods. This window is thought to be between four and six months of age, and allergy experts recommend introducing solids at this time. The most confusing thing for parents now is that two conflicting guidelines exist: One saying delay introducing solids until after six months (and exclusively breastfeed until that time) and the other saying to go ahead and start feeding solids to your baby at four to six months. One way to satisfy both criteria is to simply aim to introduce solids around the four- to six-month mark while continuing to breastfeed.

Let babies get down and dirty

As we discuss in Chapter 2, some evidence exists that people in Westernised societies need to expose themselves to more (healthy) bugs rather than stay too clean. Evolving evidence suggests that children exposed to a broad range of 'good bugs' may be protected against food allergy.

Good germs on the outside

Although scientists talk about exposure to 'good bugs' in the environment, we should emphasise that this is based on very little evidence — mostly small observational studies. Research to date has mostly examined how the development of asthma was affected by living on a farm in Germany during pregnancy and the first years of life for the baby, so translating these findings to food allergy and our lifestyle in Australia is difficult.

With those caveats in mind, here are a few things we think might help to get some good bacteria into your children's lives:

- **Let your child muck about in the dirt.** Encourage your child to play outside and don't worry if your child rolls about in the dirt — playing outside is certainly better than staying inside watching television or playing computer games. Of course, children should wash their hands before eating so they don't get worms.

- **Avoid using antibacterial cleaners to clean kitchen benchtops and surfaces.** Cleaning benchtops and surfaces with soap and water is a good way to remove harmful bacteria, and your child is very unlikely to catch a serious infection from your own home. Mums have been cleaning benchtops this way for many years!

Researchers haven't been able to work out whether having a pet in the home when you're growing up can protect you against allergic disease. Studies examining this question have found conflicting results, with some studies showing beneficial effects and others showing no effect or increased allergic disease symptoms. So, for the time being, allergy experts don't recommend either buying a pet or getting rid of your family pet for the purposes of preventing food allergy or other allergic diseases.

Good germs on the inside

The jury is still out on whether prebiotics and probiotics can prevent food allergies or other allergic conditions (refer to Chapter 2 for more on these). The effects of probiotics and prebiotics on preventing allergic conditions can vary dramatically — depending on the type of bug or prebiotic fibre used, the dose, and when it's given (whether to the mother during pregnancy or to the baby in the first months of life, or both).

TIP

Restoring healthy microbiota may help allergic conditions

Probiotics and prebiotics can modify the intestinal *microbiota*, or bacteria, providing a more healthy balance of bugs in the gut. Because of this, they have been tested as a way to prevent or treat allergic conditions. *Probiotics* are live microbial organisms that benefit the host by improving intestinal microbial balance. A *prebiotic* is an indigestible fibre taken in the diet that can selectively stimulate the growth and/or activity of good bacteria in the gut microbiota.

Lactobacilli and Bifidobacteria are the most frequently used probiotics. The lactobacillus bacteria love to live off lactose (the main sugar in milk), which is why they're called lactobacillus. Probiotics are available from most health food stores and probiotic drinks are available at supermarkets. Doctors argue about whether refrigerated versions of probiotics are better than those stored on the shelf because refrigerated versions are more likely to include bugs that are still alive. However, some evidence suggests that even dead probiotic bugs have a protective gut colonising effect, possibly because they act like prebiotics and encourage the healthy growth of bugs already residing in your gut.

Studies show that probiotics may be able to prevent allergic disease, but researchers are still trying to work out which bacteria work best, when they need to be taken and the dose that's needed. So at this time, they can't be recommended for the prevention of allergic conditions. However, the studies that have been published suggest that giving probiotics to mothers during late pregnancy as well as to babies in the first six to twelve months of life is important for benefits to be seen.

Prebiotics are important nutrients for the beneficial bacteria in the intestine. They're broken down by the good bacteria into short chain fatty acids, which can have important effects on your immune system. Breast milk has high levels of oligosaccharides (prebiotics) that may help to promote a healthy immune system in your baby. Baby formula companies sometimes add either probiotics or prebiotics to their infant formulas. High levels of prebiotics are found in chicory root, Jerusalem artichoke and dandelion greens; lower levels are found in whole grains. Prebiotics are also available as supplements.

Fewer studies of prebiotics for preventing allergic conditions are available — just three studies look at the effects of prebiotic supplements given to babies in the first six months of life on eczema and other allergic problems. Two of these studies showed beneficial effects, while one did not. Different prebiotic fibres and different doses were used in the various studies. So, for both probiotics and prebiotics, experts still have a lot to learn before they understand if these agents work to prevent allergic problems and, if so, how they do this.

Most studies that used probiotics starting in pregnancy and then continuing on into the first six to twelve months of the baby's life showed beneficial effects on preventing the development of eczema — although the effects on food allergy are still unknown. On the other hand, most studies that gave probiotics only to babies after they were born for the first six to twelve months of life (and not to mothers during pregnancy) didn't protect against developing eczema or other allergic conditions and one study actually resulted in increased sensitisation (positive skin prick test) in the babies.

Mimi's own study, which looked at whether giving a probiotic (LGG) to mothers during the last weeks of pregnancy (without treating the babies) might protect their babies from developing eczema, found no beneficial effects. This tells us that treating both the pregnant mother and the baby (or mother if breastfeeding) for the first six to twelve months of the baby's life is important for beneficial effects.

Further studies are needed to work out which bugs or prebiotics should be used, as well as the dose and the best timing for treatment, before these can be used to prevent allergic disease. (See the sidebar 'Restoring healthy microbiota may help allergic conditions' for more.)

Get some sunshine in your life

Evolving evidence suggests that children without enough vitamin D (either through insufficient sun exposure or through a deficient diet) are at increased risk of food allergy.

Humans can't produce vitamin D — it's made in your skin when you're exposed to sunlight and is also found in foods like eggs and fish. As well as being an essential substance for life, vitamin D appears to have a number of important specific functions in the body, including keeping the immune system in good shape.

If you had low vitamin D when you were pregnant (and didn't take supplements before your baby was born), your infant has a good chance of having low levels also. In Australia and New Zealand, about 20 per cent of mothers are low in vitamin D. This is most likely due to the success of the sunscreen campaign, which has been great for decreasing rates of malignant melanoma but perhaps has had an unexpected impact by increasing food allergies in children — although this is highly contentious and only indirect evidence is available to support this hypothesis.

Try to optimise your child's exposure to sunlight and increase vitamin D intake through diet. The Osteoporosis Society of Australia recommends that to get enough sunlight to produce vitamin D you need to expose your hands, face and arms (around 15 per cent of body surface) to sunlight for about six to eight minutes, four to six times per week (before 10 am or after 2 pm Australian Standard Time in summer, for moderately fair people). Dark-skinned people need longer exposure times of around 15 minutes. So encourage outdoor activity and plenty of sunshine during the early to mid-morning and late afternoon.

Exposure to sunlight between 10 am and 2 pm in the summer months (11 am to 3 pm during Daylight Saving Time) isn't recommended due to the cancerous effects of sunlight at that time, which outweigh any possible benefits from vitamin D production. Make sure children wear appropriate hats and sunscreen to prevent burning during the peak risk hours of the middle of the day in summer.

Figure 3-1 summarises the possible prevention measures for food allergy.

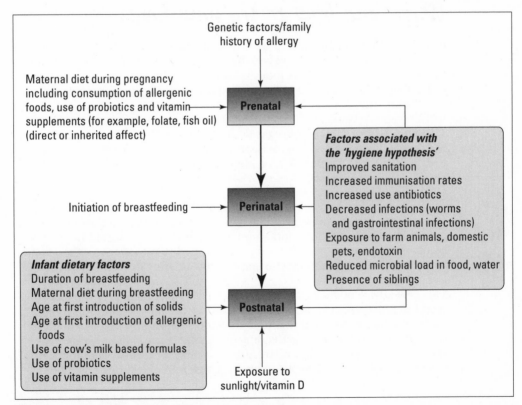

Figure 3-1: Food allergy and possible prevention measures.

Introducing Foods into Baby's Diet

Starting a baby on solids is a very exciting milestone for parents. Unfortunately, a lot of confusion surrounds the decision about the ideal time to introduce foods into an infant's diet. This is not a new phenomenon: Experts have been arguing about this for decades and, as such, over the last 40 to 50 years, quite a dramatic change has taken place in the recommended start time. (Refer to the sidebar 'Working out the ideal time to start solids' for more.)

So where does that leave you as parents or carers trying to decide when to start introducing solids into your baby's diet? And are all foods the same or should you follow a special order of introduction? The following sections offer some guidelines.

When and how to try new foods

In the past, parents and carers were told to delay introduction of foods that commonly cause allergy. However, the recommendation now is to continue breastfeeding for at least six months and to introduce complementary foods (including those that are common causes of food allergy) from four to six months of age.

This advice is for all babies, regardless of whether they have a family history of allergic disease (babies with a family history of allergic disease have a higher risk for developing allergic disease). Even babies with eczema should follow this advice.

In our HealthNuts study of 5,000 infants in Melbourne, we found that about 45 per cent of the population is introducing solids at four to five months and a further 45 per cent at around about six months. So you would be in good company if you were to introduce solids around four to six months — a time when your baby is probably starting to show interest in food anyway.

This new advice might be confusing because it contradicts the current World Health Organization recommendations for infant feeding, adopted by the Australian National Health and Medical Research Council, which recommends exclusive breastfeeding of all infants for at least six months. However, in the setting of a Westernised country with good sanitation, where low risk exists of babies becoming sick from infectious diarrhoea due to poor sanitation, and where allergic diseases are the most common chronic illnesses affecting children, advising earlier introduction of complementary solid feeds from four to six months onwards is reasonable.

Introducing solids is an important milestone in your baby's life and in yours. Start introducing foods into your infant's diet only when she's ready. This might be when your baby is grabbing food off your spoon. Babies don't need to read books — they know when they're hungry and when they're ready!

Stay calm, keep your sense of humour and, most importantly, have a camera or DVD recorder close by to record some of the outright hilarious things babies do when they're learning that most basic skill of eating.

Here are some tips on how to introduce solids to your baby:

- ✔ Make sure your child is sitting comfortably and isn't too hungry (not too many hours have passed since the last breastfeed or bottle-feed).

- ✔ Start with a single food rather than a mixture. Try half to one teaspoon after a milk feed.

- ✔ If your baby refuses the first time, try again in a day or so.

- ✔ Introduce a new food every few days, waiting until a food is tolerated before you introduce the next, so that you can watch for any adverse reactions.

  If your baby develops redness around the mouth, an itchy skin rash (such as hives, which are bumps that look like mosquito bites) or vomiting within a few minutes of ingestion, stop and seek medical advice.

- ✔ Avoid small hard foods such as nuts and uncooked vegetables, due to risk of choking. But nut products such as peanut butter or nut pastes are fine.

- ✔ Be prepared for mess as your baby learns to eat. Babies love to explore the food they're eating, which can include throwing it on the floor to see what happens. Stay with your baby during a feed, and sit your baby with the family during meal times so your baby can watch and learn feeding skills.

Expect to see a change in bowel habits when your baby starts eating foods other than just milk.

Which foods to introduce in what order

Once you've made the decision to start introducing solids to your baby, your next question may be what foods you should start with, and when and how you should start building up variety. Here's an outline of our recommended process:

1. **Start by introducing pureed vegetables, fruit or rice cereal to your baby by spoon.**

   You can serve these with added liquid — either expressed breast milk, boiled cooled water or the baby's complementary formula.

   Breast milk or an appropriate infant formula should remain the main source of milk until 12 months of age, although cow's milk can be used in cooking or with other foods.

2. **Slowly expand baby's diet, as tolerated.**

   Offer fresh fruits and a wider variety of cereals and legumes. You can then follow this with the introduction of yoghurt, egg custard and nut pastes. (Introduce a new food every few days, watching for signs of an allergic reaction — see the preceding section for more.)

3. **Keep increasing the variety, as tolerated.**

   Include bread, crackers, pasta, wheat-based breakfast cereals, cow's milk on cereal, cheese, egg, fish, other seafood, nut products and foods containing nuts.

Part II
Defining Food Allergies

Glenn Lumsden

*'Sorry, but the doctor says you aren't allergic
to broccoli, homework or making your bed.'*

In this part ...

Most people have heard about food allergies but many people are confused about what exactly a food allergy is and what has gone wrong to cause it. Many people have experienced an unpleasant reaction to a food at some time, and some think that this is a food allergy. But that isn't correct — most reactions to foods aren't food allergies. So, what is a food allergy and how do you know if you have one? If you're confused by all of this, don't worry — you're not alone.

In this part, we explain what a food allergy is, and how it's different to a food intolerance. Also, we describe the different types of food allergy — the immediate, IgE mediated, food allergies and the delayed, non-IgE mediated and mixed IgE/non-IgE mediated, food allergies — and examine the common foods that cause allergies in children. Diagnosing food allergies can be tricky and we look at the different allergy tests that can help your doctor diagnose food allergy.

Chapter 4

Identifying Immediate Food Allergies

*F*ood allergies are now much more common than they were 50 years ago, so most people are familiar with the term. But food allergies are not all the same. Two main types of food allergy are known — immediate and delayed allergy — and each is caused by different immune responses and, therefore, results in quite different symptoms. As well, the symptoms of an immediate food allergy can differ, depending on how severe the allergy reaction is (whether mild or more severe). And the age at which a food allergy develops can vary, depending on the specific food allergy (whether egg, milk or peanut and so on).

In this chapter, we focus on immediate food allergies. These allergies, which most people are more familiar with, usually cause easily recognised symptoms such as hives or swelling very quickly after the food is eaten. You find out what can happen to people when they eat a food they're allergic to, and what symptoms they can develop. You discover how a mild to moderate allergic reaction is different to a severe allergic reaction (anaphylaxis), and how to recognise a severe allergic reaction. You also learn about the foods involved in immediate allergies — and the similarities and differences between the common immediate food allergies.

Note: Delayed food allergies mainly cause gut symptoms many hours after a food is eaten. These allergies are discussed in Chapter 5.

Explaining Immediate Food Allergies

When Mimi tells someone she's just met that she's a doctor who specialises in food allergies, the person often says something like, 'Oh yeah — that's when a person eats a food and gets hives, swells up and dies!' Most people know about the immediate food allergies and may have read about anaphylaxis and how the condition can kill you. So parents often become anxious and terrified on hearing about their child's condition. But this extreme level of worry isn't really justified — to quote former Australian prime minister John Howard, being 'alert, but not alarmed' is important.

In Chapter 1, we talk about how an allergy develops when the immune system recognises something as harmful and mounts a reaction to it. In the case of an immediate food allergy, the immune system recognises a food you've eaten as harmful and generates allergy antibodies (IgE) against that food. Each subsequent time you eat that food, the IgE antibodies recognise the food and activate specialised allergy cells, called *mast cells*, to release allergy factors (histamine, leukotrienes and others) that cause the rapid development of symptoms (see Figure 4-1).

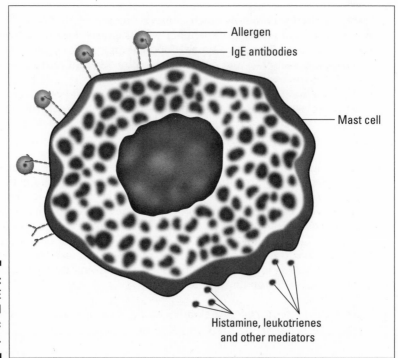

Allergen
IgE antibodies
Mast cell

Figure 4-1:
An IgE
mediated
allergic
response.

Histamine, leukotrienes
and other mediators

The key features of an immediate food allergy reaction are, firstly, that symptoms develop rapidly after eating the food (typically within ten minutes and usually within one hour) and, secondly, that changes can affect just four parts of the body — your skin, intestines, airways and circulation. Immediate allergic reactions to foods can range from mild skin reactions to severe anaphylaxis, which is life-threatening. The parts of the body that become involved in an immediate allergic reaction are what determines whether a reaction is classified as mild, moderate or severe.

The majority of immediate allergic reactions are mild or moderate with skin symptoms — severe reactions (anaphylaxis) are uncommon. So if your child accidentally eats a food she's allergic to, a mild or moderate reaction is most likely. Knowing this can help to allay unnecessary anxiety. Of course, you must be alert and prepared, and know about how to minimise the chances of your child having a severe reaction and how to recognise and deal with a severe reaction (we discuss these aspects in Chapter 7). But being constantly anxious and fearful of the possibility of a severe reaction isn't necessary.

Understanding mild to moderate allergic reactions

Immediate food allergy reactions affecting your skin or intestines are considered mild to moderate because they don't pose a risk to a person's life. Skin symptoms include redness, itching, hives and/or swelling of the skin tissue. These changes in the skin are most commonly seen around the mouth and on the face, but can involve the entire body. Hives, also referred to by doctors as *urticaria*, look like welts or mosquito bites on the skin (see Figure 4-2). Swelling of the skin tissue, referred to by doctors as *angioedema*, is most frequently seen affecting the face, especially the eyes and lips (see Figure 4-3) but can also be more widespread.

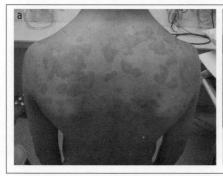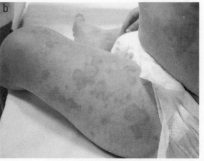

Figure 4-2:
Hives on a patient's skin.

Source: Images courtesy of medicalpix.com

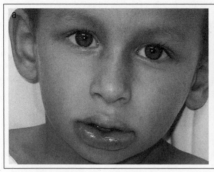

Figure 4-3:
Swelling
of the eye
and lip.

Parents are understandably terrified when they see these changes developing within just a few minutes — for example, their child's face can become swollen and distorted to such an extent that the child is unrecognisable. However, we can assure you that these changes in the skin, while disfiguring and frightening, don't put your child's life at risk.

When the intestines are involved, you can develop vomiting, nausea, tummy pain and sometimes even diarrhoea. As is typical for the immediate food allergies, these symptoms develop soon after you eat the food you're allergic to, usually within one hour. The gut reactions that occur with immediate food allergy can be very distressing for the person experiencing them but aren't life-threatening.

Being able to recognise how severe your child's allergic reaction is means you can then work out what you should do to manage the reaction, and how rapidly you need to take action, using the action plan you have developed with your child's doctor (see Chapter 11).

Demystifying anaphylaxis

If your child's allergic reaction affects the airway, your child's ability to get oxygen can be compromised. If the reaction affects the circulation, the delivery of blood (and, therefore, oxygen) to the brain and heart can be reduced. These serious reactions are called *anaphylaxis* and they can pose a risk to life.

A severe anaphylaxis reaction caused by foods usually affects the airways and only rarely involves the circulation. If the airway is involved, you can experience persistent coughing, hoarse voice, wheezing, noisy breathing or difficulty breathing. If the circulation is involved, loss of consciousness and collapse may occur.

Signs of mild to moderate allergic reactions and anaphylaxis

The following list provides a summary of the symptoms of mild to moderate allergic reactions, and of anaphylaxis.

Signs of a mild to moderate allergic reaction (listed in order of frequency of symptoms in cases):

✔ Hives

✔ Swelling of the lips, eyes or face

✔ Vomiting and abdominal pain

Signs of anaphylaxis — any of the above signs together with any one of the following (listed in order of frequency of symptoms in cases):

✔ Persistent coughing

✔ Hoarse voice

✔ Wheezing or noisy breathing

✔ Difficulty breathing

✔ Pale and floppy (infants and young children)

✔ Loss of consciousness or collapse

Babies and young children usually don't collapse when their circulatory system becomes involved during a severe anaphylaxis reaction. Instead, they appear pale and floppy. See the sidebar 'Signs of mild to moderate allergic reactions and anaphylaxis' for more about warning signs.

The accepted expert definition of anaphylaxis is 'a systemic allergic reaction that is life-threatening'. The Australasian Society of Clinical Immunology and Allergy (ASCIA) further defines anaphylaxis as a systemic allergic reaction that involves (i) the skin or gut *and* (ii) the respiratory or cardiovascular systems or both. The fundamental principle is that if the airway or circulation is involved then the reaction is potentially life-threatening and is classified as anaphylaxis, but the ASCIA definition also requires that the skin or gut be involved. (See the sidebar 'Criteria for diagnosing anaphylaxis' for more.)

In Mimi's study of anaphylaxis admissions to the Royal Children's Hospital, most children with food anaphylaxis presented with skin and airway involvement (hives and/or swelling of the lips or eyes together with wheezing or hoarse voice), and only rarely did the symptoms indicate involvement of the circulation (pale or floppy, low blood pressure or collapse).

Deaths from food allergy are very rare. Cumulative data from studies of anaphylaxis in Western countries has found that the prevalence of anaphylaxis is approximately five to ten per 100,000 patient years, and the estimated prevalence of anaphylaxis deaths is one to three per million patient years. This compares with a rate of food allergy in childhood of around eight per 100 children (around 8 per cent). Around 1 per cent of all food allergy reactions are anaphylaxis, and of these 0.5 to 2 per cent are fatal. In Mimi's study of all anaphylaxis deaths in Australia from 1997 to 2005 inclusive, only seven deaths occurred due to food anaphylaxis. Of course, any death of a child due to food allergy is a tragedy, and doctors, researchers and families alike must make every effort to prevent such a devastating outcome.

Criteria for diagnosing anaphylaxis

An international expert group has developed a set of criteria for the diagnosis of anaphylaxis to help doctors more quickly identify a patient who might have anaphylaxis.

The first definition is exactly the same as the ASCIA definition of anaphylaxis, which stipulates that the skin or gut *and* the respiratory or cardiovascular systems or both must be involved. But, in addition, two other situations have been included where, if exposure to a known allergen for the patient is likely, clinicians can make a diagnosis of anaphylaxis and so start treatment.

Here's a listing of what these additional situations are regarding clinical criteria for diagnosing anaphylaxis. *Note:* Anaphylaxis is likely when one of the following two criteria is fulfilled:

✔ **Two or more of the following that occur rapidly after exposure to a likely allergen for that patient (minutes to several hours):**

- Involvement of the skin-mucosal tissue (for example, generalised hives, itch, flush, swollen lips/tongue/uvula)

- Respiratory compromise (for example, dyspnea, wheeze-bronchospasm, stridor, reduced PEF, hypoxemia)

- Reduced BP or associated symptoms (for example, hypotonia (collapse), syncope, incontinence)

- Persistent gastrointestinal symptoms (for example, crampy abdominal pain, vomiting)

✔ **Reduced BP after exposure to known allergen for that patient (minutes to several hours):**

- Infants and children: Low systolic BP (age specific) or greater than 30 per cent decrease in systolic BP

- Adults: Systolic BP of less than 90 mm Hg or greater than 30 per cent decrease from that person's baseline

The clinical criteria outlined in the preceding list are very useful for doctors who are treating patients in an emergency, and help doctors identify situations when anaphylaxis may be likely so that they can start treatment as early as possible. On the other hand, these criteria may also over-diagnose anaphylaxis, because patients could be classified as having anaphylaxis when they may not even have been exposed to the allergen in question.

For example, if a patient with a known food allergy developed low blood pressure, or hives and vomiting for other reasons without having eaten the food he is allergic to, he might be diagnosed by the doctor as having anaphylaxis and treated immediately, to avoid the potentially dangerous situation of waiting for more symptoms to develop before starting treatment.

While these international criteria help doctors manage patients better in an emergency, they are less helpful in other clinical care settings and in research because they may diagnose anaphylaxis incorrectly. In the end, the specific criteria that doctors and research- ers use depend on whether they are trying to diagnose anaphylaxis in order to treat a patient in an emergency or whether they are trying to accurately diagnose anaphylaxis for ongoing patient care or a research study.

Contemplating Common Food Allergies

Most people eat many different types of food, yet the healthy immune system is programmed to ignore these antigens and not react to them in a harmful way. And among the hundreds of different foods available in the world, only a handful of foods commonly cause food allergy.

In Western countries such as Australia and New Zealand, for example, just eight food groups cause 90 per cent of all immediate food allergies — these foods are egg, cow's milk, peanut, tree nuts, wheat, soy, fish and shellfish. Even more intriguing is the finding that the types of food causing allergy in children are different to those in adults. The most common food allergies in children are egg, milk, peanut, tree nuts, followed by wheat and soy, whereas the commonest food allergies in adults are peanut, tree nut, fish and shellfish.

Food allergy is more common in children than in adults. Children grow out of most food allergies by the time they are ten to fifteen years old.

In the following sections, we look at the more common food allergies: Egg, cow's milk and peanut.

Examining eggs

Egg allergy is the most common food allergy in children. Egg allergy is usually discovered in the first year of life or shortly afterwards, which is the time when egg is usually introduced into an infant's diet. As is the common course for all food allergies in children, an allergic reaction to egg typically occurs the very first time a child eats some egg. Children with immediate egg allergy have IgE antibodies that react to certain proteins in egg, or *egg allergens*.

The prevalence of egg allergy depends on age and geographical location, and is highest in early childhood and in countries with a Westernised lifestyle. In Westernised countries, egg allergy affects 1 to 2 per cent of children.

Our population-based HealthNuts study of food allergy in Melbourne found that around 8 per cent of 12-month-old infants had challenge-proven egg allergy, which is the highest reported prevalence in the world.

The most common egg allergens are found in the egg white: Ovomucoid, ovalbumin, ovotransferrin and lysozyme, with ovomucoid being the most common allergen that children are allergic to. Some children also have IgE antibodies to allergens in the egg yolk but being allergic to egg yolk and not the egg white is rare.

Eggs are commonly found in the following foods:

- Custard and marshmallows
- Mayonnaise, béarnaise sauce and hollandaise sauce
- Meringue and pavlova
- Quiche, frittata and omelette

The majority of immediate allergic reactions to egg are mild, with common symptoms including the following:

- Hives around the mouth or generalised over the body
- Swelling of the eyes or lips that develops within minutes to an hour after eating egg
- Vomiting and abdominal pain

More severe reactions can cause (in order of most common)

- Persistent coughing
- Hoarse voice
- Wheezing
- Noisy breathing
- Difficulty breathing (in more severe reactions)

In the most severe allergic reactions, the circulation is involved, meaning infants and young children can go pale and floppy while older children can have loss of consciousness and collapse. But keep in mind that death from egg allergy is rare. Mimi's recent study of anaphylaxis deaths in Australia over a nine-year period found no recorded cases of death from egg allergy.

Egg allergens are *heat labile*, which means that the structure of the egg protein is rapidly changed by heat from cooking. This explains why some children who are allergic to egg may be able to eat cooked forms of egg, such as in quiche, without having an allergic reaction, but react to raw or less well cooked forms of egg, such as scrambled egg, cake batter, or mayonnaise. Ask your doctor about whether your child should avoid baked foods that contain small amounts of egg, or if these foods are safe to eat.

Vaccines: May contain egg protein

Children with egg allergy can react to vaccines that contain low amounts of egg protein. The influenza vaccine (the flu vaccine) and the yellow fever vaccine are made by growing the vaccine in eggs, and small amounts of egg protein are present in the final vaccine. The flu vaccine is the main vaccine of relevance in our Australian and New Zealand setting, and the actual amount of egg protein can vary from batch to batch.

Nevertheless, most children with egg allergy can safely receive the influenza vaccine — although this should be supervised by an allergy specialist or a specialised immunisation centre that's familiar with administering the vaccine to children with egg allergy. Children with egg allergy who need the flu vaccine can usually have the vaccine without any further testing, provided this is done in a specialist centre. However, if your child has had anaphylaxis to egg, your child usually needs to undergo skin testing to the vaccine, and the vaccine can then be administered according to a careful schedule to minimise the risks of a reaction if one develops.

Most allergic reactions to the vaccine are actually to other components of the vaccine, and occur in people who don't have egg allergy.

Note: The measles mumps rubella vaccine (MMR) doesn't carry the same concern as for the flu vaccine or yellow fever vaccine. The measles and mumps components are grown in chicken embryo cell cultures (not chicken egg). Studies have proven that children with egg allergy don't have an increased risk of reaction to the MMR compared to children who don't have egg allergy. This means MMR can be given to children with egg allergy without any special testing.

If your child is allergic to egg, avoid both cooked and raw forms of egg because being sure how well cooked the food that contains egg will be is difficult.

If your child is allergic to hen's egg, she's likely to also be allergic to eggs from other birds such as duck, goose or quail. However, egg allergy isn't the same as being allergic to chicken, so children with egg allergy can eat chicken without difficulty.

Most children grow out of their egg allergy by the time they are in high school, with one study reporting that two-thirds of children with the condition no longer have egg allergy by 16 years of age.

Cakes and biscuits and other similar delights

One issue that remains controversial is whether children with egg allergy need to exclude from their diet foods that contain small amounts of baked egg, such as cakes and biscuits.

The baking process involves very high temperatures and most baked foods contain very small amounts of egg (for example, a whole cake often contains just one egg), so most children with egg allergy can tolerate baked foods such as cakes and biscuits.

Nevertheless, the reason for the controversy is that being sure how much egg is in a baked food is difficult — with mud cakes, for example, containing up to eight eggs. On top of this, researchers don't know if eating small amounts of egg can delay the disappearance of egg allergy.

Therefore, some doctors recommend that if your child is allergic to egg, you should exclude all forms of egg from your child's diet, including small amounts of egg in baked goods, arguing a risk of allergic reaction always exists if you're unsure how much egg is contained within the baked food and that you may delay your child growing out of their egg allergy.

Other doctors recommend that you can continue to include baked foods if your child is already tolerating these, contending that this approach is more convenient for the family and that no strong evidence really exists that eating such small amounts of egg delays the disappearance of egg allergy.

Our own recent research into this showed that eating small amounts of egg in baked cakes and biscuits didn't slow down the disappearance of IgE antibody to egg in children with egg allergy, suggesting that the inclusion of such foods in the child's diet shouldn't slow down the resolution of egg allergy. However, a formal study examining the effect of eating baked foods on resolution of egg allergy is required to confirm these findings.

Considering cow's milk

Cow's milk allergy is one of the most common immediate food allergies in children, affecting around 2 per cent of children in Westernised countries. The condition usually presents in the first 6 to 12 months of life, when cow's milk is most commonly introduced into the infant's diet in the form of cow's milk–based formula.

Like egg allergy, most children outgrow their allergy to cow's milk by the time they are 10 to 15 years old, and having cow's milk allergy as an adult is uncommon.

Cow's milk is a common cause of both the immediate type of food allergy and the delayed type of food allergy (see Chapter 5 for information on delayed food allergies). Children with immediate allergy to cow's milk have IgE antibodies that recognise various proteins (allergens) in cow's milk. The antibodies bind to the proteins and activate a host of allergy factors that lead to an immediate allergic reaction. The main allergenic proteins are the caseins and beta-lactoglobulin. The caseins are contained in the milk *curd* and account for most of the protein in cow's milk. Beta-lactoglobulin is contained within the *whey*, the watery part of milk that's left after the curd is removed.

The allergens that cause cow's milk allergy are also found in other animal milks, such as goat's milk or sheep's milk, so children with cow's milk allergy will also be allergic to goat's milk and sheep's milk.

Food types that commonly contain cow's milk or cow's milk products include

- Biscuits and cakes
- Butter and cheese
- Chocolate
- Cream, ice-cream and yoghurt
- Infant rusks and bread

The majority of immediate allergic reactions to milk are mild, with symptoms including the following:

- Hives around the mouth or more generalised on the body
- Swelling of the eyes, lips or face, developing within minutes to an hour after taking milk
- Vomiting and abdominal pain

More severe reactions can cause

- ✔ Persistent coughing
- ✔ Hoarse voice
- ✔ Wheezing
- ✔ Noisy breathing
- ✔ Difficulty breathing (in more severe reactions, which are less common)

Food anaphylaxis usually presents with airway involvement rather than circulatory involvement, but milk allergy sometimes causes loss of consciousness and collapse or paleness and floppiness (all key symptoms of anaphylaxis). Mimi's research on anaphylaxis fatalities in Australia over a nine-year period found no food anaphylaxis deaths due to cow's milk.

Lactose intolerance is a distinct condition from cow's milk allergy. Lactose intolerance doesn't cause hives or swelling of the lips, eyes and face, which are typical symptoms of immediate food allergy. See Chapter 5 for more information about distinguishing between cow's milk allergy and lactose intolerance.

Picking out the peanuts

Peanut allergy is common, affecting around 1 per cent of children in Western countries (putting the condition behind egg allergy and milk allergy in terms of prevalence). Our recent HealthNuts study in Melbourne found that almost 3 per cent of infants aged 12 months had a challenge-proven peanut allergy, which is the highest prevalence reported worldwide. This higher rate may reflect better identification, rising rates of peanut allergy over time, or higher rates in infants.

Peanut allergy commonly presents in the first few years of life, when a child is offered peanut-containing foods such as peanut butter. Like other food allergies in childhood (such as to eggs and cow's milk — see preceding sections), children with peanut allergy usually have their first allergic reaction to peanut when they eat peanut for the first time. But this is where the similarity with egg and milk allergies ends.

Unlike the other common food allergies in childhood, the majority of children don't outgrow their peanut allergy. Around 80 per cent of children with peanut allergy still have peanut allergy as adults. In a study of peanut allergy in children that Katie was involved with, it was found that the chances of growing out of peanut allergy were greatest in early childhood, and most children who outgrew their peanut allergy did so before they were five years old. The factors that make you more or less likely to grow out of peanut allergy are poorly understood.

Investigating the rise in peanut allergy

The prevalence of peanut allergy has been shown to vary in different countries with similar Western lifestyles. A recent study comparing rates of peanut allergy in the UK and Israel found that rates of peanut allergy among children in the UK were ten times higher than rates of peanut allergy in children living in Israel. The researchers suggested that this dramatic difference in prevalence of peanut allergy may relate to differences in the timing of introducing peanut into the diet — at the time of the study, the UK policy was to delay introduction of peanut into the infant's diet until after three years, compared to the common practice in Israel of offering peanut snacks to babies in infancy (refer to Chapter 3 for more on preventing food allergies). A number of studies are now underway to investigate this further.

The way that peanut is processed in Westernised countries such as the US, UK, Australia and New Zealand may also be contributing to the high prevalence of peanut allergy in these countries. Most peanut products in these countries are made with roasted peanuts and roasting has been shown to increase the binding of peanut proteins to peanut IgE antibodies. In contrast, in developing Asian countries where peanut is a common food in the diet from an early age yet prevalence of peanut allergy is low, peanut is usually boiled or shallow fried rather than roasted.

One of Katie's recent studies suggests that children who have higher levels of peanut IgE antibody on a skin prick test (SPT) are less likely to outgrow peanut allergy. The study also showed that those whose peanut SPT remains elevated between the age of one and four years had a poorer prognosis — although whether this was confounded by the fact that those with a persistently large SPT wheal are less likely to be offered a food challenge to diagnose tolerance isn't clear. Those children who have many food allergies may be less likely to outgrow their peanut allergy; however, the evidence for this isn't strong.

Foods commonly containing peanuts include

✔ Asian meals

✔ Baklava

✔ Cakes, biscuits and muesli bars

✔ Peanut butter

✔ Satay sauce

Most reactions to peanut are mild, with common symptoms including the following:

- ✔ Hives around the mouth or generalised over the body
- ✔ Swelling of the eyes, lips or face
- ✔ Vomiting within minutes to one hour after eating peanut.

Peanut allergy is more likely to cause a severe allergic reaction (anaphylaxis) than is cow's milk allergy or egg allergy. Around 40 per cent of reactions to peanut may involve the airway (such as persistent coughing, hoarse voice or wheezing), compared to around 1 per cent of reactions to egg or milk. Looking at this another way, peanut allergy is the most common cause of food anaphylaxis in children, even though egg and milk are the more common causes of immediate food allergy overall.

Mimi's study of anaphylaxis deaths in Australia and similar studies in the UK and US have consistently found that peanut and tree nuts are the most common food allergies causing death. In addition, eating food prepared outside the home was an important risk factor for death, highlighting that if your child is allergic to peanut, knowing what's in the food your child eats when not at home is especially important. (See Chapter 7 for more on managing food allergies.)

Children with peanut allergy may develop airway symptoms if they inhale airborne peanut allergen. This might occur when a bag of peanuts is opened in a closed environment (such as on an airplane), or in dining venues when peanuts are being cracked open from their shells. However, airway symptoms don't occur from breathing near peanut butter, and severe reactions involving the airway or circulation aren't triggered by casual skin contact with peanut butter.

Studying the Not-So-Usual Suspects: Other Food Allergies

The other common food allergies include wheat, soy, fish, shellfish and tree nut allergy. In the following sections, we cover the common immediate allergic reactions caused by these food types, as well as the products they are commonly found in and when children usually outgrow the allergy.

Threshing out wheat allergies

Similar to the other IgE mediated immediate food allergies in childhood, wheat allergy usually presents in the first years of life when foods containing wheat are introduced into the diet. Wheat is a common component of the Western diet, being used to make bread, cakes, biscuits as well as being an ingredient in a variety of meat, fish and vegetable dishes. While no good data is available on the percentage of children affected by wheat allergies, most children outgrow their allergy to wheat by 10 to 15 years of age.

The predominant allergens in wheat are the *glutenins* and *gliadin*, and IgE antibodies against glutenin subunits are most commonly associated with immediate wheat allergy. IgE antibodies against gliadin have also been detected and may correlate with more severe immediate reactions. (Wheat can also cause delayed food allergy reactions — see Chapter 5.)

The majority of immediate reactions to wheat are mild, including

- ✔ Hives
- ✔ Swelling
- ✔ Vomiting and abdominal pain (less common)

Most children with wheat allergy are able to tolerate other gluten-containing grains, such as barley and rye, because these grains don't contain glutenins. However, children who are allergic to components of gliadin can have symptoms with other gluten-containing grains and may also need to avoid these.

Some people can develop anaphylaxis if they eat wheat and exercise within several hours of each other; this condition is called *wheat-dependent exercise-induced anaphylaxis* (WDEIA). People with WDEIA can tolerate wheat and exercise separately, but the combination within a certain time period results in an allergic reaction. IgE antibodies to a component of gliadin, ω-5 gliadin, are commonly found in this condition.

Many people think that coeliac disease is a form of wheat allergy. This isn't correct. Although coeliac disease is triggered by eating gluten (proteins found in wheat, rye and barley), the condition is more like an autoimmune disease. See Chapter 5 for more information about coeliac disease.

Sorting out soy allergies

Soy allergy is less common than allergies to egg, milk and peanut but is still one of the more common food allergies. Soy is a common cause of both immediate food allergies and delayed food allergies (see Chapter 5 for more on delayed food allergies). (No good data is available on the percentage of children affected by soy allergy.)

Soy allergy usually presents in the first 6 to 12 months of life, when soy formula is introduced into the diet. Soy is also a prevalent component in manufactured processed foods, such as sausages and processed meats, so reactions may develop in childhood when such foods are introduced.

Soy is commonly found in the following foods:

✔ Edamame

✔ Most vegetarian meat-substitutes

✔ Miso soup

✔ Soy milk, soy cheese and soy ice-cream

✔ Tofu and tempeh

✔ Other products containing soy flour, such as cakes, biscuits, pastries, sauces, soups and baby cereals

Immediate allergic reactions to soy are usually mild, including the following:

✔ Hives around the mouth on more generalised over the body

✔ Swelling of the lips, eyes and face

✔ Vomiting and abdominal pain within an hour of taking soy

Severe reactions are less common. IgE mediated allergy to soy can be present in up to 15 to 20 per cent of children with IgE mediated cow's milk allergy. Most children outgrow their soy allergy during childhood; however, the condition may persist into adulthood.

Although soy beans and peanuts are both from the legume family of plants, no evidence suggests that children with peanut allergy are more likely to be allergic to soy or vice versa. Moreover, taking soy products doesn't increase the chances of developing peanut allergy. In our study of food allergy in infants, we found no association between soy allergy and peanut allergy.

Hooking up with fish allergies

Fish allergy affects up to 1 per cent of the population. The condition is primarily seen in adults and is a less common cause of food allergy in children, but does occur. Populations that eat a lot of fish in their diet, such as Asian cultures, have higher prevalence rates of fish allergy. Most people don't outgrow fish allergy, with only 20 per cent of fish allergies resolving over time.

The most common allergen causing fish allergy is *parvalbumin*, a protein present in most species of fish — meaning that children with an allergy to one type of fish are usually (but not always) also allergic to other types of fish. Some children are able to tolerate a number of species of fish while being allergic to others, presumably because they have IgE antibodies to proteins that aren't common across species.

If your child has a fish allergy and you would like to still include some fish in her diet, you can ask your doctor to perform testing to individual species of fish to identify any that your child can tolerate.

While tuna is thought to be less allergenic than other fish, this species still causes many food allergies. Here is a list of the most common fish species that cause food allergies:

- ✔ Anchovy
- ✔ Cod
- ✔ Eel
- ✔ Haddock
- ✔ Herring
- ✔ John Dory
- ✔ Mackerel
- ✔ Salmon
- ✔ Sardine
- ✔ Tuna
- ✔ Trout

Foods that commonly contain fish products include the following:

- Fish dips and mousses
- Fish paste (commonly used in Asian cooking)
- Pizzas and pasta sauces (which sometimes include anchovies)

Fish allergens are usually relatively heat stable — meaning they don't degrade with heat from cooking. However, some children are able to tolerate tinned tuna that has been processed at high heat, while being allergic to less well cooked tuna. Some people have also reported reacting to cooked fish but not the raw fish. This is likely to relate to the emergence of allergens during the cooking process.

The allergens in fish are different to the allergens in shellfish, so many children who are allergic to fish are still able to tolerate shellfish.

Most reactions to fish are mild, with symptoms including the following:

- Hives
- Swelling
- Vomiting and abdominal pain developing within one hour of eating the fish

More severe reactions — such as coughing, hoarse voice, wheezing, loss of consciousness and collapse (or paleness and floppiness in infants and young children) — are less common.

Occasionally, people with fish allergy can develop breathing difficulties (anaphylaxis) from inhaling fumes when seafood is being cooked, and in seafood processing factories. This is mainly seen with fish and shellfish allergies and isn't a feature of egg or milk allergies.

Allergy to a fish parasite called *Anisakis simplex* can masquerade as fish allergy. This parasite is a known allergen and can cause allergic reactions like any food allergen. Reactions can range from mild to severe — including anaphylaxis. *Anisakis* larvae can be killed by freezing or cooking, but the allergen can still be present and cause an allergic reaction. Because fish and shellfish commonly carry the *Anisakis* parasite, people who are allergic to *Anasakis* should avoid all fish and shellfish. If your child has had an allergic reaction after eating fish but allergy testing to fish is negative, he may have an allergy to the parasite *Anisakis simplex*.

Prying into shellfish allergies

Unlike most food allergies, shellfish allergy usually develops in adults rather than in young children. Indeed, shellfish allergy is the most common food allergy in adults, affecting around 1 to 2 per cent of adults in Western countries. Only about 0.1 per cent of children have shellfish allergy, and more commonly teenagers. Shellfish allergy is more common in countries where shellfish is a common food in the diet, such as in Asian countries. Most people don't outgrow shellfish allergy.

Shellfish are divided into two families, and both can cause allergies, as follows:

✔ **Molluscs**, including

- Clams

- Mussels

- Oysters

- Scallops

- Squid

✔ **Crustaceans**, including

- Crab

- Crayfish

- Lobster

- Shrimp

Foods that commonly contain shellfish products include the following:

✔ Bouillabaisse and seafood stews

✔ Prawn paste (a common ingredient in Asian cooking)

✔ Seafood dips and sauces

✔ Tempura (which commonly includes prawns)

Many reactions to shellfish are mild, including the following:

✔ Hives

✔ Swelling

✔ Vomiting and abdominal pain

Shellfish allergies can be severe, particularly in adults with asthma. Shellfish allergy is a common cause of anaphylaxis and follows closely after peanut and tree nut allergies as a cause of death from food anaphylaxis. Occasionally, people with shellfish allergy can develop breathing difficulties (anaphylaxis) from inhaling fumes when the shellfish is being cooked. This is also seen with fish allergies.

The main allergenic proteins in shellfish are called *tropomyosins*. All shellfish are closely related, so the tropomyosins in all shellfish are similar; however, those from the same family (either crustaceans or molluscs) are especially alike. Therefore, if you're allergic to one variety of shellfish, you're probably allergic to most or all types of shellfish from that family. On the other hand, you may or may not be allergic to members of the other family, depending on whether the allergenic protein you're allergic to is present only in the one family of shellfish or cross-reacts with the other family of shellfish as well.

No simple method is available to identify whether a person who's allergic to a particular species of shellfish in one family is going to also be allergic to members of the other family of shellfish. If your child has a shellfish allergy, the safest way to find out whether she can eat other shellfish is for her doctor to perform skin testing relating to the different crustaceans and molluscs.

Food allergen labelling laws in Australia and New Zealand require crustaceans to be listed as an allergen on food packaging if they're an ingredient in the product, but this doesn't apply to molluscs. This means that manufacturers aren't required to list the presence of clams, oysters, mussels, scallops or other molluscs in ingredient lists. If your child is allergic to crustaceans, you should work out with his doctor whether he is also allergic to molluscs because, if he is, you need to take extra care in reading ingredient labels to avoid foods that contain shellfish from the mollusc family. (See Chapter 7 for more on managing food allergies and Chapter 8 for more information on food labels.)

Shellfish and iodine allergies

If your child has an allergy to shellfish, you may wonder whether she may also be allergic to iodine and iodine-containing materials such as antiseptics (betadine) or radiocontrast dyes. In the past, doctors incorrectly thought that if a person was allergic to shellfish a cross-reaction with iodine and iodine-containing materials was possible. But this isn't the case. A person can develop an allergic-type reaction to iodine or radiocontrast material, but such reactions are not allergies and aren't related to shellfish allergies. If your child is allergic to shellfish, she doesn't need to avoid iodine or radiocontrast material.

Shellfish is one of a small group of food types that can cause food-dependent exercise-induced anaphylaxis — where you can develop anaphylaxis if you eat a certain food and then exercise within several hours of doing so. Refer to the section 'Threshing out wheat allergies' for more information.

Cracking open tree nut allergies

The term *tree nuts* refers to all nuts that grow on trees. While tree nuts are among the eight common foods causing allergies, tree nut allergies are less common than peanut allergy, affecting around 0.2 per cent of children. Similar to peanut allergy, the condition usually presents in the first few years of life, and the first allergic reaction to a tree nut typically occurs when a child eats that nut for the first time. The most common tree nut allergies are to cashew and walnuts. Most children with tree nut allergy have their allergy for life, with only 10 per cent growing out of their tree nut allergy.

Types of tree nuts include the following:

- Almonds
- Brazil nuts
- Cashews
- Hazelnuts
- Macadamia nuts
- Pecans
- Pine nuts
- Pistachios
- Walnuts

Note: Tree nuts don't include peanuts, which are a type of legume, and also referred to as ground nuts.

Foods that commonly contain tree nuts or tree nut products include

- Baklava (made from various tree nuts)
- Cakes, biscuits, breakfast cereals and muesli bars
- Middle Eastern and Asian cooking
- Nut pastes and nut butters
- Pralines (usually made from hazelnuts), flourless cakes and marzipan (usually made from almond meal) and Nutella (made from hazelnuts)
- Sweets such as chocolate, nougat and fudge

Many reactions to tree nuts are mild, including the following:

- ✔ Hives
- ✔ Swelling
- ✔ Vomiting

Similar to peanut allergy and shellfish allergy, however, allergic reactions to tree nuts tend to be severe. Tree nuts are a common cause of food anaphylaxis, and tree nut and peanut together represent the most common cause of fatal food anaphylaxis.

Most people with a tree nut allergy are not allergic to all tree nuts; only about one-third of children who are allergic to one tree nut are also allergic to another tree nut. This means that more than half of the children who are allergic to a tree nut aren't allergic to other nuts.

High cross-reactivity occurs between some tree nut families. The most common cross-reactivity is between cashew and pistachio and between walnut and pecan. So children who are allergic to cashew are commonly also allergic to pistachio, and children who are allergic to walnut can be allergic to pecan.

Predicting whether someone who's allergic to a tree nut is also going to be allergic to other tree nuts or peanut requires allergy testing. Similarly, predicting whether a person who's allergic to peanut is also going to be allergic to tree nuts requires allergy testing. If your child has a tree nut allergy, allergy testing can help to reveal which of the tree nuts he's allergic to and, therefore, identify those tree nuts that he should avoid.

Exploring rare allergies

Although food allergies predominantly involve a small number of foods, developing an allergy to just about any food is theoretically possible. A person can develop IgE antibodies to many different protein or carbohydrate components within foods, and an increasing number of foods have been reported to cause allergy; allergies to a variety of fruits, vegetables, meats (beef, lamb, pork and chicken) and cereals (rice) have all been described. In addition, allergies to additives in foods such as spices and gelatine, and natural remedies (such as royal jelly and echinacea) have also been reported.

Searching out sesame seed allergy

Sesame seed allergy has become an increasingly common food allergy in recent years. In Australia, the condition is thought to be the next most common food allergen after the most common eight food allergens (egg, milk, peanut, tree nuts, wheat, soy, fish and shellfish). Sesame is a common ingredient in Middle Eastern and Asian foods, which are now increasingly available in the Australian diet, so sesame allergy is increasing. Our own recent HealthNuts study found that just under 1 per cent of 12-month-old infants in Melbourne have a sesame seed allergy confirmed by food challenge. Sesame allergy is much more common in Israel where sesame is a major ingredient in cooking — in Israel, sesame allergy is the third most common food allergy. Children with a sesame seed allergy need to avoid sesame seeds in their diet, but these children can avoid this food and still have a balanced, healthy diet.

In Australia and New Zealand, food manufacturers must state the presence of sesame in a product, because sesame is included with tree nuts as one of the major allergens that must be declared on food labeling. This is also the case in the United Kingdom, European Union and Canada — although the United States doesn't include sesame in its list of allergens that must be listed because experts there still consider sesame seed allergy to be an emerging food allergy.

Note: Benne, benniseed, gingelly seeds, simsim and til are all terms sesame seeds are also known by. So any products using these as ingredients, such as benne oil or til oil for cooking, also need to be avoided if your child is allergic to sesame.

Ingredients and foods to avoid if your child is allergic to sesame include the following:

- Hummus
- Pasteli
- Sesame oil
- Sesame paste
- Sesarmol
- Sesomolina
- Tahina
- Tahini

Products which may contain sesame include

- Asian foods
- Bakery goods
- Crackers
- Dips
- Dressings
- Halvah
- Herb mixes
- Marinades
- Middle Eastern foods
- Nutritional snacks
- Patés
- Pretzels
- Salads

Nevertheless, these other food allergies altogether account for less than 10 per cent of food allergies, so a sensible approach is to offer your child a broad, healthy diet.

No good tests are yet available to help us accurately predict whether someone is going to have an allergy to less common causes of food allergy — the best test is to eat the food. Introduce any new foods to your child's diet slowly, so that if your child is allergic to a food, any reactions are likely to be mild. If a reaction develops, take your child to see the doctor. (See Chapter 6 for more on testing for more common causes of food allergy.)

One food that's unlikely to be the cause of food allergy is chocolate! Parents often tell us they think their child is allergic to chocolate because their child has developed allergic symptoms, such as hives or swelling, after eating chocolate. In fact, allergy to the cacao bean in chocolate is extremely rare. The most likely cause of allergic reactions to chocolate is an allergy to one or more of the common allergens contained within chocolate — such as milk, egg or nuts.

Oral Allergy Syndrome

In *oral allergy syndrome,* local symptoms in the mouth develop when eating raw fruits and vegetables. This is typically seen in people with pollen allergy, because some allergens in grass and tree pollens are cross-reactive with allergens contained within fruits and vegetables. For example, the major birch pollen allergen cross-reacts with allergens in apple. So some people who are allergic to pollen allergens that cross-react with allergens in fruit or vegetables can experience symptoms in their mouth and throat when they eat fruits and vegetables.

While no good data is available on the percentage of children affected by oral allergy syndrome, the condition is uncommon in children and is more likely to affect adults (and sometimes adolescents).

The most common local symptoms of oral allergy syndrome are itching and swelling in the mouth. Less commonly, swelling and tightness of the throat may occur, or a more significant involvement of the airway.

The allergens involved in oral allergy syndrome are usually heat labile, which means that they're destroyed by heat during cooking, so symptoms are usually only experienced when eating the raw food and not when the food is cooked.

Chapter 5

Discovering Delayed Food Allergies

- -

In This Chapter

▶ Working out which symptoms are associated with delayed food allergies

▶ Discussing which foods are likely to cause stomach upsets

▶ Finding out the difference between being allergic to cow's milk and intolerant of lactose

▶ Deciding whether your child has a delayed food allergy

- -

*D*elayed food allergy is a term used for the food allergies that don't result in an immediate reaction to a food. The term covers a whole range of food allergies — from well-described diseases such as eosinophilic esophagitis to less-defined conditions such as food-induced colic. The general belief among researchers is that delayed food allergies are on the rise and further research needs to be done to better define them and help to improve their management.

Symptoms of delayed food allergy tend to centre on the gut, and include vomiting, diarrhoea, tummy pain or difficulty with feeding such as food refusal or choking during feeding. So, if your child has symptoms that don't seem immediately related to the ingestion of a food but have occurred since the introduction of a new food in their diet, this is the chapter for you!

In this chapter, we discuss the differences between delayed and immediate allergies, and cover the common symptoms, and the timing of symptoms, of delayed allergies in more detail. We also look at the foods that may cause delayed allergies, and whether conditions that commonly occur during infancy (such as colic, reflux and eczema) may, or may not, be related to food allergy.

Explaining Delayed Food Allergies

Delayed food allergies are a poorly defined group of allergies about which, unfortunately, allergists know very little. One thing we do know is that delayed food allergies are a very different set of diseases from immediate food allergies (which we cover in Chapter 4). We know that symptoms are usually associated with gastrointestinal upset and occur several hours after ingesting a food (or can build up over several days of repeated ingestion). While delayed food allergy can affect adults, the condition is most likely to occur among infants and children.

In the following sections, we describe delayed food allergies in more detail, and look at methods of diagnosing related conditions.

Understanding the difference between IgE and non-IgE allergies

Allergists like to think about food allergy in terms of IgE versus non-IgE food allergy, and good reasons exist for this practice. The main reason is to distinguish patients who are at risk of anaphylaxis (patients with IgE mediated, or immediate, food allergy — discussed in Chapter 4) from those who aren't at risk of anaphylaxis (non-IgE mediated and mixed IgE/non-IgE mediated, or delayed, food allergy). This is important from a safety point of view — patients at risk of anaphylaxis shouldn't try home challenges with foods to test for and confirm allergies. (See Chapter 6 for more on testing for food allergies.)

Defining delayed food allergy terms

The diagnosis of delayed food allergy usually brings with it a host of medical terms. Here's what some of the more common terms mean:

✔ **Colitis:** Inflammation of the *colon* (large intestine)

✔ **Enteropathy:** Inflammation of the small intestine. More extensive inflammation can lead to damage of the intestinal lining.

✔ **Eosinophilic esophagitis (EoE):** Inflammation of the esophagus involving allergy inflammatory cells called *eosinophils*

✔ **Food-protein-induced enterocolitis syndrome (FPIES):** Inflammation of the small and large intestine, which causes severe vomiting.

✔ **Proctocolitis:** Inflammation of the rectum and colon

Really, the definition of delayed food allergies as being 'non-IgE mediated' or 'mixed IgE/non-IgE mediated' is simply an admission by clinicians and scientists alike that, although we know that these conditions aren't caused by IgE antibodies, we really don't understand the mechanisms that cause them! So, in a (slightly disappointing) way, delayed food allergies are defined simply by what they're not — that is, they're not IgE mediated.

Looking for the right symptoms

Delayed food allergies are most commonly associated with gastrointestinal upset. In fact, food allergens can affect every part of the gut from the top to the bottom, and delayed food allergies have been defined to match every part of the intestinal tract affected.

The type of symptoms that a person develops can predict where the food allergy is affecting the intestine. These types of *gut reactors* are often seen by paediatric gastroenterologists rather than allergists because endoscopy can be used to better distinguish whether the symptoms are caused by a food allergy or some other unrelated condition.

An infant with FPIES

Food-protein-induced enterocolitis syndrome (FPIES) can present as a very frightening condition — the excessive vomiting that accompanies it can result in a form of low blood volume shock. Luckily, no deaths from FPIES have been reported, but the condition is very under-recognised. The example of Sam is common with this condition.

Sam was a healthy six-month-old baby boy. He'd happily breastfed and, after just starting solids, was really enjoying apple, pear and pumpkin puree. His mother, Sally, decided to introduce rice cereal into his diet for the first time at lunch. He ate two teaspoons of the cereal but didn't seem interested in eating any more. Two hours after lunch, Sam started vomiting profusely and became pale and floppy. Sally raced Sam to the emergency department at the local hospital, where the doctors ran a number of blood tests and did an abdominal ultrasound. The tests were all clear and, after a few hours, Sam seemed to pick up and return to his old self. The next day he was overall well, although his mother noted he had one loose bowel action. The next week, Sally tried some rice cereal again and the same symptoms, although not as severe, occurred.

Sally thought the symptoms could relate to the rice cereal, and asked the emergency department doctors whether this could be possible. The doctors thought the connection was highly unlikely but agreed to refer Sam to the hospital's allergy department, where a diagnosis of FPIES was indeed made. Because most children outgrow this condition by the time they're two or three years old, the allergist recommended that Sam avoid rice until he was two years old and that Sam then come back for a careful hospital-based food challenge.

Starting from the top of the body, food allergies can cause reactions in the

✔ **Esophagus:** Food allergies that affect the esophagus can cause *gastroesophageal reflux* (vomiting and frequent regurgitation) or *eosinophilic esophagitis* (EoE — sometimes thought of as eczema of the esophagus), resulting in food refusal, failure to thrive, vomiting and food sticking in the throat during eating.

Children with EoE are often very slow eaters and are often the last to leave the meal table. Sometimes they have learnt to push the food down their inflamed esophagus by drinking lots during a meal.

Occasionally children with EoE can develop esophageal strictures, which mean they start to avoid foods that are difficult to swallow, such as meat or bread. Food can even become impacted if the esophagus is severely damaged. Sometimes parents don't notice the subtle signs of EoE and diagnosis is made during an endoscopy to remove a food bolus obstruction.

✔ **Small intestine:** *Food-induced enteropathy* occurs when food proteins cause damage to the lining of the small intestine, resulting in diarrhoea, abdominal pain, bloating and irritability.

Irritability can present as colic in the first four months of life (see the section 'Contemplating colic', later in this chapter, for more). Secondary lactose intolerance can result from allergy-induced damage to the intestinal lining (covered in the section 'Distinguishing Between Cow's Milk Allergy and Lactose Intolerance', later in this chapter).

✔ **Small and large intestine:** *Food-protein-induced enterocolitis syndrome* (FPIES) usually presents in the first year of life and is associated with profuse vomiting approximately two to four hours after eating a newly introduced food. Infants who are affected can go into shock from very severe vomiting and often present to the emergency room extremely unwell. Doctors often mistakenly diagnose such infants as suffering from a severe infantile infection such as sepsis or meningitis. FPIES really only presents in children in the first year of life and often results from less common food allergens such as rice, oats and meat in addition to the more common causes of food allergy such as to cow's milk and soy. (See the sidebar 'An infant with FPIES' for more.)

✔ **Lower intestine:** Irritation of the lining of the lowest part of the intestine (or colon) results in *proctocolitis* and causes diarrhoea that can be streaked with blood. Interestingly, babies with this condition are usually happy and thriving. So, although sounding nasty, this condition is actually usually more concerning for the parents than for the infant.

Inflammation of the intestine may also in theory affect its motility and result in constipation, which is a less commonly recognised symptom associated with delayed food allergies. This is especially associated with cow's milk protein allergy in young infants.

Other than gut reactions, delayed food allergies can result in other less well defined symptoms, such as headaches and non-specific abdominal pain as well as eczema flares. Very little is known about these non-gut related delayed food allergy reactions, but keep in mind that non-specific symptoms like headache are highly unlikely to be related to food allergy. If your child displays atypical symptoms, seek advice from your doctor so that other causes can first be safely excluded.

Watching the timing of symptoms

Delayed food allergies can occur several hours after ingestion of a food but can also take days of repeated ingestion to become obvious. Because the timing can vary so widely with each child, pinpointing whether a symptom is caused by food can be very difficult.

What is coeliac disease and is it a food allergy?

Coeliac disease is not usually categorised as a food allergy; however, by definition it could be because the condition involves an abnormal immune-based reaction to a food protein. Coeliac disease is caused by an abnormal reaction by the body to dietary gluten, found in wheat and other cereal grains, including barley and rye. The condition is becoming increasingly common and affects up to 1 in 200 people of Northern European descent.

Doctors know that gliadin, a component of gluten, is the cause of the immune reaction in coeliac disease, but the precise mechanisms leading to this are still not fully understood. When a person with coeliac disease eats gluten, the gliadin components enter the intestinal lining and form a complex with an enzyme in the intestinal lining called *tissue transglutaminase* (tTG). The immune system recognises this complex as harmful and makes antibodies against gliadin and tissue transglutaminase (as well as anti-endomyseal antibodies), which initiate an inflammatory response that damages the intestinal lining.

Before coeliac disease was found to be due to gluten, children with this condition would literally waste away and many died. Now coeliac disease is easily identified and just as easily treated by following a gluten-free diet (this is the only treatment for the condition). As long as kids with the condition avoid gluten, they can expect to be completely symptom-free with an excellent prognosis.

Although coeliac disease is most commonly diagnosed in the first couple of years of life, the condition can present at any age in life — Katie knows of one case where a woman was diagnosed at 80 years of age! While adults being diagnosed with coeliac disease is certainly not uncommon, in some of these cases the sufferer has had low-grade symptoms for a long time. Often parents of older children diagnosed with coeliac disease have become used to these low-grade symptoms, saying something like, 'My son has had loose smelly bowel actions for such a long time we thought that was just him'. Amazingly, some children have learnt to partially self-treat and just don't eat sandwiches put in their lunch boxes.

(continued)

(continued)

The most common signs and symptoms of coeliac disease are

✔ Diarrhoea

✔ Poor weight gain

✔ Vomiting

Less common signs of coeliac disease include

✔ Abnormal liver function tests

✔ Arthritis

✔ Iron deficiency (*anaemia*)

✔ Kidney disease

✔ Osteoporosis

The good news is that excluding the possibility that coeliac disease is the cause of the symptoms outlined in the preceding lists is easy. A coeliac screen (which screens for anti-tissue transglutaminase and anti-gliadin antibodies) is a simple blood test that usually shows an abnormal result if coeliac disease is present.

If the screening test is positive, your local doctor refers your child to a paediatric gastro-enterologist for a confirmatory gastroscopy. In order to join your local patient support group (for example, in Australia, the state branches of Coeliac Australia, which provide a wealth of information and support) your child needs to provide a letter from your gastroenterologist confirming that biopsies taken during the gastroscopy were consistent with coeliac disease.

For more information on coeliac disease, see *Living Gluten-Free For Dummies*, Australian Edition, by Donna Korn and Margaret Clough (Wiley Publishing Australia).

Most of the delayed food allergies cause a low level irritation of the intestine, and only after the food has been eaten often do the symptoms actually rear their head. Some children have a more aggressive reaction, presenting with symptoms after eating the food once or twice and with the symptoms occurring within hours of eating the food.

For example, some children with delayed food allergies develop abdominal pain, nausea and diarrhoea within a couple of hours of eating their allergen. Other children with delayed food allergies can be sneaking their allergen into their diet for days or weeks before they develop symptoms (well, symptoms that they admit to anyway!). Experts believe the reason for the difference in timing of symptoms is more to do with the severity of the reaction.

Identifying the age when delayed food allergies begin

Delayed food allergies can present at any age; however, similar to IgE mediated food allergies, they are more common in young infants and children. These types of allergies are more likely to be missed or the diagnosis delayed compared to immediate food allergies — partly because the symptoms are often reasonably non-specific and can be mistaken for other conditions (such as reflux or colic). The body is also pretty good (and pretty amazing) at working out what foods are upsetting it, and sometimes children have learnt to avoid the foods that aggravate the symptoms.

Fussy eating is common to almost all young children and only a very small proportion of them actually have food allergy. So be aware that some kids say they're allergic to greens to get out of eating brussels sprouts! However, some children with conditions like EoE have such bad symptoms when they eat that they may end up self-treating these symptoms by only eating foods that don't aggravate the condition — most commonly, soft and pureed foods such as mashed potato, cereal and milk.

Because children with delayed food allergies often self-regulate by only eating particular foods, certain themes emerge. For example, when parents say to Katie that their child 'only eats white food' she always makes sure she thinks about whether these symptoms are parading as an undiagnosed EoE.

Diagnosing delayed food allergies

Very few diagnostic tests are available that help us to distinguish that food allergy is causing tummy upsets. Endoscopy to obtain intestinal biopsies is essentially the only way to diagnose EoE and coeliac disease (since the diagnosis is based on pathological criteria). However, for the vast majority of delayed food allergies, the only diagnostic test we have at our disposal is the elimination/rechallenge test. (See Chapter 6 for more on diagnosing food allergies and this type of testing.)

Finding Out Which Foods Cause Tummy Upsets

Delayed food allergies are most commonly caused by cow's milk, with a smaller percentage of people also having co-existent soy intolerance. Other foods such as wheat, egg and nuts (common causes of immediate food allergies — refer to Chapter 4) less commonly cause delayed food allergies.

Conditions such as EoE and FPIES (see the preceding section) are caused by a more diverse range of foods. For example, the top four foods associated with EoE are cow's milk, soy, wheat and egg; meat, grains and corn are the next most likely causes. For FPIES, quite an unusual range of foods can cause the syndrome. Although 50 per cent of FPIES cases are due to cow's milk (and, in some cases, combined cow's milk and soy allergy), the other 50 per cent are caused by rice, meats (including beef and chicken), oats (and other grains), fish and even fruit.

Distinguishing Between Cow's Milk Allergy and Lactose Intolerance

Cow's milk is made up of three main components: Protein (of which several components are present, such as beta-lactoglobulin), sugar (lactose) and fat. Protein and lactose are the components that can cause problems in cases of cow's milk allergy and lactose intolerance, but for different reasons.

Considering how cow's milk allergy leads to lactose intolerance

Milk is the perfect early food for infants but, as people sometimes say, 'While breast is best for babies, cow's milk is for calves'. The protein in breast milk is more easily digested — infants and children with cow's milk allergy are reacting to the protein component of the milk. Cow's milk proteins can cause irritation to the lining of the small intestine and the resulting damage means the intestine is not as good at doing its job of digesting and absorbing food nutrients.

The small intestine does an incredibly complex job of sorting through all of the food that your child ingests and working out how to break each bit down to its component parts so that the digested food can get into the blood stream and be taken to the liver for processing.

Interestingly, the one process that is most sensitive to irritation from food proteins in children with food allergy is the production of the enzyme *lactase*, which breaks down the milk sugar, lactose. Lactase resides in the tips of the villi that line the small intestine (see Figure 5-1). When the small intestine is damaged, the tips of the villi are the first to be affected and parts of the intestinal lining can become worn down — like an old shag pile carpet with bald patches. The loss of lactase means that lactose is not properly digested.

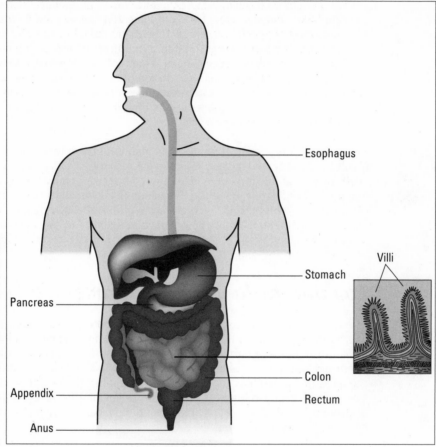

Figure 5-1:
The digestive tract with detail showing villi in the lining of the small intestine, where lactase resides.

Esophagus

Villi

Stomach

Pancreas

Colon

Appendix

Rectum

Anus

Lactose digestion is critical for life in infancy (lactose is one of the main components of breast milk). Congenital lactase deficiency (that is, being born without lactase) is rare in Caucasians (but common in Asians) and, before the advent of medicated formula, these children would have died soon after birth.

Non-digested lactose has two effects:

✔ Acting like a sponge, non-digested lactose takes water with it down the intestinal tract and causes diarrhoea (termed *osmotic diarrhoea*).

✔ Providing a great big juicy meal for all of the lactose-loving bacteria in the colon, non-digested lactose cause bacteria in the gut to increase. Sometimes the bacteria grow up as high as the lower part of the usually sterile small intestine (known as *small bowel bacteria overgrowth*). This excess of sugar can result in fermentation, similar to what occurs in a vat of wine — when you throw in more sugar, you get more fermentation. (A similar effect happens when someone eats baked beans, except the non-digested sugar is not lactose but poorly digested fibre, which feeds intestinal bugs.) The final common pathway of bacterial fermentation is, however, the socially unacceptable production of gas — sometimes from both ends of the intestinal tract! In babies, the build-up of gas can cause bloating and irritability and symptoms similar to colic (see the section, 'Contemplating colic', later in this chapter) often accompanied by excessive burping and flatulence.

Cow's milk allergy is only one of many insults to the intestine that can result in non-digested lactose (lactose intolerance). Coeliac disease and gastrointestinal infections are also important reversible causes of this condition. Fortunately, once the provoking insult resolves (such as removal of cow's milk protein from the diet in cow's milk allergy or gluten in coeliac disease), the intestinal lining grows back and ability to digest lactose returns. However, cases of permanent lactose non-digestion do occur.

Looking at lactose intolerance

The enzyme lactase is commonly absent in people of Asian descent, as well as in many other adults. The absence of lactase results in lactose intolerance. In these circumstances, lactose intolerance is due not to an abnormal immune response to cow's milk but to the lack of lactase in the intestinal lining (see the preceding section for more on this enzyme). The enzyme can also become transiently deficient after an episode of gastroenteritis due to the gut lining being damaged, a particularly common situation in young children.

The symptoms of lactose intolerance are

- ✔ Abdominal pain
- ✔ Bloating
- ✔ Diarrhoea
- ✔ Flatulence

These symptoms can be difficult to differentiate from the delayed form of cow's milk allergy.

Lactose intolerance can be tested formally by either a breath hydrogen test (BHT) or by an endoscopic biopsy to test how much enzyme is actually in the lining of the intestine. During a BHT, the patient is given a drink of liquid lactose after providing a sample of breath into a bag (just like a breathalyser for alcohol). Then four to five further breath samples are taken over a period of two to three hours. If the breath hydrogen climbs over that period, that signals that the bacteria in the lower intestine is making an excess of hydrogen because they're feeding on undigested lactose (the lactose that was ingested at the start of the test and has passed down into the large intestine). The hydrogen produced by the bugs is absorbed into the blood stream and then comes out in your breath — so the test is pretty nifty and, obviously, much less invasive than an endoscopy. Endoscopies require a general anaesthetic in a child; however, these tests can also provide more information about what might be causing the lactose intolerance in the first place.

The Irritable Infant

For many people, a crying infant can be one of the most distressing and anxiety-provoking aspects of being a parent. Unfortunately, babies don't come with handbooks and, for all parents, working out what's normal and what's not can be difficult — especially in this age of information explosion. Sources of information and advice are numerous — from the internet to friends and family — but sometimes knowing what source to trust is hard. This is not just a problem for new parents. Even those who have been through the mill before still need to get to know the specific temperament of a new addition.

Babies can cry for all sorts of reasons including hunger, tiredness, pain or even boredom. In our parents' generation parenting was much more 'by the book', with feeding and sleeping routines far more highly scheduled than is usually the case nowadays. So many different schools of thought about the best way to care and settle for a baby are now available that sometimes parents can feel very confused.

Sometimes, however, an irritated infant isn't hungry, tired, in pain or bored — instead, conditions such as colic, reflux, constipation or eczema may be the cause. In the following sections, we look at these conditions and the role food allergy plays in them.

Contemplating colic

Colic is defined as a condition of a healthy baby in which periods of intense, unexplained fussing or crying occur, lasting for more than three hours per day, on more than three days per week and for more than three weeks. The condition usually starts at around two to four weeks and usually resolves by about four months of age. Most babies with colic don't have food allergy and symptoms spontaneously resolve without any medical help.

A common symptom of colic is the baby drawing up the legs, as if in pain or discomfort. Although this can also be a symptom of food allergy, sometimes the baby swallowing air during excessive crying or not getting rid of air due to poor burping can result in similar discomfort and cause the drawing up of the legs.

Some signs are more likely to be suggestive of food allergy-related colic than others. Certainly colic continuing past 16 weeks of age should be investigated for the possibility of food allergy. Colic associated with other signs and symptoms such as excessive reflux, diarrhoea or eczema should also be investigated further.

Cow's milk proteins are secreted through breast milk and the amount of cow's milk allergen within breast milk can be sufficient to cause a whole range of delayed food allergies. The one exception is FPIES (see the section 'Looking for the right symptoms'), which has never been reported in an exclusively breastfed baby — probably because the concentration of cow's milk protein in breast milk is too low to trigger an FPIES reaction.

Some families wonder whether family history increases the risk of food allergy related colic and anecdotal evidence seems to suggest it does (although not in a very strong way). Katie has often recorded a patient history where a parent says something like, 'Yes, Mum said I was a really irritable infant and I had to be given a special formula as a baby'.

If a baby has new onset of colic-like symptoms when introduced to cow's milk formula, a cow's milk allergy should be considered — cow's milk allergies commonly cause food allergy reflux. In this case, your doctor is likely to recommend a trial of cow's milk elimination from both the mother's and the baby's diet; this elimination should be usually undertaken for two weeks. Even if improvement is detected, the two-week elimination should be followed by a *rechallenge step* (where cow's milk is reintroduced to the diet), to prove that the reintroduction causes the symptoms to re-occur and that the improvement in colic was not just a coincidence related to natural resolution with time.

As well as eliminating cow's milk from their diet, some mothers also need to exclude soy and other foods such as egg, wheat and nuts. However, before eliminating food, you should always be assessed by an allergist and engage dietitian support to ensure that you're getting adequate nutrition to maintain your breast-milk supply.

Reflecting on reflux

Lots of babies spit up or reflux feeds, and feeling like you're constantly wiping down your back after every feed can be very disconcerting. More concerning is if you feel that your child is vomiting so frequently that he's not getting enough nutrients to grow.

Watch out for certain 'red flags', or signs that your baby's reflux is severe. If you notice any of the following symptoms in your baby, contact your medical practitioner for referral to an allergist or gastroenterologist:

- ✔ Blood or bile in the vomit
- ✔ Food refusal
- ✔ New onset of symptoms that seem related in particular to the introduction of cow's milk formula or cow's milk containing foods
- ✔ Poor growth (or failure to thrive — see the sidebar 'Identifying babies who aren't thriving')

Concerning constipation

Controversy remains about whether food allergy can cause constipation — research is divided about whether the phenomenon exists and, if it does, how common it is. However, in our experience in allergy treatment, some connection does seem to exist — and, again, cow's milk and soy appear to be the main potential culprits. In our experience, some patients' constipation resolves once cow's milk is removed from the diet for two to four weeks, and the symptoms return if cow's milk is reintroduced to the diet.

Identifying babies who aren't thriving

In your baby's early weeks, months and years, regular attendance at your child and maternal health nurse is important. These visits allow your nurse to check your baby's general well-being and development, and measure your baby's weight and height. Weight and height measurements are then used to determine your baby's centile, which is a way to compare your baby to the rest of the population. Centile charts use accumulated averages — for example, for a baby with a weight on the tenth centile, 90 babies in a normal population of 100 babies are heavier and ten babies lighter. So being on the 50th centile for weight or height means your baby is right on average for her age.

In the first 12 months of life, babies often 'find their centile'. That is to say they may gradually cross one or two centiles and then find a new steady rate of weight gain and growth. (Note that if your baby was premature, your nurse should use age-correction techniques when recording your baby's centile.)

However, if your baby is rapidly crossing two or more centiles or, even worse, not gaining any weight at all (referred to as *flat lining* of growth by doctors, because the line on the growth chart is a flat line), this is cause for concern. In this situation, your baby may be diagnosed as failing to thrive, and may need referral to a specialist for further investigations.

Certainly, if the constipation only occurs when formula is introduced, we are more likely to suggest an elimination/rechallenge sequence for cow's milk (see Chapter 6 for more on this type of testing). However, many infants are introduced to formula at around the same time they are introduced to solids, and solids can certainly increase the firmness of the stools (as, indeed, can formula generally) without a food allergy being present. In older children presenting with long-standing constipation, we recommend elimination/rechallenge to cow's milk and soy if they have symptoms that have arisen in early infancy.

Thinking about eczema and eating in infancy

Eczema is a persistent rash characterised by extreme dryness and itching of the skin. The condition typically begins early in life, with children at age one year being the most commonly affected. In our Melbourne-based HealthNuts study of 5,000 12-month-old infants, up to 40 per cent of children were affected by eczema in the first year of life.

Eczema can be associated with a whole range of triggers and causes (see Chapter 1 for more on eczema). Eczema that starts early in life (that is, less than six months of age) is more likely to be related to food allergy, especially if symptoms are severe. Most infantile eczema starts to settle in the second year of life. Eczema that starts after the age of two years is much less likely to be associated with food triggers — most obviously because the child has been exposed to a wide and varied diet, usually including the foods most commonly associated to eczema.

Other factors that can contribute to eczema's onset and severity include the following (listed in order of most important contributing factor):

- **Genetic susceptibility:** Eczema runs strongly in families.

- **Contact irritants:** Look for items such as synthetic clothing and nappies as well as wool.

- **Heat:** Some children are worse in winter with dry indoor heating; others are worse in summer with increased humidity.

- **Bacteria on the skin:** Children with eczema have higher loads of bacteria on their skin than children without eczema. These bacteria can activate the immune system and worsen eczema. Controlling bacterial loads on the skin by using non-soap cleansers can improve eczema symptoms dramatically. Allergy specialists often recommend weak bleach baths (similar to the chlorine content in swimming pools) to reduce staphylococcal bacteria on the skin!

✔ **Infection:** Often caused by excessive scratching, infection is caused when staphylococcal bacteria is introduced into the damaged skin.

✔ **Soaps and detergents:** Avoid soap and products that include harsh chemicals, such as some baby bath washes. Use soap-free products to wash your baby or child. But keep in mind that cleansing to reduce bacterial loads on the skin is an important part of eczema care.

Moisturisers can be used to treat dry skin and may even be useful in preventing progression to eczema — and some studies are trying to investigate this approach. Use hypoallergenic products, such as Ego, QV Skincare or Dermeze, without perfumes or colouring, and avoid moisturisers with nut-oil emollients.

Evidence suggests that about 40 to 50 per cent of children with moderately severe eczema have food allergy — mostly an IgE mediated food allergy, although the condition can be associated with both mechanisms of allergy. While that still means a reasonable chance exists that eczema isn't associated with food allergy, many doctors believe testing for the possible association between food allergy and eczema is worthwhile — particularly an IgE mediated food allergy, but a delayed food allergy could also be considered.

In a child regularly eating a food but in whom food-related eczema flares are suspected, a trial of elimination of that food is a reasonable thing to do — provided that the proof in the pudding (so to speak) of the diagnosis is established by re-introducing the food back in to the diet to see whether the same symptoms of eczema flare come back.

The most common types of delayed food allergy that can flare eczema include cow's milk, soy, wheat and occasionally egg. Nut allergy (including peanut allergy) associated with eczema is almost always IgE mediated.

Understanding that your breast milk is composed of what you eat

In addition to carbohydrate, protein, fat and water, breast milk also provides vitamins, minerals, digestive enzymes and hormones — all of the things that a growing infant requires. As such, breast milk is regarded as a complete and perfect food for infants in the first six months of life. Breast milk also contains antibodies and other immune cells and factors passed from the mother that help the baby to fight infections.

Understanding why some children get eczema

Many factors appear to be associated with either the development of eczema or making your child's eczema flare. One of these is diet but the other is your child's genes. A recently discovered gene, *filaggrin*, appears to be the cause of eczema in about 20 per cent of cases. And while you can't do anything to change your genes, researchers are hopeful that understanding the genes involved in eczema may give them some tools for better prevention or treatment. Filaggrin is a gene involved in ensuring optimal function of the skin barrier. So those who have an abnormal filaggrin gene develop very dry skin and eczema. Gene testing for filaggrin isn't a routinely available test that can be ordered by your doctor but is widely used in studies as researchers seek to understand more about the reasons eczema develops.

The principal proteins of breast milk are casein, alpha-lactalbumin, lactoferrin (an iron-storage protein), IgA, lysozyme and serum albumin. The carbohydrate in breast milk is lactose.

Lactose is higher in the foremilk of breast — the hindmilk is richer in fats that are more satiating. If the breast isn't given enough time to fill with hindmilk or the baby doesn't drain the breast when feeding, babies can be at risk of a relative lactose intolerance (refer to 'Distinguishing Between Cow's Milk Allergy and Lactose Intolerance', earlier in the chapter).

Lots of foods ingested by the mother appear to make their way into breast milk. While little is known about how long food takes to makes its way into the breast milk after eating, we do know fully breastfed babies can have reactions to the food allergens in the breast milk.

In the past, breastfeeding mothers of infants with a high risk of developing allergic disease (due to a family history of allergic disease) were told to avoid common food allergens, such as nuts and eggs, when pregnant and breastfeeding to try to minimise the risk of food allergy. This recommendation has now been reversed because no evidence exists that avoidance of these foods during pregnancy or lactation in either the mother's or infant's diet prevents food allergy (refer to Chapter 3 for more on this).

See Chapter 7 for more on removing food you know your child is allergic to from your diet if you're breastfeeding.

Chapter 6

Testing for Food Allergies

- -

In This Chapter

▶ Understanding why different tests are used for different types of food allergy

▶ Learning about what type of testing is used for IgE mediated food allergy

▶ Knowing what to expect when your child requires testing for non-IgE mediated food allergy

▶ Talking about scientifically unproven allergy testing

- -

*F*ood allergy testing has come ahead in leaps and bounds over the last 20 years and we now have very good and reliable tests for most food allergies (although more work needs to be done for some of the less common types of food allergies). In particular, experts understand an awful lot more about how to diagnose *IgE mediated food allergies* (food allergies that cause immediate reactions; see Chapter 4 for more) in a safe and reliable way. Testing for *non-IgE mediated food allergies* and *mixed IgE/non-IgE mediated food allergies* (delayed food allergies) has also been developed, mostly in the form of home-based elimination/rechallenge tests.

In this chapter, we cover testing options available for immediate and delayed food allergies, to help you work out where to go to get testing and understand what testing needs to be undertaken for your child with suspected food allergy. We also cover other tests available that aren't supported by scientific analysis and aren't recommended.

Some of the allergy tests covered in this chapter can only be undertaken in specialist allergy clinics. Because research into allergies, and the validation of appropriate, scientifically proven testing is really only a recent thing, a time lag has occurred between the release of the research and the updating of practising GPs on the research and tests available. With the information in this chapter, you can have a fully informed discussion with your GP about your child's health.

Comparing Testing for Immediate and Delayed Food Allergies

The simple answer to understanding what test should be used to diagnose food allergy is that if your child has symptoms that occur within minutes of ingesting a food, your child should have doctor-based testing for an IgE mediated food allergy. Allergen-specific IgE testing is very reliable — if your child has a negative allergen-specific IgE test, this result effectively rules out the chance that your child can develop food-induced anaphylaxis.

However, a negative allergen-specific IgE test result doesn't rule out a food allergy altogether — as discussed in Chapter 5, other, non-IgE mediated and mixed IgE/non-IgE mediated, forms of allergy can also occur. What's reassuring about a negative test is that your doctor can guide you in the diagnosis of other forms of food allergy safely at home. This involves a process of eliminating particular foods from the diet and, if symptoms seem to go away because of the removal of the food, then reintroducing the food to the diet to see if the symptoms come back. (See the section 'Checking for Delayed Food Allergies' for more information.)

Home elimination/rechallenge tests should be done together with your doctor because working out if symptoms have in fact improved with elimination and worsened with reintroduction of foods can be difficult.

Testing for IgE Mediated Food Allergies

The most important part about working out whether your child has an IgE mediated food allergy is for your doctor to take a thorough history. Doctors are like detectives when they are assessing your child for a food allergy, and they love to hunt out what part of your child's diet might have provoked a reaction — so be prepared for being cross-examined! Your doctor asks about aspects such as how soon after eating the food your child developed allergic signs and symptoms, and what those signs looked like. Your doctor also asks lots of questions about the food that your child ate — whether the food was fully cooked, partially cooked or raw, and how much was eaten.

By the time you take your child to your doctor, any signs of an allergic reaction are highly unlikely to be still remaining. So the doctor has to rely almost entirely on history rather than examination, unlike other medical conditions where examination findings can help to discover the cause of the problem.

As well as going over the symptoms of the presumed allergic reaction, your doctor also asks you whether your child has tolerated the food in question either before or since the reaction. Parents are often surprised to discover that, although typically IgE mediated reactions occur to small amounts of food, the amount that causes a reaction can vary from person to person — so some children can have small amounts without reacting while others react to very small amounts of the food.

Your doctor examines your child but doesn't really look for signs of food allergy. Rather, your doctor looks for other signs of allergic conditions such as eczema and asthma because these diseases tend to run in packs — if children have one form of allergic disease they're more likely to have another. The same is true for asking questions about a family history of allergy — allergy does run in families (as discussed further in Chapter 2).

Once your doctor is satisfied your child's symptoms may have been caused by food allergy, various tests may be ordered, such as skin prick tests, blood tests and hospital-based food challenges. The following sections cover these tests in more detail.

Using skin prick tests

The mainstay of testing for IgE mediated food allergy is to test whether the immune system has produced IgE antibodies to the food allergen in question (allergen-specific IgE — refer to Chapter 4). If your child has a history of an immediate allergic reaction to a food and the allergen-specific IgE test to that food is positive, this confirms that your child has IgE mediated food allergy to that food.

Traditionally, the simplest way to test whether a person makes IgE antibody to a food is to do a skin prick test (SPT). The test procedure is as follows:

1. **A drop of allergen is placed on the child's back or forearm.**

   The allergen is a commercially prepared product containing the food protein in question, held in a liquid suspension of glycerol.

2. **A small lancet or prick device is gently pricked through the drop.**

   This prick introduces the allergenic protein into the superficial layer of the skin.

3. **A drop of histamine and a drop of saline are also applied as a positive control and negative control for the test.**

4. **The test is allowed to develop for 15 minutes and is then read.**

   The histamine test should come up as a bump, to show that your child is not taking any medications that can block the SPT reaction; the saline test should cause no reaction, to show that the skin is not over-reactive and causing a bump to the prick action itself. (See the following section for more about control methods used in skin prick tests.)

See Figure 6-1 for how a SPT is performed (either on the arm or back).

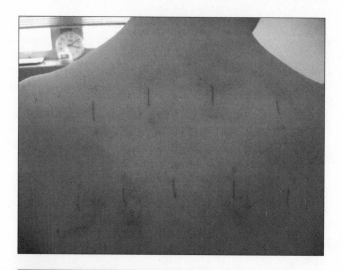

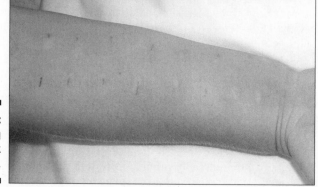

Figure 6-1:
Receiving a skin prick test.

The pricks that occur during a SPT are more like pinches than pricks. While the pricks are a little uncomfortable, the most annoying thing about the test is that, as the lumps develop, they can be very itchy. Cold compresses on the lumps after the test or sometimes antihistamines can help your child feel more comfortable.

The most common adverse event from SPT is fainting, but this is more likely to occur in older children and is very uncommon in young children. Rarely, your child can have a generalised allergic reaction to the SPT procedure, which is why these tests should only be done by doctors or nurses who have experience with such tests and where facilities are available to treat an allergic reaction if one develops.

Reading skin prick test results

Reading the SPT involves measuring the diameter of any lump (or *wheal*) that appears at the site of the testing. (Redness can also result around the lump, but this is not measured as part of the test result.) The basic outcomes are as follows:

- ✔ **Negative:** This outcome is recorded if no itchy lump occurs, or if the lump is less than 3 millimetres in diameter.
- ✔ **Positive:** This outcome is recorded if the diameter of the wheal size is 3 millimetres bigger than the negative saline control (or more).

Sometimes, a wheal of 2 millimetres diameter can indicate a positive test, and your doctor will discuss with you what this means.

If your child has had antihistamines in the previous 48 to 72 hours, the body won't make a wheal response and the results of the tests will be inaccurate (more scientifically speaking, the positive control of this test will be negative). So, make sure you don't administer any antihistamine medications such as Zyrtec or Phenergan for at least four days before your child has a SPT. (If you forget to tell your doctor that you have accidentally given such a medication to your child, your doctor can still work out that your child has had antihistamine from the test results.)

Doctors also use a negative control in the form of saline — just to make sure that the child's skin isn't reacting to the physical action of the SPT. If a child does make a wheal to a negative control, we call that *dermatographism*, which literally means that the skin forms a lump if it's scratched or drawn on. Dermatographism is harmless and most parents already know that their child has sensitive skin — with lumps forming if things are rubbed against the child's arm, for example.

If your child's skin does react to the negative control, the SPT is repeated at a later stage or a blood test to check for allergen-specific IgE antibodies is ordered.

Interpreting skin prick tests

SPTs are very reliable when they're negative — if they're negative, your child is highly unlikely to have an IgE mediated food allergy.

However, SPTs are more difficult to interpret when the results are positive — the presence of a positive test only means that your child has made allergen-specific IgE to the food but may or may not indicate clinical food allergy. Many children with allergen-specific IgE to a food are not clinically allergic and are only 'sensitised' (refer to Chapter 1 to read about sensitisation and allergy). For example, about 50 per cent of children with a positive SPT to a certain food are able to tolerate that food. The reasons some children who have made allergy antibodies to a food aren't allergic to that food aren't yet understood — although researchers are working hard to discover them. Understanding the mechanisms that prevent allergy in this situation could lead to new ways of treating food allergy.

If a child has a positive skin prick test but has never eaten the food, we say that this child is *sensitised* to that food. Unless children have eaten and reacted to the food, we can't say that they're definitely allergic to that food.

We don't recommend that SPT be used in a screening situation because a positive result may not necessarily mean an allergy to a food — it only means that your child has made allergy antibodies against the food. So, if your child has never eaten the food, we don't recommend doing a SPT for that food to see if they might be allergic.

The main exception to the rule of not using SPTs as screening tests is those children who already have an allergy to one food: we need to understand if they're allergic to other common food allergens, because these children have a 25 to 30 per cent chance of being allergic to more than one food. (Refer to Chapter 4 for more on the common foods that cause food allergy.) For instance, in children with a history of an allergic reaction to peanut, we do a SPT to confirm that they're peanut allergic and also screen for other tree nuts (because about 25 per cent of children with peanut allergy also have an allergy to another nut, such as cashew). SPT may also be used as a screening test in a child who has never eaten a food but has a strong risk factor for food allergy (such as severe eczema in babies). SPTs are great when you want to confirm a food allergy but doctors need to be cautious about using them to screen for food allergies.

Although positive SPT (or blood allergen-specific IgE tests — see following section) don't always indicate food allergy, researchers have found that the chances of an allergy being present increase progressively as SPT wheal sizes (or the level of allergen-specific IgE in the blood) increase.

Researchers have established 95 per cent threshold cut-offs — above which a 95 per cent chance exists that food allergy is present. These 95 per cent thresholds can be used to diagnose food allergy in children who haven't eaten the food. For example, a wheal diameter of 8 millimetres is the 95 per cent threshold for predicting the presence of peanut allergy. (Similar 95 per cent thresholds have been established for cow's milk and egg allergies, but not the other foods.) The size of a SPT wheal can vary depending on the person doing the test, the device used, the time of the day, and where on the body the SPT is performed. So the 95 per cent thresholds for SPT really only provide a guide for doctors in making a diagnosis of food allergy when the child hasn't yet eaten the food. Allergists have also established 95 per cent thresholds for the blood allergen-specific IgE tests to peanut, egg, milk and fish. These are more accurate because the levels of IgE don't tend to fluctuate the way the SPT wheal size can.

If a child with a strong risk of food allergy who has never eaten peanut has a wheal size to peanut of 10 millimetres, we can say the child has a 95 per cent chance of having peanut allergy rather than just being sensitised to peanut — that is, if the child were to eat peanut, an allergic reaction to peanut is more than 95 per cent likely.

Understanding that skin prick tests can't predict the severity of reactions

The first question parents often ask when they receive the SPT results is, 'Does this test tell us whether our child will have anaphylaxis?'. Unfortunately, the answer to this question is emphatically 'No'.

No allergy tests can predict the severity of a future allergic reaction — available tests can only predict the likelihood of a reaction occurring. So while the bigger the wheal size the more likely it is that your child is allergic to the food, doctors just can't predict what type of reaction your child is likely to have — your child's reaction could be a few hives or it could be a more full-blown reaction.

The only known predictor of anaphylaxis is a previous episode of anaphylaxis, and even this isn't absolute — although 80 to 85 per cent of children who have had an anaphylaxis have another severe reaction, up to 40 per cent of children who have an episode of anaphylaxis have had a milder reaction on previous exposure.

If your child's test results for an immediate food allergy are positive, your child may or may not be allergic to the food. But the bigger the SPT, the more likely your child is to have food allergy.

Checking blood samples for allergen-specific IgE antibodies

Some doctors choose to do a blood test for food-specific IgE antibodies.

Traditionally, a technique called RAST (radioallergosorbent test) was used to detect allergen-specific IgE antibodies (using radioactive reagents), and this acronym has now become the colloquial term for these types of tests (since it's easier to say than the alternatives!). However, the main methods used nowadays are immunoassays for allergen-specific IgE, which don't involve any radioactive reagents (the tests are called *ImmunoCAP* and *IMMULITE*).

To do the blood tests for food-specific IgE antibodies, your child's doctor orders a small blood sample to be taken and sent to the laboratory. You need to return to your doctor's clinic for review, or contact the doctor to obtain the results.

The main reason that allergists prefer SPTs (see preceding section) over blood allergen-specific IgE tests is that patients can be told the results on the day of testing and a management plan implemented immediately.

Table 6-1 outlines the pros and cons of SPT versus blood allergen-specific IgE tests.

Table 6-1	Pros and Cons of SPT versus Allergen-Specific IgE Tests	
	SPT	*Allergen-Specific IgE Tests*
Results provided on the day	✔	✗
Risk of an allergic reaction	Generalised allergic reactions; anaphylaxis is rare	✗
Well-tolerated	Some children faint	Some children have needle phobias
Undertaken by allergy specialists	✔	✔
Undertaken by general practitioners and general paediatricians	✔	✔
Number of foods that can be tested	As many as required and/or tolerated	Only four foods tested on one blood sample, performed up to 3 times within a 12-month period, can be claimed through Medicare per year
Can be performed when skin is affected by eczema	✗ SPT can only be done on healthy skin — if the skin on the back or arms are affected by eczema, the SPT can't be done	✔
Can be performed when skin is affected by dermatographism	✗ SPT are difficult to interpret if dermatographism is present	✔
Can be performed while using antihistamines	✗ The SPT can't be done if your child is on antihistamines; some children aren't able to stop their antihistamines due to severe hay fever or eczema	✔

Challenging food allergies in hospital

Hospital-based food challenges are undertaken when a food allergy diagnosis is in question. Referral to an allergist is required if a food challenge is needed. The allergist may arrange for a hospital-based challenge when

- ✔ Symptoms and test results don't correspond with each other — for example, an allergic reaction has occurred but the test is negative and parents are sure that the food caused the reaction.

- ✔ The SPT or allergen-specific IgE blood test is positive but the child hasn't eaten the food previously, and the test result is below the 95 per cent threshold cut-off for food allergy.

- ✔ Parents aren't sure which particular food has caused the reaction when eaten as part of a meal.

- ✔ Symptoms of the allergic reaction have been unclear.

- ✔ Your child has reached an age when she's likely to have developed tolerance to her allergy. (For more about prognosis of food allergy, see Chapter 12.)

In a hospital-based challenge, increasing amounts of the food are given to your child, usually at 15 to 20 minute intervals. The first dose is usually a very small amount touched to the inside of the lip, and then larger amounts of the allergen are given (usually mixed with a food that the child routinely tolerates, such as apple puree or yoghurt) until a standard serve of the food is reached (for example, 100 millilitres of milk, or one egg). Your child then continues on this highest dose once a day for a week after the challenge. Sometimes the food needs to be hidden so that your child can't be influenced by whether he thinks he has eaten the food and develop suggestible symptoms. (See Chapter 3 for more about food challenge tests and how these tests are controlled scientifically.)

Children are monitored throughout the challenge to check what type of allergic signs and symptoms are developing. Once the first clearly objective allergic sign is identified, the challenge is stopped. Children are usually observed for a minimum of one to two hours after the last dose (if they don't react to the challenge) or after an objective allergic reaction (a positive challenge). And a staff member usually calls the next day and after one or two weeks to check that your child hasn't developed a late reaction.

Sometimes your child might develop an allergic reaction either on the way home from the clinic or later in the day or even in the following week when taking the food at home. Most clinics ask you to contact them if this occurs. If the symptoms are a generalised allergic reaction, you should take your child immediately to the closest hospital emergency room. If anaphylaxis occurs, call an ambulance.

Some doctors use food challenges to try to work out whether a child is *exquisitely sensitive* to a food (meaning the child may react to very low doses of the food). If your child is exquisitely sensitive to an allergen, doctors are more likely to prescribe more stringent avoidance of precautionary labelling (see Chapter 8 for advice on reading ingredient labels). However, this practice isn't universally used because, unfortunately, the type of reaction on one exposure may not always predict how severe future reactions are going to be — although a severe reaction (anaphylaxis) usually means that your child is likely to have further anaphylaxis reactions. Also, the severity of a reaction can depend on other things such as exercise or whether your child has a virus at the time — allergic reactions can be more severe if your child exercises heavily after eating the food, or is unwell with a virus or asthma. So although in the clinical setting a child might tolerate a larger dose with a small reaction, this doesn't reliably transfer to the real-life scenario. In some instances, a child might vomit following an unexpected food allergen exposure and yet, at another time, the child may develop hives and *angioedema* (swelling beneath the skin) to a similar dose of the same allergen. Many undetermined factors other than allergen dosage are likely to be important in the variation in reactions that can occur in the same child over time.

Checking for Delayed Food Allergies

If your doctor has eliminated the chances that your child has an IgE mediated (or immediate) food allergy and believes that your child's symptoms are more suggestive of a non-IgE mediated or mixed IgE/non-IgE mediated (or delayed) food allergy, the next step is to consider whether testing for delayed food allergy might be required. Most delayed food allergies cause some form of gastrointestinal symptoms such as diarrhoea or vomiting. The main ways to test for these allergies are home-based food elimination challenges and patch tests. Both these methods are covered in the following sections.

Some signs and symptoms require further investigation by a gastroenterologist or an allergist before you move to home allergy testing for the delayed food allergies; these signs and symptoms are listed in the sidebar "Red flag' symptoms that may require further investigation'.

'Red flag' symptoms that may require further investigation

Some gastrointestinal signs and symptoms are more serious than others and warrant more formal investigation of the problem by either a general paediatrician or gastroenterologist. The gastroenterologist may undertake an *endoscopy* (which includes a *gastroscopy*, or inspection of the interior of the stomach, with or without a colonoscopy) to rule out other conditions such as coeliac disease, or more specific syndromes associated with presumed delayed food allergy such as eosinophilic esophagitis, gastro-esophageal reflux or allergic proctocolitis (discussed in Chapter 5).

The symptoms to watch for in your child include the following:

✔ Chronic diarrhoea

✔ Failure to thrive (poor weight gain or weight loss)

✔ Iron deficiency anaemia

✔ Persistent rectal bleeding

✔ Vomiting that doesn't respond to anti-reflux medication

✔ Vomiting that produces stomach contents that look like coffee grounds

Undertaking a home elimination and challenge test

A home-based food elimination and challenge simply consists of removing all foods containing the suspected offending protein (for example, cow's milk or wheat) from all aspects of the diet and watching to see if symptoms improve, then reintroducing the food to see if symptoms return. Undertaking this sort of test involves careful reading of labels (see Chapter 8 for help with this) and also excluding of allergens from the maternal diet if the baby is breastfed (refer to Chapter 5).

Home testing is usually done for a total of four to eight weeks, and parents are often advised to keep a diary during this time to record whether the child has any symptoms linked to the allergen being tested. For instance, if the child presents with diarrhoea or constipation, parents are asked to keep a diary about the nature and frequency of bowel actions throughout the home challenge test.

Food elimination and challenge testing at home involves two phases:

✔ **Elimination phase:** During the elimination step of the test, avoid giving your child the suspected allergen (or refrain from eating the allergen yourself, if you're breastfeeding).

You may notice an initial improvement in the first few days, although sometimes complete resolution of the presenting symptom can take several weeks. Sometimes symptoms may only improve after a few weeks, so usually the elimination phase is continued for a minimum of two weeks — and some doctors recommend four weeks.

✔ **Rechallenge phase:** Once you're comfortable that the symptoms have resolved (or at least improved considerably), you need to reintroduce the food in question to your child's diet. We always recommend our patients start with small doses of the food and increase the dose each day — mainly so that we don't precipitate a nasty reaction, but also so we can see at what dose threshold symptoms occur.

When reintroducing a food, we suggest starting with one teaspoon daily of the allergen being tested; double the dose each day until a full serve is achieved or your child develops symptoms — at which point, the challenge should be stopped. Typically with liquids (such as cow's milk and soy milk) we start with 10 millilitres on the first day and double the dose daily (so 20 millilitres given on day 2, 40 on day 3 and so on) until 200 millilitres is tolerated. Starting with the most pure source of the food (for example, a cereal such as Weetbix for wheat or cow's milk for cow's milk protein) is best so we can confirm that other aspects of the food preparation aren't producing the symptoms. Once the child is tolerating the allergen regularly, we then suggest that other related products be tried in the diet — for example, with a child allergic to cow's milk, once milk is being tolerated, we'd try other dairy products such as cheese and yoghurt.

Knowing the difficulties involved with home elimination and challenge testing

Home food elimination and challenge tests can present some difficulties for parents, including the following:

✔ **Time frame:** Sometimes a clear answer isn't achieved from the first elimination–rechallenge cycle and the whole process needs to be repeated.

✔ **Incomplete diet:** If parents are over-zealous with excluding food from their child's diet, this type of testing can result in a more broadly restricted diet than is necessary and can thus place the child at risk of micronutrient deficiencies.

We always recommend that a parent speak with a dietitian trained in safe elimination diet implementation if more than two or three foods require elimination — your child's doctor can provide a referral. We also always provide calcium supplementation advice for those avoiding cow's milk.

✔ **Incomplete testing:** Many parents attempt elimination testing for their child but most miss the critical step of reintroducing the food, which is necessary in order to prove that the food in question does indeed continue to illicit symptoms.

Keeping safe during home challenges

Obviously, the risks of home-based challenges are the recurrence of the symptom that you're concerned about in the first place. So if your child's symptoms were diarrhoea or vomiting, you can expect these symptoms to recur when the food is reintroduced.

However, since home testing is the gold-standard method for diagnosing delayed food allergy, the benefits outweigh the risks. A hospital stay to diagnose this condition is impractical (because symptoms occur hours to days after eating) and, more importantly, isn't required since home challenges are essentially safe if undertaken carefully.

When reintroducing a food to your child's diet, if you notice more severe symptoms or signs of an immediate reaction, such as hives, swelling or vomiting within minutes, stop the food challenge and call your doctor or allergy centre. Of course, if your child has any unexpected signs of anaphylaxis (coughing, wheezing, breathing difficulties or collapse) call an ambulance immediately. Tests can be wrong — just because the SPT was negative, the risk of an IgE mediated food allergy isn't 100 per cent excluded unless your child is already regularly tolerating the food.

A challenge should not be done at home if the SPT or allergen-specific IgE blood test is positive because a possibility exists that your child can have an IgE mediated food allergy reaction, which can be dangerous.

Using patch tests

Patch tests, often referred to as atopic patch tests (APT), are a new type of allergy test still in development. They have been investigated particularly for use in eosinophilic esophagitis and other delayed food allergies.

Essentially, the principle of the patch test is to insert a small amount of purified food into special chambers within the patch, which is then attached with adhesive tape to your child's back and left in place for 48 hours. The foods are chosen based on the child's current diet, knowledge of common allergens, and previous reactions. The doctor removes the patch at 48 hours and then reads the result at 72 hours — the area where the patch was attached shows obvious signs of irritation if the test is positive; the area is unaffected if the test is negative.

Unfortunately, the early promise of these tests has not translated into reliable testing in the clinical setting — although research into this form of testing continues.

Scrutinising Unproven Tests

The delay that often occurs while waiting to see allergists has driven the development of alternative health practitioners (who in some cases are doctors). Many of these practitioners offer a range of unproven allergy tests, often at great expense to the consumer.

Here's a list of the most dubious tests to watch out for:

- Cytotoxic testing
- Food-specific IgG and IgG4 tests
- Hair analysis/toxicology tests
- Kinesiology
- VEGA testing

These tests have not been shown to be predictive of food allergy. Some of them are based on concepts that are ill-informed and clearly incorrect when checked against known medical knowledge.

Others take advantage of the ill-informed consumer — in the case of IgG testing, for example, the practitioner is relying on the consumer not picking up that IgE testing, which is valid and reproducible for the diagnosis of food allergy, is unrelated to IgG testing, which is neither. By using a known medical term, IgG, these tests are masquerading as the real thing, when in fact they're phony. A positive IgG test just reflects that your child has been exposed to the food in the past — not that your child is allergic to that food. Allergen-specific IgG doesn't lead to symptoms.

Part III
Living with Food Allergies

Glenn Lumsden

'We made sure your cake was mouth-watering, not eye-swelling or skin-itching.'

In this part ...

Managing your child's food allergies is a big responsibility and many parents can feel overwhelmed and anxious about how to keep their child safe. Because severe allergic reactions to food (anaphylaxis) can be life-threatening and result in death, parents are understandably extremely worried by the possibility that their child may accidentally eat their food allergen. Staff in schools and childcare centres are similarly fearful of the responsibility of managing your child's allergy while at school or child care. While being alert to the possibility that your child can accidentally eat a food that contains a known allergen is good, being overly anxious about it isn't healthy — for you or your child.

The best way to gain a more balanced attitude and reduce this unnecessary anxiety is to increase your knowledge of how to manage your child's food allergies — and that's what Part III is all about. Becoming familiar with the information in this part can empower you and your family to manage your child's food allergies. You can gain greater confidence in helping your child avoid food allergens and in acting quickly should your child accidentally eat a problem food.

In this part, we outline the four key steps to managing your child's food allergies. Staff in schools and childcare services are required to do many things in order to provide a safe and supportive environment for children with food allergies. So, for these staff, we provide information to help you manage a child's food allergies while under your care. We also offer some tips for older children with food allergies to encourage these children to take some responsibility for their food allergies as they mature. Finally, we explain the information in your child's medical emergency action plan for allergic reactions or anaphylaxis. This is one of the most important resources that you and your child can refer to when your child has an allergic reaction.

Chapter 7

Managing Food Allergies

- -

In This Chapter

▶ Finding out about the four steps to manage your child's food allergy

▶ Avoiding food allergens by reading ingredient labels and using alternatives

▶ Identifying situations when accidental ingestion of food allergen is more likely

▶ Knowing how to recognise and treat allergic reactions, including anaphylaxis

▶ Being aware of risk factors

▶ Getting help from a dietitian

- -

*P*arents are often quickly overwhelmed when we tell them that their child has a food allergy and now needs to avoid that food. At first, they may think handling the situation is easy — they can just remove the food from their house. But then they start thinking about other aspects, such as what their other children like to eat, or how they can protect their child outside of the home. All of these worries flood into their minds, and they start feeling extremely anxious about the responsibility of managing their child's food allergy.

Feeling anxious about having to manage your child's food allergy is very normal. But the good news is you don't have to feel anxious — you just need to take control of the situation and become familiar with what you can do to help manage your child's food allergy. In fact, you don't have to remove the food from your home, your child's siblings can still enjoy the food, and you can take control to help keep your child safe even when not at home.

In this chapter, we cover the four basic elements of managing your child's food allergy. We also look at enlisting a dietitian to help you with possible food replacements and new recipe options that suit your child's particular requirements.

Knowing the Four Elements of Food Allergy Management

You need to be familiar with four basic elements when managing your child's food allergy:

- ✔ **Avoid food allergens:** Replace your child's known food allergens with safe alternatives and help your child to avoid allergens. Teach your child how to read ingredient labels.

- ✔ **Minimise the chance of accidental exposure:** Reduce the chances of your child eating the food (or foods) she's allergic to by mistake. Also known as *risk minimisation*, you and your child becoming familiar with high-risk situations is important, as is developing ways to avoid accidents in these situations.

- ✔ **Know how to recognise and treat an allergic reaction:** Be familiar with your child's emergency action plan. If your child has been prescribed an adrenaline auto-injector, ensure your child carries this at all times.

- ✔ **Ensure your child takes his asthma medicine:** Uncontrolled asthma is the most important risk factor for severe or fatal allergic reactions.

Avoiding the Foods that Cause Troubles

No cure yet exists for food allergies. Researchers are working hard to discover new curative treatments (see Chapter 13), but any effective therapy is likely to be at least five to ten years away, probably longer. So if your child has been diagnosed with a food allergy, the only way to manage your child's food allergy is to exclude that food from your child's diet.

While this may sound like a fairly simple instruction to follow, avoiding the common food allergens isn't easy, because these allergens are used extensively in cooking and are ingredients in food from almost all cultures around the world. Egg, cow's milk, wheat and nuts, in particular, are prevalent in both Eastern and Western foods, while shellfish and fish (as well as peanut) are especially common as ingredients in Asian cooking. So avoiding the common food allergens requires you to take great care when you're doing your shopping and when you and your family are eating out. (In Chapter 8, we look at the topic of eating in restaurants with your child with food allergy more closely.)

Although avoiding allergenic foods isn't straightforward, you and your child can do a number of things to make avoiding food allergens easier, starting with reading ingredient labels and finding alternatives to replace the foods your child is allergic to. If your child is still breastfed, removing known allergens from your diet may be required for some food allergies — your doctor can advise you on whether this is important for your child's allergy.

Avoiding food allergens and finding replacements means changing the way you, your family and your child think about eating, preparing food and eating out. We offer you some tips and advice in the following sections that can help to make this process easier.

Reading ingredient labels

One of the most practical things you can do to help avoid a food allergen is to closely read ingredient labels on packaged foods, because this helps you work out whether an allergen is present in that food.

Being familiar with reading food labels can help prevent allergic reactions due to accidental ingestion. In a recent study by Food Standards Australia New Zealand (*Consumer Study on Food Allergen Labelling: Follow on survey 2008–2009*), almost half the respondents reported that the person in their household with the most serious allergy had experienced a reaction since diagnosis, and this was significantly more common (55 per cent) among respondents who were always or often unsure about food items or ingredients when reading labels to ascertain whether or not the product was safe to eat.

Manufacturers in Australia and New Zealand can label their products in two ways: Mandatory statements about the product ingredients and voluntary statements about potential allergens.

Here's a summary of the two types of statements:

- ✔ **Mandatory statements:** These are governed by requirements set down by the Australia New Zealand Food Standards code. Customers must be able to identify any potential allergens, including products made from an allergen.

- ✔ **Voluntary statements:** These include statements such as 'may contain traces of . . .', or 'made in a facility that also makes products on the same production line containing . . .', and are sometimes listed on food labels by manufacturers to indicate the possibility of cross-contamination with allergen during the production process. Such statements are voluntary and aren't based on any testing or measurement of allergen levels in the food.

Instead of using voluntary statements, the Australian Food and Grocery Council Guidelines recommend that Australian and New Zealand food manufacturers adopt Voluntary Incidental Trace Allergen Labelling (VITAL) to help provide a clear and consistent message about food allergens to consumers.

See Chapter 8 for more on reading labels and shopping for your child.

Sidestepping allergens with alternative foods

Trying to remove a particular food from your child's diet is never easy. So much of what we eat these days is already prepared or pre-packaged and most of these foods contain one or more of the common allergens. Everyday items like breakfast cereal, bread, crackers and sweet biscuits all usually contain milk, egg and wheat, and often peanut or tree nuts as well. So managing your child's food allergy diet can be quite challenging.

But you can still offer your child a broad diet that's healthy and delicious through using alternative foods in place of the food allergen that your child is avoiding. In this section, we provide you with some readily available alternatives for the three common food allergens that are most prevalent as staple foods in the Western diet — milk, egg and wheat.

Avoiding most other common allergens (such as peanut, tree nuts, fish and shellfish) is more straightforward, so we haven't discussed these here. But flick over to Chapter 15 for more information on replacing these, and other, common allergens.

Cow's milk

Milk is a staple food in the Western diet and is an important source of protein and calcium in your child's diet, so alternative foods must offer sufficient amounts of protein and calcium.

The most appropriate alternative depends on your child's age and what sort of milk your child is likely to drink.

Most milk formulas are cow's milk-based so if your baby is not fully breastfed and has been diagnosed with cow's milk allergy, you need to consider other forms of formula milk. You need to know a few things about alternative milk formulas:

- Babies under six months old with cow's milk allergy and babies with non-IgE mediated allergy to cow's milk (refer to Chapter 5) should have a hydrolysed cow's milk formula as an alternative to standard cow's milk formula. These formulas can only be provided on prescription from your doctor. (Options available in Australia include Alfare and Pepti-Junior; in New Zealand, only Pepti-Junior is available).

Partially hydrolysed cow's milk formulas (HA formulas) are only partly digested and still contain significant amounts of cow's milk allergens. Because of this, they're not suitable as an alternative to cow's milk formula in babies with cow's milk allergy. They may, however, be used to prevent allergic conditions in babies at increased risk of allergy problems (refer to Chapter 3).

✔ Between 80 and 90 per cent of babies with immediate IgE mediated cow's milk allergy can tolerate soy milk and be placed on a soy milk formula; however, most doctors don't recommend soy formulas for babies under six months of age. Between 10 and 20 per cent of babies with cow's milk allergy are also allergic to soy milk. Babies who are allergic to both cow's milk and soy require an extensively hydrolysed formula (eHF) such as Alfaré or Pepti-Junior, only available on prescription.

✔ Up to 10 per cent of babies with cow's milk allergy can't tolerate eHF (they react to the small amount of cow's milk allergen remaining in eHF) and require an amino acid–based formula (such as Neocate, Elecare), which are also only available on prescription.

Toddlers and older children have more options for milk replacements, including the following:

✔ **Soy milk:** Whole soy milk (as compared to soy milk formula) isn't suitable for babies under 12 months, but can be taken from one year of age (if your child isn't also allergic to soy). Be sure to choose a brand that has added calcium (so the product has the same amount of calcium as cow's milk).

✔ **Rice milk:** Rice milk isn't suitable for children under two years of age because it's low in protein and fat, but can be used as an alternative to cow's milk in children older than two years. Again, make sure to choose a brand with added calcium.

✔ **Oat milk and potato milk:** These milks are more expensive and not as readily available. However, if you can find them, these alternative milks can be used for children from two years of age onwards, for drinking or as replacement ingredients in cooking.

If your child is drinking less than 600 millilitres per day of calcium-fortified soy or rice milk, he may need to take a calcium supplement. Your doctor, dietitian or pharmacist can help you find an appropriate supplement.

Milk products that offer different levels of milk proteins (such as A2 Milk) and lactose-free cow's milk are partially modified but still contain the allergenic cow's milk proteins. So they're not suitable for your child with cow's milk allergy. Other milks, such as goat's milk, sheep's milk, horse's milk aren't suitable alternatives for children with cow's milk allergy either, because they contain proteins that are very similar to cow's milk and children with cow's milk allergy can react to them.

Egg

Egg, like milk, is a widely used ingredient in foods from almost all cultures, so can be a difficult food to avoid. Obviously, avoiding egg means not eating dishes like scrambled egg, omelette or quiche. But, perhaps not so obviously, egg is also in foods such as mayonnaise, custard and marshmallows. Finding an alternative to egg that can be used in cooking makes your life and your child's life more enjoyable.

Several alternatives to egg are available that allow you to continue to make tasty foods:

- ✔ **Egg replacer:** This can be bought at most supermarkets. Just be careful not to mistake egg substitute for egg replacer, because egg substitute is still made using egg whites (the product is for people who are on low-cholesterol diets).

- ✔ **A simple mixture of baking powder, water and oil:** This mixture can replace egg in recipes. Mix one and a half tablespoons of oil with one and a half tablespoons of warm water and one teaspoon of baking powder, then whisk until foamy. This is a good option if you can't get to the supermarket to buy egg replacer — chances are, you already have these ingredients in your house.

Some controversy surrounds whether your child with egg allergy should avoid foods that contain small amounts of baked egg, such as cakes and biscuits (refer to Chapter 4 for more on this issue in egg allergy). We suggest that if your child hasn't had any reactions to such foods, your child can continue eating these foods; however, you should discuss the issue with your doctor. Your child should still avoid any foods that contain larger amounts of egg (such as mud cakes, custard, meringue and mayonnaise) and, of course, whole eggs (such as quiche and scrambled eggs).

Wheat

Wheat can seem difficult to avoid; this food appears to be in everything. Staple foods such as bread and pasta are made from wheat, and wheat is present in most snack foods, including crackers, sweet biscuits, cereals and snack bars.

Wheat allergy should not be confused with coeliac disease (discussed in Chapter 5). People with coeliac disease must avoid all gluten-containing foods (including wheat, but also barley and oats) while people with a wheat allergy don't necessarily have to avoid gluten.

People with a wheat allergy can usually tolerate other grains, such as oats, rye and barley. So these grains, along with rice, corn and quinoa, can be used as alternatives to wheat, as follows:

- ✔ **Oat, rye, barley and rice flours** are good alternatives to wheat flour.
- ✔ **Rice, corn and quinoa pastas** are available in place of wheat pastas.
- ✔ **Rice bread, corn bread, and gluten-free bread** are all readily available alternatives to wheat bread.
- ✔ **Rice cakes, corn chips, potato chips, popcorn, corn puffs** are good options for snacks.
- ✔ **Rice- or corn-based cereals** can be used in place of wheat cereals.

Minimising the Risk of Accidental Exposure

Reading ingredient labels and buying foods that are safe for your child to eat are important ways you can help prevent your child having an allergic reaction to a food allergen. But situations do occur when your child isn't with you and you're not available to offer guidance on what to eat or drink. Your child may be at a friend's house, at a party or at the movies, and someone may offer her something to eat or drink without realising that she's allergic to a food allergen in that meal.

These situations are when your child is at a greater risk of accidentally eating the food she's allergic to, because not everyone knows that your child has a food allergy, and the person responsible for looking after your child at these times may have lots of other things to deal with (such as children running havoc at a party!) so your child's food allergy may not be foremost in that person's mind. (See Chapter 11 for information on emergency action plans, which are written for situations just like these!)

Recognising when your child may be in one of these higher risk situations is, therefore, very important for you, your child, and others who care for him. Knowing how to minimise the risk of your child mistakenly eating a food he's allergic to in these situations is equally important. (We provide more detailed information on risk minimisation in Chapters 8, 9 and 10.)

Knowing when accidental exposure occurs

So, when would your child be most likely to eat a food she's allergic to by mistake? The obvious situation is when your child's at a friend's birthday party or at the movies — when you're not around to help her work out what's safe to eat.

But other high-risk situations can also occur, and these may not be as apparent, such as when your family is visiting friends in their home, when you're eating out together at a restaurant or cafe, or even buying ice-cream at the ice-cream shop. In all of these circumstances, a high chance exists of cross-contamination of foods with allergen because other people (rather than you) are preparing food for your child and may use cooking or serving utensils that have also been used to serve foods that contain the allergen your child is allergic to.

Mixing foods means danger

Cross-contact is what happens when a small amount of an allergenic food is unintentionally mixed with another food during the cooking process or when the food is being served.

For example, if utensils aren't cleaned properly between use and or if they're used to cook or serve multiple different dishes, utensils that have been used with allergen-containing foods can transfer allergenic proteins to other foods which don't contain the allergen. Such cross-contact with allergen can cause an allergic reaction if enough of the allergen is transferred across.

Cross-contact with allergen is very likely when cooking with fryers or blenders, or when using the same chopping surfaces, because cleaning these sufficiently to avoid cross-contamination is difficult.

Cross-contact can also occur during the manufacturing process of a food ingredient or food product — for example, during harvesting of raw ingredients and transportation of ingredients or foods, as well as during manufacturing, processing and packaging of ingredients or food products.

While cross-contact during food manufacturing is difficult to predict or avoid, food producers will hopefully adopt the VITAL program, which can provide consumers with more information on the likelihood of cross-contact during the manufacturing process. (See Chapter 8 for more on the VITAL program.)

Accidental exposure can also occur in the following situations:

- **School camps and other school trips:** These are particularly high-risk situations for children with food allergy because they may feel pressured by other children into eating a food they know they shouldn't eat or they may simply be too embarrassed to refuse. (See Chapter 9 for specific tips on preparing your child for camps and other school trips.)

- **Cafeterias and buffets:** Also particularly risky for your child with food allergy. The risk with cafeterias and buffets arises because usually little or no labelling of ingredients is provided for the prepared foods, and customers who may not understand the importance of cross-contact can be careless when using utensils to take their food. (We explain more about the effect that cross-contact can have on food in the sidebar 'Mixing foods means danger'.)

Unfortunately, despite everyone's best efforts, accidents do happen and your child mistakenly eating a food he's allergic to at some point is likely. Because of this, being able to recognise and manage an allergic reaction is just as important as knowing how to avoid allergenic foods. See the section 'Treating Allergic Reactions', later in this chapter, for more on the signs and symptoms of an allergic reaction and how to deal with one. (Also see Chapter 11 for more information on emergency action plans and how these can help you treat allergic reactions.)

Dodging accidental allergens

When your child is in any high-risk setting (such as parties, picnics or movies), you or the person responsible for your child (or your child if she's old enough), should be sure to speak to the people preparing and serving food to let them know that your child has a food allergy and needs to avoid a particular food allergen.

In the case of cafes, restaurants and friends' homes, letting the kitchen and/or serving staff and your friends know ahead of time about your child's food allergy is best, so they have time to prepare your child's meal, taking care to avoid any cross contamination with allergen. Another thing you and your child can do to minimise the risk for your child in these situations is to be alert for early signs of an allergic reaction.

Some allergists recommend that, as a precaution before eating a food, older children and adults with food allergy can touch a small amount of the food to the outside of their lip to see if they experience any signs of an allergic reaction (such as tingling or itching). These signs tell them some allergen may be present in the food. This isn't recommended for younger children who may not be able to pick the signs of an allergic reaction every time.

Unfortunately, at some eating places you may not be able to speak with the staff preparing or serving the food, or they themselves may not be able to avoid cross-contact between foods that contain food allergens and those that are allergen free. In these cases, avoiding eating at these places is best.

Situations where your child may need to avoid eating at include the following:

  ✔ **Buffet restaurants**, because the risk of cross-contact (see the sidebar 'Mixing foods means danger') can't be controlled by the kitchen and serving staff.

  ✔ **Ice-cream shops**, because the ice-cream scoops are generally dipped into a common pot of water between customers, and both the ice-cream scoops and the tubs of ice-cream not being cross-contaminated with various food allergens is very unlikely.

Other situations will arise when you're not with your child and your child needs to take responsibility for avoiding the food he's allergic to. In order to prepare your child for such times, you can teach him to always look for the ingredient label on food products, read the ingredient labels looking for the food allergen he's allergic to, and only eat food products or meals that he can be absolutely certain don't contain the food allergen he's allergic to.

If your child follows these simple rules, he can be confident in knowing how to avoid foods that are more likely to be affected by cross-contact with allergens — for example, foods that don't have an ingredient label, or don't have an adequate ingredient label, and foods or meals prepared by friends or their parents where your child can't be certain of all the ingredients.

The likelihood of inadvertent cross-contact with an allergen depends on the level of quality control processes in place in the facility where the food is manufactured. Foods that are produced in small overseas factories, particularly in Asia (where peanut and nuts are commonly included as ingredients in food), are more likely to be affected by accidental cross-contact than commercial grade foods prepared in large facilities in the US, UK, parts of Central Europe, Australia or New Zealand, which are regulated by stringent and reliable quality control measures.

Chapter 10 is specially directed at kids with allergies, so if your child is old enough to read and understand this chapter, why not offer this book, open at Chapter 10?

Being cautious without imposing too many restrictions

Different people have varying comfort levels in their approach to avoiding food allergens, and your level of comfort in part depends upon how severe your child's food allergy is. However, in general, being cautious without imposing too many restrictions on your child and your family's life is best. Food is a big part of enjoying life and, although making sure your child can avoid the food allergen is of the utmost importance, minimising the impact on other aspects of your child's life and also on your family's diet and lifestyle is equally important.

One situation when taking a balanced approach is important is when thinking about whether you should ban a particular food from your home because your child is allergic to that food. Many parents, for example, feel that they should have a 'nut-free' house because their child has a peanut or tree nut allergy. However, this isn't necessarily the best approach — either for the child who has the food allergy or for other members of the family who don't have nut allergy. Continuing to have the allergy-causing food in the home so that other family members can still eat foods that they enjoy is generally better — but just take extra care in ensuring that such foods are placed well away and out of reach of your child who has the allergy while that child is still young.

As children approach school age, they need to start taking some responsibility for themselves in avoiding the food they're allergic to. They begin to spend more time away from home and away from your care — they may be invited to play at a friend's home or to birthday parties, when you can't be there to help them avoid the food they're allergic to. In order to prepare your child for these situations, you can start to teach her how to be careful around the home and how to check whether an allergen might be in a food she has been offered before eating the food. By growing up in a home that has the allergy-causing products around, your child with food allergy becomes familiar with how to be careful about what she eats, and she's better prepared for situations when you're not around. (See Chapter 8 for more on managing food allergy in the home.)

Medical experts and parent support groups also don't recommend food bans in schools. Instead, children should learn how to manage their food allergies in situations where they may be exposed to a food they're allergic to, and be familiar with ways to minimise the chances of accidental ingestion. Schools can help children to manage their food allergy by developing individualised allergy management plans for all students with food allergy, and ensuring that teachers and staff have received training in the management of allergic reactions and anaphylaxis and can initiate emergency treatment should a child experience an allergic reaction at school. (See Chapter 9 for more on risk minimisation in schools.)

Another situation to consider is whether your child should avoid other food allergens in addition to the known allergens. If your child is allergic to peanut, should he also avoid the tree nuts? Or if your child is allergic to cashew, should she also avoid peanut? In the past, some allergy specialists may have recommended that children who are allergic to one of the nuts, whether this was peanut or a tree nut, should avoid all nuts. Specialists thought that avoiding a food might prevent the development of allergy to that food and that total avoidance of all nuts was simpler.

However, this approach was not based on any scientific evidence, and recent studies are suggesting quite the opposite. What we now know is that avoiding a food doesn't help to prevent you developing an allergy to that food; in fact, you need to eat a food in order to become tolerant to it. So, if your child is allergic to peanut and allergy testing shows that he's not allergic to the tree nuts, he can have tree nuts in his diet, provided that the tree nuts aren't cross-contaminated with peanut. Similarly, if your child has been diagnosed with cashew allergy and she's already eating peanut butter without difficulty, she can continue to eat peanut butter. The best evidence that your child isn't allergic to a food is if your child is eating that food without any problem.

However, in some situations your child may need to avoid all nuts, even though he's only allergic to one or a few nuts. For example, your child should avoid all nuts if you or your child can't distinguish the different nuts due to language barriers, or if the chance of cross-contamination between types of nuts is high.

Your child only needs to avoid the foods she's allergic to. Your doctor can help you work out what your child can or can't eat. In general, if your child is already eating a food without having an allergic reaction, your child isn't allergic to that food and can continue to eat it.

Treating Allergic Reactions

Even if you and your child take the utmost care to avoid your child's food allergens, accidents can happen and your child is likely to inadvertently eat an allergy-causing food. Studies show that up to 50 per cent of children with food allergy accidentally eat the food they're allergic to within five years, and 75 per cent mistakenly eat the food they're allergic to within ten years. These figures mean that, on average, each child with food allergy has one accidental ingestion every three years. The chances of an accidental exposure are even higher if a child has peanut allergy, with 50 per cent of these children having an allergic reaction to peanut within two years. So more likely than not, your child is going to have an unexpected allergic reaction at some time, and you need to be ready to take action when that happens.

A large part of managing your child's food allergy is recognising when your child is having an allergic reaction and knowing how to treat your child's reaction, which we cover in the following sections. Your doctor can also help with this, and provide you with an emergency action plan, which clearly outlines this same information. (See Chapter 11 for more information on emergency action plans.)

Your child's doctor also assesses whether to prescribe an adrenaline auto-injector for your child and teaches you (and in some cases your child) how to use it if it's prescribed.

Recognising allergic reactions

Being very familiar with what happens to the body during an allergic reaction helps you pick up the early signs of a reaction in your child. Chapter 4 describes the symptoms of an allergic reaction, and we strongly recommend that you read that chapter, if you haven't already. For the safety of your child, you should be able to distinguish a severe allergic reaction (anaphylaxis) from a mild to moderate one.

Your child's sensitivity to the food allergen and the amount of allergen that's eaten affects the severity of an allergic reaction. Severity can also depend on the following:

- ✓ **Cooking:** This can make some allergens (such as those found in egg) less allergenic.

- ✓ **Doing exercise soon after eating the allergen:** This can make a reaction more severe.

- ✓ **Eating a food allergen mixed with other foods:** This can delay absorption.

- ✓ **Having asthma:** This condition can lead to more severe food allergy reactions.

Deciding on your treatment options

The approach you take to treat your child's allergic reaction depends upon the severity of the reaction — that is, whether the reaction is mild or severe.

Treating mild symptoms of allergic reaction

A mild to moderate reaction that causes itching, hives, swelling of the face and/or vomiting can be treated with over-the-counter antihistamines — such as loratidine (marketed as Claratyne), cetirizine (Zyrtec), fexofenadine (Telfast) and desloratidine (Aerius).

Use the newer antihistamines now available because the older preparations can cause drowsiness — which can cause confusion because drowsiness is also seen as a symptom of more severe allergic reactions.

If you think your child is developing an allergic reaction, you must stay with your child and watch her closely to see if she's developing any of the signs of a severe reaction (anaphylaxis). You shouldn't leave your child at any time. If you need to get your child's medication, ask someone else to do that so you can stay with your child.

Treating severe symptoms of allergic reaction

A severe reaction that involves the airway or circulatory system (anaphylaxis) can cause persistent coughing, wheezing or noisy breathing, hoarse voice, paleness or floppiness in a young child, or collapse. Anaphylaxis is life-threatening and requires immediate medical treatment. If your child develops any one of these severe symptoms, you must respond immediately.

If anaphylaxis occurs, keeping your child lying down is important — moving about can make an allergic reaction more severe and can be dangerous. So don't ask your child to move to the sofa in another room or to walk to a quieter place in the restaurant — keep your child lying wherever he is.

If your child is drowsy, pale or floppy, you can raise the legs to help maintain the circulation to the heart and brain. (Keep in mind that most children with anaphylaxis due to foods have symptoms affecting their airways rather than their circulation.) If your child is having difficulty breathing, you can sit her up slightly while still keeping the legs flat because this can help make breathing easier.

The only medicine effective in treating anaphylaxis is adrenaline (antihistamines and corticosteroids don't help). If your child has been prescribed an adrenaline auto-injector, you should use it; if an adrenaline auto-injector isn't readily available, you must call the ambulance without delay. The ambulance and paramedics have adrenaline as well as oxygen and any other medicines or equipment that might be needed to treat your child.

Even if you treated your child yourself with an adrenaline auto-injector, you must still call the ambulance after you have used the adrenaline, because your child may need additional care. Once your child has been treated with adrenaline, your child must always be taken to hospital for further care. Sometimes an allergic reaction can improve but then return after one or more hours and require more treatment. This is called a biphasic reaction, and happens in about 10 to 15 per cent of children with anaphylaxis.

The only injectable antihistamine available in Australia is promethazine. This shouldn't be used in cases of anaphylaxis because the drug causes drowsiness.

Table 7-1 summarises the common symptoms of allergic reactions and how they should be treated.

Table 7-1	Symptoms and Treatment of Allergic Reactions
Symptom	*Treatment*
Mild to Moderate Reaction	
Hives	Stay with your child
Swelling of lips and/or eyes	Antihistamines
Vomiting and/or abdominal pain	Watch for signs of anaphylaxis
Severe Reaction (Anaphylaxis)	
Wheezing and/or noisy breathing	Lay your child down
Hoarse voice	Give adrenaline (EpiPen or Anapen), if available
Tongue swelling up	
Persistent cough	Call ambulance
Pale or floppy	
Collapse	

Adrenaline auto-injectors

An adrenaline auto-injector is a device that has been designed to deliver a single pre-measured dose of adrenaline. They're used for the emergency treatment of anaphylaxis in the community setting, and allow a person without any medical training to treat anaphylaxis quickly and easily without having to draw up medicine with a syringe and needle, which can be confusing and fiddly, particularly in an emergency.

Two types of devices are available: The EpiPen and the Anapen. The two devices work by different mechanisms, so the method for using them is also quite different. Basically, the Anapen is activated by pressing the end of the device, whereas the EpiPen is activated by pushing the device onto the thigh. (Chapter 11 covers the use of EpiPens and Anapens in more detail in relation to emergency action plans.)

The different methods of activation can be confusing for parents but, to be practical, you can just familiarise yourself with whichever device your doctor has assigned for your child, if your child has been prescribed one. Everyone, including doctors and nurses, needs some training in order to use these devices correctly but most people (even children, if they can follow instructions) can be trained. (Keep in mind, however, that studies have shown that regular training every year is very important, because people can easily forget how to use them.

Both the EpiPen and the Anapen come in two doses of adrenaline — 0.15 milligrams for children under 20 kilograms, and 0.3 milligrams for children over 20 kilograms. The Anapen also comes in a higher 0.5 milligram dose.

Working out who should have an adrenaline auto-injector

Really, anyone who has an anaphylaxis reaction would benefit from early treatment with adrenaline. Unfortunately, working out who should be prescribed one isn't that simple. Although as many as 1 in 15 children can have a food allergy, only 1 in 1,000 are likely to have anaphylaxis — so a lot of children with food allergy won't have anaphylaxis. And, no reliable test or marker is yet available that we can use to identify these 1 in 1,000 children who are going to have anaphylaxis.

But we do have some leads. We know that if a child has already had a severe food allergic reaction (anaphylaxis), any allergic reactions that child has in the future are also likely to be severe. Studies have also shown that anaphylaxis is more likely to develop in people who have peanut or tree nut allergy, and in people who also have asthma, particularly if their asthma is uncontrolled. In addition, researchers have found that being allergic to peanut, having uncontrolled asthma, being a teenager or young adult aged 15 to 35 years, and delay in receiving treatment of anaphylaxis with adrenaline can significantly increase the risk of food anaphylaxis resulting in death.

Where did auto-injectors come from?

The first auto-injector device was developed for the military to treat soldiers in the field who were poisoned by nerve gas. The device was designed by a man called Sheldon Kaplan to be injected through army fatigues and deliver an antidote that rapidly reversed the effects of nerve gas. Sheldon Kaplan later adapted this device to deliver adrenaline, taking advantage of its simple design, which allowed a person without any medical training to deliver a set dose of emergency medicine in the field setting — and giving rise to the EpiPen.

Using all of this information, experts from the Australasian Society of Clinical Immunology and Allergy (ASCIA) have suggested that adrenaline auto-injectors should be provided to those children with food allergy in the following manner:

✔ **Recommended:**

- Previous anaphylaxis

✔ **May be recommended:**

- Adolescent or young adult

- Peanut allergy

- Remote geographic location

- Uncontrolled asthma

✔ **Usually not recommended:**

- Positive allergy test without any allergic reactions in the child

- Anaphylaxis in the family without any allergic reactions in the child

- Asthma without food allergy

These recommendations have been adopted by the National Pharmaceutical Benefits Scheme (PBS) in Australia, and subsidised access to adrenaline auto-injectors through the PBS scheme is available for these children on authorised restricted prescription.

Of course, these recommendations only provide a guide for when to prescribe an adrenaline auto-injector, and doctors consider each individual child's circumstances when making a decision whether or not to prescribe an adrenaline auto-injector.

Any decision to prescribe an adrenaline auto-injector isn't set in stone and can be changed at any time if circumstances change. For example, we may choose not to prescribe an adrenaline auto-injector to five-year-old Daisy who has peanut allergy and mild asthma, but lives in Melbourne with ready access to medical care; however, we may decide to prescribe one when Daisy turns ten and has to go on a school camp (see Chapter 9 for more information on managing food allergies in school).

Getting your adrenaline pumping

Adrenaline is a natural hormone produced by the adrenal gland and is usually released in higher amounts during a fright–flight response. So, for example, you may get a rush of adrenaline just before you run a race or sit an exam.

Adrenaline opens up your airways and causes your heart to beat harder and faster, which helps you to breathe better and raises your blood pressure.

These effects counteract the changes in your body caused by anaphylaxis. The symptoms of anaphylaxis usually improve very quickly after treatment with adrenaline, and parents are often surprised at how soon their child can look and feel much better after adrenaline is given.

What happens when your child is prescribed an adrenaline auto-injector

If your doctor has decided to prescribe an adrenaline auto-injector for your child, you usually receive two devices. This is so you can give one device to your child's school or child care, and keep the other one with your child at all times. Your child must carry the adrenaline auto-injector wherever he goes — the auto-injector is no help to your child if it's sitting in a handbag or briefcase when he has an allergic reaction at his friend's house after accidentally eating a chocolate bar containing peanut.

Your doctor also gives you an anaphylaxis action plan to keep with your adrenaline auto-injector, so you can refer to the plan if your child has an allergic reaction.

See Chapter 11 for more on action plans and adrenaline auto-injectors.

Managing Conditions and Medicines That Can Make Allergy Reactions Worse

Not only must you manage your child's food allergy, but you also need to manage any other conditions or medicines that can make an allergic reaction more severe, or make treating your child if she has a severe allergic reaction (anaphylaxis) more difficult.

Asthma is the most serious risk factor for making an allergic reaction more severe and for anaphylaxis to result in death. Children with food allergy who have asthma also have more severe asthma exacerbations.

So if your child has food allergy and asthma, your child's asthma must be well controlled. This means your child needs to take his asthma medicine according to the asthma action plan provided by his doctor. If your child is on a preventer, she must continue to take this every day. Your child's asthma should also be reviewed by the doctor every three to six months. This way, the doctor can monitor your child's asthma and make sure that the condition stays well controlled.

Children with food allergy who don't have asthma when they're first diagnosed with food allergy can develop asthma later. Even if your child doesn't have asthma now, watch out for any signs of asthma, such as getting a wheeze with colds or exercise, or a persistent cough in the mornings or at night. If any of these symptoms develop, take your child to your doctor.

Some medicines can also make treating anaphylaxis more complicated. Medicines such as beta blockers and ACE inhibitors can make reversing the changes in the body that develop during anaphylaxis more difficult, and should be avoided if possible. For example, beta blockers are used to lower blood pressure and work by blocking the beta receptors that adrenaline acts on to open up the airways. These beta blocker medicines are rarely used in children, but if your child has a heart condition that requires medicines as part of the treatment, you must let your doctor know that your child also has a food allergy, and you can ask if an alternative medicine is available that could be used in place of a beta blocker.

Enlisting the Help of a Dietitian

Once your doctor has diagnosed your child with a food allergy, a dietitian becomes a very important person in your lives. A dietitian who specialises in the dietary management of food allergy can help you to manage your child's food allergies with confidence and independence, and can be an indispensible source of information and support to you in managing your child's food allergies.

A dietitian can help you and your child

- Learn how to read ingredient labels with more self-assurance and knowledge.
- Make sure that your child's diet is nutritionally adequate when different foods have been taken out.
- Offer you simple recipes that exclude food allergens.
- Provide practical advice on replacing food allergens with alternative ingredients.

Ensuring your child's diet is adequate is probably the most important thing a dietitian can offer, because the nutritional content of your child's diet can be dramatically affected by having to eliminate even just one food allergen. For example, cow's milk and cow's milk products such as yoghurt and cheese are the major sources of calcium in the Western diet, so if your child is allergic to cow's milk and is avoiding all foods that contain cow's milk (and products made from cow's milk), your child is highly likely to be lacking calcium in her diet and to need an alternative source of calcium to meet the daily requirement. Your dietitian can confirm whether your child's diet is lacking in nutrients such as calcium and suggest ways to increase the amount in your child's diet, which may include taking supplements.

The issue of nutritional adequacy is even more relevant if your child is allergic to more than one food allergen and so is avoiding a number of different foods. This is not an uncommon situation, since up to a third of children who have one food allergy have a second food allergy. For example, babies are commonly allergic to both egg and milk, and avoiding both of these foods is not only very challenging for mums but can also possibly reduce the nutritional value of the baby's diet. Getting practical advice from a dietitian on how to avoid these foods while keeping a healthy diet for your baby is both informative and ensures your baby's wellbeing.

Dietitians, just like doctors, usually specialise in a particular area of care, so try to find a dietitian who has had experience working with food allergies in children, and has worked alongside an allergist who looks after children with food allergy. A dietitian who specialises in diets for the management of metabolic conditions, for example, may not have the necessary experience to answer your questions and assist you with your child's food allergy.

Your doctor should be able to identify an appropriate dietitian in your area and refer you and your child to that person. You can also contact the Dietitians Association of Australia (DAA — www.daa.asn.au) or Dietitians New Zealand (DNZ — www.dietitians.org.nz) for help with finding a qualified dietitian in your area who has experience with kids' food allergy diets.

Make sure the dietitian you see is an Accredited Practising Dietitian (in Australia) or registered with the Dietitians Board (in New Zealand).

Chapter 8

Caring for Kids at Home and On the Go

Kids are busy people — and parents are even busier trying to keep up with the joyous, exciting, boring, challenging, evolving time of life that is childhood. Parents of kids with food allergies have an extra set of considerations when it comes to working out how to help their child eat and enjoy food safely.

When your child is first diagnosed with food allergy this might seem an overwhelming hurdle — after all, eating is an essential activity for life that we simply can't avoid. Luckily, help is at hand and a vast array of information is now available for parents. Armed with information, you can feel empowered to enable your child to go out and participate in the multitude of activities that every child has the right to enjoy.

In this chapter, we discuss the fraught area of food shopping for children with food allergies, how to keep your home safe for children with food allergies, and how to minimise the risk of allergic reactions when eating away from home — whether on an overseas trip or just in a local restaurant.

Shopping for Kids with Allergies

Shopping for kids with food allergies can be a real headache, because it's hard to know exactly what manufacturers are putting into their products. Luckily, the situation is changing fast. With the rapid rise in food allergy prevalence and the wider acceptance that keeping kids with food allergies safe is paramount, options for families have improved dramatically. The good news is that mandatory labelling of common food allergens is now in place in Australia and New Zealand. That means that what you read on the label of a food is what you get. And new legislation insists that information and warnings are in language that everyone can understand.

What remains a difficult area is that of precautionary labelling — or the 'may contain traces of …' type statements. People hold varied opinions on what this type of labelling means and whether avoiding these foods is worthwhile. Importantly, though, manufacturers and the food industry are continuing to work with consumers and allergists to find the best solutions.

We look at the tricky area of product labelling in the following sections, as well as detailing what sorts of products are likely to be contaminated.

Mobile phone apps are also being developed to help you check labels and get more information about the food you're purchasing. So, instead of having to ring the company to find out a specific detail about a food that perhaps couldn't fit into the space on a label, you'll soon be able to flash your phone at the product and have information instantly at your fingertips.

Making sense of ingredient labels

Information about possible food allergens in food sold in Australia and New Zealand can be listed on labels in two ways: Mandatory statements about the product ingredients, and voluntary statements about potential allergens. We discuss both in this section.

Mandatory statements

In 2003 legislation was introduced in Australia and New Zealand that requires the mandatory labelling of the most common food allergens — peanuts, tree nuts, milk, eggs, sesame, fish, shellfish, soy and gluten — as well as ingredients derived from those foods. This labelling is mandatory and regulated, providing clear information for the consumer about whether a potential allergen is an intended added ingredient. (By law, manufacturers must use wording that's clear to the consumer.) For example, listing a constituent of cow's milk, such as casein, on a label is no longer allowed — 'cow's milk' must be the description used. Similarly, labels that used to list *ovalbumin* or *albumin* (taken from egg whites) or *lecithin* (found in egg yolks) now must also list 'egg' in the allergen section of the label.

Food labelling formats in Australia and New Zealand

In Australia and New Zealand, the labelling of allergenic foods and ingredients is regulated by the Australia New Zealand Food Standards Code. The code specifies the mandatory declaration of certain substances and their products on the ingredient list of packaged foods. The substances that must be declared are as follows:

✔ Cereals containing gluten — namely, wheat, rye, barley, oats, spelt

✔ Cow's milk and cow's milk products

✔ Crustaceans (shellfish) and their products

✔ Egg and egg products

✔ Fish and fish products

✔ Peanut and peanut products

✔ Soybean and soybean products

✔ Sulfites if present at 10 milligrams per kilogram or more (sulfites can trigger asthma symptoms in some people)

✔ Tree nuts and sesame seeds and their products

Note: In the case of cereals, hybridised strains must also be listed on the product label (other than where these substances are present in standardised preparations of beer and spirits). Any cereal that contains gluten must also be listed in order to provide adequate information for people with coeliac disease (who must avoid all gluten). However, as discussed in Chapter 4, most people with wheat allergy are able to eat the other cereals without reaction.

In some situations, products may be exempt from this mandatory labelling requirement — for example, where the size of food packaging imposes limits on what the label can contain (such as chewing gum packets) or where expectations are lower for labelling, such as fund-raising events. Nevertheless, if a food is exempt from labelling but is for retail or catering purposes, the required allergen information must be displayed on, or in connection with the display of, the food, or provided to the consumer upon request.

One example of a recommended labelling format for such mandatory declarations is shown in the following figure. It is recommended that allergens are listed in bold in the ingredient list and a summary statement, which includes all the allergenic ingredients in a separate list, is provided. The use of VITAL precautionary labelling ('may be present') is also recommended in place of other voluntary statements (such as 'may contain traces of'), as VITAL precautionary labelling is based upon testing for allergen in foods. (See the sidebar 'Deciphering Voluntary Incidental Trace Allergen Labelling (VITAL)' later in this chapter.)

(continued)

(continued)

INGREDIENTS

Tree nuts specifically identified.

Allergenic ingredients & derivatives declared in **bold** each time they appear.

Water, vegetable oil, vinegar, cane sugar, tomato paste (5%), salt, parmesan **cheese** (2%), **egg** yolk, maize thickener (1412), **almonds**, red capsicum, **soybean** oil, garlic (1.0%), vegetable gum (415), spice, herbs, **wheat** cornflour, flavour (**wheat** maltodextrin, **sesame** oil), antioxidant (320).

Gluten source (grain source) qualified in ingredient list.

Contains milk, egg, almonds, soy, wheat and sesame.

Summary statement lisiting all allergenic ingredients in the product.

May be present: xxx.

Precautionary statement declared if appropriate. This statement must only be used in conjunction with VITAL.

Similar laws are in place in the United States, United Kingdom and European Union, but aren't in place in other countries. So you can't rely on food labelling to help identify food allergens in packaged foods when you travel to countries outside of these areas, and need to be extra careful about what your child eats. (See the section 'Travelling with Food Allergic Kids', later in this chapter, for more.)

The Australia New Zealand Food Standards Code also recommends that food allergens in the ingredient list are highlighted by bolded text and that a separate summary statement of the allergenic ingredients used to make the product is provided alongside the ingredient list. (For further details about the mandatory labelling requirements, see the sidebar 'Food labelling formats in Australia and New Zealand').

Voluntary statements

Mandatory statements (see preceding section) marked a major step forward in ingredient labelling for the allergy community in Australia and New Zealand — but listing possible allergens on labels has opened a can of worms that has yet to be satisfactorily addressed. The major question is this: How to label foods that might be cross-contaminated with allergens during the manufacturing process through use of shared equipment and facilities, and during the supply chain?

Manufacturers have attempted to address the issue of cross-contamination by voluntarily introducing precautionary labelling, or voluntary statements, which include such lines as 'may contain traces of' or 'made in a facility that also makes products on the same production line containing ...'. These statements are intended to advise consumers that a chance exists that cross-contamination with allergens can occur during manufacturing.

Food can also be accidentally contaminated with allergens through packaging errors. While you can't protect against this last form of error (unless a manufacturing plant and the supply chain from which it receives constituent ingredients is completely free from the allergen), some manufacturers use precautionary labelling to signal to consumers that although trace contamination is unlikely the possibility of mislabelling accidents still exists — and 'made in the same facility as ...' labelling is often used in this instance.

Because voluntary statements aren't regulated, manufacturers have developed a huge variety of statements that are often ambiguous. (See the sidebar 'Variations of precautionary labelling statements' for more information about the different types of labelling, and what the statements really mean.)

Voluntary statements aren't based upon any testing or measurement of allergen levels in the food, so no-one can tell which foods have been cross-contaminated with allergen/s. And no guarantee exists that foods that don't declare such statements are free from cross-contamination with allergens. For these reasons, voluntary statements don't help people with food allergies understand the risks associated with eating the food — they just confuse people.

To combat such confusion, the Australian Food and Grocery Council Guidelines instead recommend that food manufacturers in Australia and New Zealand adopt Voluntary Incidental Trace Allergen Labelling (VITAL) to help provide a clear and consistent message about food allergens to consumers.

VITAL requires food producers to analyse the risk of allergen cross-contact during the manufacturing process, take all steps possible to minimise this risk, and then determine if a precautionary statement is required using the VITAL action level grid. VITAL uses the standard precautionary statement, 'may be present', which means something quite different to the other voluntary statements in use. VITAL precautionary statements provide information on the actual risk of allergen cross-contamination for a particular food product, based on a formal risk assessment — so they provide more information to help you choose whether to buy a particular food product for your child with food allergy. (See the sidebar 'Deciphering Voluntary Incidental Trace Allergen Labelling (VITAL)' for more on the specifics of the labelling protocols.)

Using precautionary labelling in Australia

Recent research (jointly authored by Katie) has highlighted how ubiquitous precautionary labelling has become. The research shows that more than 55 per cent of all edible packaged goods in Australia has some form of precautionary labelling. The research also found that the categories most likely to have precautionary labelling were snack products, with up 93 per cent of sweet biscuits surveyed declaring precautionary peanut or tree nut labels.

The widespread use of precautionary labelling in Australia appears to have resulted in decreased confidence in the reliability of these labels. Certainly, if followed closely, precautionary labelling severely limits choices for allergy sufferers. We hope that new VITAL labelling (currently under discussion) might help avoid unnecessarily restrictive diets in food allergic children.

Evolving evidence in Australia at least indicates that an increasing number of consumers with food allergy are ignoring advisory labels. While some doctors are very worried by this development, others try to shape their advice around what is a reasonable approach to minimising risk for their patients.

Precautionary labelling, such as 'may contain traces of . . .', doesn't necessarily provide complete security that, if your child avoids these foods, she's going to be safe. Since precautionary labelling isn't mandatory, foods without precautionary labels may be just as unsafe as those that contain precautionary labels. The only way to be sure that your child is eating a food completely free from a particular allergen is to not allow her to eat any processed or manufactured goods — which for most families is a highly restrictive and prohibitive lifestyle choice!

When interpreting voluntary statements other than those associated with VITAL protocols, take a sensible approach. The level of caution you need to take depends on how severe your child's food allergy is. So, for example, if your child is extremely sensitive and has had serious allergic reactions or anaphylaxis after eating very small amounts of peanut, be more cautious. Certain foods, such as muesli bars, health food bars, chocolate and cereals, are more likely to be cross-contaminated with peanut or tree nut allergen, so you'd need to avoid such foods and only purchase those foods that are specifically labelled as allergen-free (such as nut-free chocolate). You'd also need to avoid foods produced in countries with less reliable food regulatory standards (refer to Chapter 7).

Variations of precautionary labelling statements

In Australia and New Zealand, the labelling of food that may be cross-contaminated with allergens is, for the moment at least, voluntary, which means the wording of statements used by manufacturers (if statements appear at all) can vary — and can be ambiguous. Common statements include the following:

- **May contain traces of** (or **may contain**)

- **Made on the same equipment** (or **manufactured on shared equipment with products containing** or **processed on equipment that makes products containing**)

- **Made in the same factory** (or **manufactured in a facility that also processes** or **made in the same premises as** or **produced in a plant which manufactures products containing**)

- **Made on the same production line** (or **manufactured on a line that processes**)

- **Allergen free** (manufactured in a tree nut-, peanut- and sesame-free site, or each batch is tested to ensure that no traces of peanuts and tree nuts are found, or peanut-, egg- and milk-free, or free from wheat, gluten, dairy, lactose, eggs and nuts)

- **May be present** (statement recommended by the VITAL procedure)

In our work at the Royal Children's Hospital in Melbourne, our general advice about 'may contain traces of' statements is as follows:

> *The chances of having a significant allergic reaction through contamination are extremely unlikely in the case of foods manufactured in Australia and New Zealand (and other countries with stringent manufacturing quality assurance processes) and most families choose to ignore these statements because the only safe alternative is to not include any commercial food products in your diet. For children with severe allergic reactions, companies can be contacted directly to explore food processing, packaging and cleaning procedures. But beware of foods prepared in countries with less well defined quality assurance processes such as Asia, where the chances of cross-contamination are higher.*

Food allergy reactions can range in severity. At the moment, we have very little information to predict who's most likely to develop anaphylaxis to a trace amount of contamination from allergen. What we can say is that those with a history of anaphylaxis, or those who are exquisitely sensitive and have reacted to very low doses of allergen in the past, should be the ones who most carefully check labels. For this group, avoiding foods with precautionary labelling may be required to keep them safe.

Deciphering Voluntary Incidental Trace Allergen Labelling (VITAL)

Voluntary Incidental Trace Allergen Labelling (VITAL) is a relatively new risk-management tool developed in Australia for use by the Australian and New Zealand food industry to assist with declaring the possible presence of allergens in their products.

VITAL was developed to provide a standardised approach for food producers to assess the risk of allergen cross-contact and to provide guidance in assigning appropriate allergen precautionary labelling for their food products. Although the program is voluntary and requires added company investment of time and resources, the Australia New Zealand Food Standards Code recommends the use of VITAL in place of other voluntary precautionary statements, and many food manufacturers already see the value in taking this approach.

The VITAL procedure encourages manufacturers to undergo a more intensive investigation of the possible presence of allergens prior to a product's release to consumers. Manufacturers are required to assess production for likely sources of cross-contact with allergenic substances, such as from raw materials and the processing environment, and to then evaluate the amount of allergenic substance present. Manufacturers should then review their ability to reduce the amount of allergenic material from all contributing sources, and undertake ongoing monitoring and verification of these steps.

Once the level of risk of allergen cross-contact is determined, VITAL provides a three-level grid to allow the food producer to work out which advisory labelling is most appropriate to accurately indicate the level of allergen cross-contact in the food product.

The three VITAL action levels are as follows:

- **Action Level 1 — Green Zone:** Precautionary labelling not required.

- **Action Level 2 — Yellow Zone:** Precautionary labelling is required for each relevant allergen using the standard VITAL statement ('may be present').

- **Action Level 3 — Red Zone:** Significant levels of the allergen are likely to be sporadically present. Labelling of the allergen as an ingredient is required.

Under these guidelines, no material is included on products to alert consumers that the 'may be present' precautionary statement is specific for products that have been assessed by the VITAL process. However, the 'may be present' statement should only be used within the VITAL program — that is, after the food producer has undertaken a thorough risk assessment of the food for allergen cross-contamination. So, if you see a 'may be present' label on a food product, you can be certain the food producer has used the VITAL methodology to document cross-contact and determined that some possibility of cross-contact exists that's unavoidable and sporadic.

Unfortunately, when a manufacturer has undertaken the VITAL assessment and determined a level 1 risk, this isn't obvious, since

Action Level 1 doesn't require any labelling. Therefore, you can't tell the difference between a product that has been tested by the VITAL process and found to be safe and a product that hasn't been tested by the VITAL process. Listing this information on food labels would greatly help parents of children with food allergy, because they would then know that the food has a very low risk of cross-contamination with the relevant allergen in question.

You can read more about VITAL on the website of Food Standards Australia New Zealand (www.foodstandards.gov.au).

Recognising which products can be contaminated

Contamination with allergen can occur through cross-contamination during the manufacturing process or via accidental mislabelling of products.

Accidental mislabelling can occur through the wrong label being placed on a product or a product being placed into the wrong box — for example, a cornflakes product that's coated in peanut being packaged in a box that's supposed to contain plain cornflakes. After all, manufacturing is a human endeavour and sometimes accidents just happen. Luckily, these events are really quite rare and a mandated recall alert system is in place when they do occur.

By contrast, low-level trace contamination occurs during the manufacturing process and relates to issues such as cleaning and sharing equipment. For example, contamination can occur because the chocolate manufacturing lines weren't washed adequately. These events may be quite common — in the United Kingdom and United States, experts believe that up to 20 per cent of products may have a higher level of allergen contamination than just a trace. (Figures for Australia and New Zealand aren't known.)

Some allergists recommend that unless your child has a history of anaphylaxis or is exquisitely sensitive to a food (that is, your child reacts to very low amounts of allergen), you don't need to be too strict about avoiding foods with precautionary labelling (see preceding section for more on this). However, some foods with precautionary labelling are more high risk, and these should be avoided by children with particular allergies.

Here's a list of foods that may be high risk for your child, depending on the food your child is allergic to:

- **Chocolate:** Assembly lines for chocolate products can't be washed, and nuts are a common ingredient.

- **Ice-cream:** Many brands, especially expensive ice-creams, contain egg.

- **Muesli bars:** Nuts are often mixed together in muesli or snack bars.

- **Pesto sauces (especially deli varieties):** Cheaper peanuts might be used as a substitute for a more expensive nut, such as pine nut or macadamia.

Preparing Food in the Home

Cooking, eating and sharing food is an essential daily activity for all of us; however, when you throw food allergy into the mix, parents can be understandably concerned by how careful they have to be when preparing foods for their child.

Every child is different and your doctor or allergist is the best-placed person to help you understand your child's particular risk profile. So talk with your child's allergist about how careful you have to be with cooking meals. As one allergist said to Katie, 'I see myself as my patient's risk manager — I give the family information about the child's allergy, my summary of the risk profile and what I think is the best risk/benefit ratio for the family. But everyone is different and getting the process right can be hard'.

In the following sections, we outline some of the different methods for minimising allergen contamination that can be helpful if your family has a child with food allergy. The extent to which you utilise these options is up to you.

Cooking meals

Although experts don't recommend creating an allergen-free home (refer to Chapter 7 for more on avoiding allergens), some families choose to rid their homes of allergenic foods, and in these families, safe food storage, preparation, cooking, serving and eating in the home is of very little concern. However, most families continue to keep allergenic foods in their home, particularly the common allergenic foods such as cow's milk, egg and wheat, which are important food groups for a balanced diet in other non-allergic family members.

As well, although families can control what food comes in to the home, they can't control their whole environment, so some allergists argue teaching children about allergen cross-contamination and avoidance in the home setting is the better option — so the practice becomes second nature. Obviously, the age of your child is important in making that decision. Stopping an active toddler from grabbing at Dad's scrambled egg is more difficult than reminding your ten-year-old daughter with peanut allergy that she should use a different knife from that already used in the peanut butter jar.

Here are some tips on how to best prevent cross-contamination while cooking at home:

✔ **Preparation:** Forming safe food preparation habits is great for all families, not just those with children with food allergies. Consider these suggestions:

- Use two sets of kitchen equipment, most notably two cutting boards (one is reserved for preparation of meals for your child with food allergy if the rest of the family is eating an allergen-containing food). Plastic cutting boards are less likely to absorb the allergen and so are easier to clean than wooden chopping boards.

- Be aware of contaminating non-allergenic food storage containers with allergens through knives, spoons and measuring cups.

- Use a clean utensil or cup when dipping into storage containers as a habit to prevent cross-contamination between foods.

✔ **Cooking:** Ensuring food is cooked without cross-contamination also requires some thought. When cooking food, be aware that frying can make food allergens airborne and result in an allergic reaction. For example, your child with food allergy may develop a swollen eye if you're frying eggs or fish. Although these reactions tend not to be severe, they're certainly not pleasant for your child. Also keep in mind that, although rare, fumes from cooking shellfish and fish can cause anaphylaxis if inhaled by people with these allergies.

✔ **Serving:** Never use a utensil used to serve an unsafe food to serve a safe food. Be vigilant about keeping the serving utensil with its respective serving dish.

Storing food

Each family has a personal way of dealing with the issue of food storage. Some families remove the allergen (such as nuts) from the home; others have the philosophy that their child needs to know how to live in an environment where an allergen might present itself. (We talk more about this issue in Chapter 7.)

If you do decide to keep allergens in the home, make sure you store all allergenic foods in sealed containers. If you have a toddler with food allergy, consider storing these foods out of reach or behind a childproof latch.

Cleaning the kitchen and home

Here are some good tips for keeping your home clean and safe for any children with allergies:

- **Use soap and water (and some good old-fashioned elbow grease) to clean surfaces.** Antibacterial agents don't 'kill' allergens. Soap and water physically remove the allergen and get the job done, especially for bench-top counters, dishes, cookware and utensils.

- **Wash tea towels and dishcloths in your washing machine.** Use hot water, especially if trying to remove oil-based allergens such as nuts. Some families prefer to use plastic and vinyl tablecloths because they're easier to wipe down.

- **Search out barbeque grill trays to allow you to cook outside without worrying.** Special barbeque products are available that can be placed on your barbeque grill to prevent cross-contamination between foods. These fire-resistant products (usually made of a Teflon-like product) can be lifted off the grill easily, and even washed in the dishwasher. Alternatively, you can use a double-thickness layer of aluminium foil.

- **Watch out for toasters!** Toasters are another source of cross-contamination — make sure you empty out the crumb tray regularly.

Travelling with Food Allergic Kids

The key to travelling safely with food allergic kids is simple: Plan ahead.

Clearly, the rules about food safety change when you travel overseas, particularly to developing countries, because not only is the menu different (and may even be in a foreign language) but the medical system is also likely to be different from your own. If your child is unfortunate enough to have an allergic reaction due to accidental ingestion of a known allergen, you may face an extra degree of difficulty in seeking appropriate medical help.

Make sure you discuss with your child and the rest of the travel party what issues you think are likely to be important. If you're staying in one or only a few places, consider contacting your accommodation well ahead of time (by email or phone) to gather more local information about medical services and to scope out the size of the communication barrier.

Obviously, some travel destinations are more difficult than others — major cities in Australia, New Zealand, the United States and Europe offer similar levels of medical care, with only European destinations potentially presenting any language barriers. (Okay — some people may say even some English-speaking destinations can also present certain language difficulties for English speakers! Certainly, the way that you ask to use the conveniences in some countries can result in some blank stares due to your needs being 'lost in translation'.)

However, a real shift in the perception of food allergies has occurred around the world within the restaurant and tourist industry, and more and more facilities understand what food allergy sufferers require. So, if in doubt, don't be afraid to ask.

In the following sections, we discuss particular challenges you may face when travelling by air or in developing countries.

Flying with confidence

The airline industry has certainly come on board (no pun intended!) with dealing with food allergies — in particular, peanut allergy. This is partly due to a high-profile US case involving airborne peanut particles (see the sidebar 'Looking into the dangers of airborne food allergens on planes' for more).

Airborne food allergens, however, may not present that high a risk for your child — the most important risk to assess is what your child actually ingests on the plane. Most airlines are more than happy to provide a special allergen-free meal as long as sufficient notice has been provided, so just make sure you enter your request when booking and then confirm your request a few days before you fly.

Some parents take a 'safety pack' of food for the flight, and this can be particularly useful for toddlers. Bringing your own food — which you know is both safe and an option your child likes — means you have something to offer if your child is hungry but either no safe meal options are available or your child refuses to try something new.

Looking into the dangers of airborne food allergens on planes

The potential dangers of airborne food allergens on planes were raised after a tragic case in the United States. An adult with peanut allergy developed significant respiratory compromise after a bag of peanuts was opened in the row in front of where the person was sitting. The adult died and subsequent investigations determined that airborne peanut could be detected in the air vent of the plane, meaning exposure to peanut may have contributed to the death. Alternatively, the passenger may have suffered a massive and fatal asthma attack.

Following the case, airlines stopped providing peanut snack bags on flights for a number of years — with some airlines replacing the peanuts with other nuts such as cashews!

However, peanuts have now crept back on to the snack menu for many airlines, and most allergists believe that this isn't necessarily a problem — especially when peanut allergy is only one of the many forms of nut allergy anyway.

Although rare cases such as the US case may make you pause, keep in mind that thousands of peanut allergic people had safely flown prior to this event and, thankfully, a similar case has not been recorded since. Although in theory your child could develop a reaction from airborne peanut particles under pressure in an airplane cabin, in reality airborne particles are extremely unlikely to cause an adverse event and even more unlikely to result in a severe reaction.

The other important thing to remember is to pack your child's allergy action plan and adrenaline auto-injector (if your child has one) in the cabin of the plane. Also make sure you visit your allergist before travel to get an ASCIA auto-injector travel authority, which explains why your child needs to carry the auto-injector in the cabin of the plane. Action plans tailored to the type of auto-injector your child has been prescribed can be downloaded from the ASICA website (www.allergy.org.au).

Travelling in developing countries

When you travel to a foreign land, you're journeying into unfamiliar territory. If you add in to that a foreign language and a developing country lifestyle (which may include poor sanitation and diminished access to a secure water supply as well as a less than ideal medical system), many families agree that this isn't an undertaking for the faint-hearted — and that includes non-allergy families as well.

But travelling with a child who has food allergy to developing countries is possible, and plenty of people do it successfully. Here are some tips if you're planning to take up the challenge:

✔ **Think about the prevalence of the problem food in your destination country.** In Asian countries, you're going to be dealing with a lot of peanut and products containing peanut. In Israel, sesame is everywhere, and fish is one of the nation's staple foods in Japan. This doesn't mean that you can't travel to these countries, but you do need to think about whether you can access cafes, restaurants and hotels that provide more Westernised foods if your child's problem food is a staple diet food.

✔ **Learn some of the local language.** Before you travel, look up the words or signs that indicate the presence of your child's problem food. Find out how to pronounce them and practise a sentence that indicates your need for an allergen-free meal for your child.

✔ **Make sure you have the appropriate medication and travel insurance.** Adrenaline auto-injectors can be purchased over-the-counter in Australia so, if you're travelling to a remote region, you may want to stock up on your supply of adrenaline and know how and when to use your child's auto-injector. Have a lower threshold for action on your child's action plan (compared to your threshold for action if you're in the safe confines of your home country). Medical emergencies may not be responded to as rapidly as in Australia and New Zealand so, if in doubt, treat — don't wait. Make sure your travel insurance covers possible emergencies and/or costs of last-minute itinerary changes in the country or countries you plan to travel to — in case your child does become sick and needs to come home.

✔ **Consider Westernised hotels if your child is high risk.** If you do plan to travel with a child who is at high risk of anaphylaxis, consider booking in to a Westernised hotel or hotel chain. These hotels cater for international guests, so English is more likely to be spoken well by their staff — and chances are someone with a food allergy has visited them previously. If you're going off the beaten track and Westernised hotels aren't an option, take a letter in the foreign language explaining your child's dietary needs — just be aware that some adults in developing countries may be illiterate even in their native language.

Gastrointestinal symptoms while travelling may be related to contaminated food or water and not an allergic reaction to food. First check whether other people in your group (who may have eaten the same food or drunk from the same water source) have similar symptoms before becoming concerned your child's symptoms indicate an allergic reaction.

Eating Out with Kids with Food Allergies

Eating out with kids who have food allergies doesn't need to be difficult but it does require forward planning and a willingness to communicate your child's needs clearly and simply. Showing children with food allergy how to advocate for their needs is an important education, particularly for those unlikely to outgrow their food allergy and who need to learn to respectfully make their needs known in new situations.

The following sections cover how you and your child can handle eating out at restaurants and friend's houses.

Calling ahead to restaurants

Although calling ahead to discuss menu options can take away from the spontaneity of going out for dinner, having the discussion really is important if you wish your child to eat safely. Most restaurants are more than happy to accommodate your requests — and if they aren't, knowing this before you turn up to the venue is best.

Calling ahead also adds credence to the food allergy — if you find it important enough to plan ahead, the restaurant staff are more likely to take your request seriously. And providing some advance warning gives the restaurant staff an opportunity to strut their stuff and show you how successfully they can create alternatives.

No-one likes to have last-minute plans sprung on them — and particularly not a busy restaurant with multiple demands and many customers. Some chefs take real pride in showing off their allergy-friendly cooking skills — as long as they have the appropriate amount of time to do so. Once you've discovered which restaurants and cafes are amenable to helping your child enjoy a meal, you're likely to turn into regular customers!

Eating at friends' houses

When friends invite you and your family for dinner, ensuring your friends are aware of your child's allergies is down to you. As a courtesy, you need to give them prior warning that you have special dietary requirements.

Even if your friends forget to ask, letting them know what specific foods need to be avoided or provided is the polite and reasonable thing to do — and these days, many people have special dietary requirements, whether for medical, cultural, ethical or religious reasons, so your requests are unlikely to cause alarm.

Some people feel supplying their child with a goodie bag of 'safe food' is less complicated. Other ideas may include (depending on the circumstances) emailing a list of what your child can or can't eat, providing a copy of some safe recipes or even lending one of your own allergy cookbooks to the family.

Katie has a note by her phone to remind herself, when inviting people over for dinner, always to ask whether any guests have special dietary needs. She's made the mistake far too often of not asking and then feeling completely embarrassed and ill-prepared to host vegetarians, vegans or those with food allergy — amazing really, considering she spends her days in clinical work or research helping those with food allergy!

Educating Others

Your child with food allergy should feel safe even when you're not around to directly supervise his dietary needs. Children with allergies need to participate in all activities appropriate for their age, but you need to provide your child with the education and confidence to know when to accept the direction of another adult and when to question the situation.

Loss of direct supervision of your child can be confronting for a parent when it first happens but (as for many other situations described in this book) forward planning and good communication can minimise the anxiety and help you feel empowered to handle the situation appropriately.

Most people are more than happy to find out more about food allergy — and, of course, if they have agreed to care for your child, that also means taking responsibility for your child's health and safety.

We cover letting other people know about your child's allergy in the following sections, including the issues you should cover, who you may need to talk with, and how you should approach the discussions.

Understanding the issues you should discuss

When speaking to others about caring for your child, make sure you discuss management of the following:

- ✔ Meal times
- ✔ Snack times
- ✔ Special treats or birthday cakes

If your child has been prescribed an adrenaline auto-injector, also make sure you discuss the following:

- ✔ Storage of the auto-injector
- ✔ Responsibility for carrying the auto-injector
- ✔ Administration of the auto-injector in an emergency (including who is responsible for this and when)
- ✔ Implementation of a 'wait and watch approach' (and when this may be appropriate)

Your allergy and anaphylaxis emergency action plans provide a good structure to discuss the last two points in the preceding list in particular. Chapter 11 covers these action plans.

In addition to discussing issues relating to meals and possible administration of adrenaline auto-injectors with supervising adults, you should also discuss these issues with your child in an age-appropriate manner, so your child is also clear on all of these things as well.

Your child should be reminded to

- ✔ Check with the adult in charge that a food is safe before eating
- ✔ Not eat a food if ever in doubt about its safety
- ✔ Not share food and drinks

Also remind your child to seek help immediately if she feels unwell — she should never 'wait and see'. Some shy or younger children may need some extra coaching about what to say if they feel unwell or are uncertain about whether they have accidentally ingested a food that they're allergic to.

Situations that can be the most difficult for children are when they're not sure about something (whether it's the people, location or something else) and they don't feel confident to articulate this uncertainty. Coach your child on the importance of speaking up. Children with food allergies need to know that when they're certain they're having a severe allergic reaction, they need to communicate that clearly and urgently so appropriate action can be taken.

Talking to family members and frequent carers

When talking to other adults who look after your child, clear, calm and precise information is key. While you shouldn't sensationalise potential outcomes for your child, you also shouldn't downplay possible risks. Carefully explaining the written emergency action plan for allergic reactions or anaphylaxis as well as how and when to use an adrenaline auto-injector are all essential elements of ensuring carers are well prepared. (See Chapter 11 for more about emergency action plans.)

Obviously, handing over care to daily carers is easier than talking with occasional or irregular carers because more time is available to educate the regular carer in every nuance of food allergy management and the carer is likely to be keen to understand all of the details accurately.

The same is true for family members since family is for life — although sometimes grandparents are a little mystified as to whether the allergy is 'real' or not.

We always find sceptical grandparents are more likely to understand the seriousness of a child's condition if they come along to an appointment with the allergist.

Finding ways to discuss allergies

While discussing the needs of your child with frequent carers and schools may be relatively easy, having the time to impart meaningful information to infrequent carers or someone who's only supervising your child once can be harder. One major quandary is what to do if your child is going to a friend's house for a play or birthday party.

At parties, we often see parents leave special, allergen-free food for their child with food allergy to eat — and for children who are old enough to know not to share food, this approach is more than appropriate. However, we have also occasionally seen parents of children with allergy do a 'drop and run' at a party. These parents rush in, leave an adrenaline auto-injector and medical kit for the party child's parents and then rush out the door without any clear explanation. This can leave the hosting parents feeling confused and dismayed, which isn't really helpful to anyone — not least the child with food allergy.

If you're going to leave an auto-injector with a carer or supervising parent, you really should come early to the party or, better still, arrange a time before the party to meet with the parent and explain what's involved.

By avoiding last-minute education sessions that are hurried and often not well understood, you avoid making other parents scared and annoyed about having to deal with your child's special needs. You have also educated one more person in the community — which is a great thing in itself.

Chapter 9

School and Childcare Staff: Caring for Kids with Food Allergies

As children get older, they can spend one-third (or more) of their waking day at school, child care or kindergarten. At the start of each year, thousands of children prepare for their first day at such centres, and this can be both an exciting and anxious time for parents and children. The time can be especially worrying for parents if their child has food allergies, particularly if this is the first time their child is cared for by other people. At the same time, school and childcare staff often feel daunted by the responsibility of looking after a child with food allergies, and can feel particularly anxious about the possibility of a child in their care having an anaphylaxis reaction, even though such an event is rare.

Staff at schools, childcare centres and other children's services, such as before or after school childcare and holiday programs, have a duty of care to provide a safe and healthy environment for the children they're looking after. This chapter focuses on providing information for such staff.

In this chapter, we cover the ways you can provide a safe and supportive environment for children with food allergies at your school or childcare centre, so these children can participate equally in all aspects of their school or childcare activities. We also offer some strategies to help you manage food allergies in children under your care, covering both prevention of allergic reactions and dealing with any reactions in a timely and effective way.

If you're a parent of a child with food allergy, you may also find this chapter useful. The information we provide gives you a better understanding of not only what you can expect your school or child care to be responsible for, but also your own responsibilities.

Keeping Kids with Food Allergies Safe at Schools and Child Care

Creating a completely allergen-free environment in schools or childcare centres is impossible, and both the staff who work at these centres and parents of children with food allergies shouldn't have a false sense of security that food allergens have been or can be eliminated from any environment.

Medical experts and support groups for people with food allergy don't recommend complete food bans in schools or childcare services. (In some situations in childcare centres, a ban may be appropriate — for example, you may implement a peanut ban in one of the childcare rooms where a toddler with peanut allergy is being cared for because staff may find keeping the toddler away from peanut difficult.)

Instead, children should be encouraged to learn how to manage their food allergies in situations where allergens may be present in the environment. Even if bans of specific allergens are in place, staff at both childcare centres and schools need to implement a range of procedures and risk minimisation strategies to reduce the risk of a child having an allergic reaction while in their care.

Your school or childcare centre can do a number of things to help minimise the risks for children with food allergies while in your care. Your school or childcare centre should develop appropriate policies and procedures, and then clearly explain these in an allergy and anaphylaxis policy document.

In the following sections, we look at the policies and procedures your school or childcare centre should adopt, and give you some information about arranging your first aid rooms, responding to emergencies and taking steps after an allergic reaction.

Setting allergy policies

All schools and childcare centres should have an anaphylaxis policy document in place that outlines all of the strategies aimed at providing a safer environment for children with food allergies, and the implementation of that policy should be monitored on an ongoing basis.

In the Australian state of Victoria, government legislation mandates that all schools and children's services have an anaphylaxis management policy in place that all staff and parents of children with food allergies must be aware of. In addition, all children's services staff and the majority of school staff are required to complete accredited training in anaphylaxis management, which must be updated on a regular basis. Such legislation has helped to improve the way children with food allergies are cared for in schools and childcare centres.

The anaphylaxis policy of your school or childcare centre should include information that helps staff manage children with food allergies while these children are under their care. The key components of such a policy are the following:

- Guidance on how to identify children with food allergies, and what their food allergens are.

- Ways to develop an individualised allergy management plan for each child with food allergy. The plan should include a risk minimisation plan and an emergency action plan for each child. (See following section for more on allergy management plans — note that the allergy management plan isn't the same as the emergency action plan.)

- Advice for establishing an emergency response plan for when a child has an allergic reaction.

- Suggestions for a communication plan to inform parents and staff about the policies and procedures that are in place at the school or childcare centre in regards to allergy and anaphylaxis management.

- Contact details (including specific people to contact) for parents to let staff know about new information regarding their child's allergy.

In the section 'Communicating Food Allergy Policies', later in this chapter, we give you some advice on discussing allergy management policies with other staff members, parents and other students.

Keeping health records

After writing the allergy policies (refer to the preceding section), the next step your school or child care needs to take to provide a safe environment for children with food allergy is find out who these children are. This can be done at the start of each year (at the same time other health information is collected for all children), and must be repeated annually. As well, your school or child care can ask parents for information about whether their child has food allergies on enrolment.

Your school or childcare centre is responsible for requesting information relating to food allergy (together with other health information) from children enrolled in their services. On the other hand, parents are responsible for informing the school promptly if their child is newly diagnosed with food allergy during the school year. (See the sidebar 'What schools and childcare centres are responsible for' to understand who takes care of specific allergy-related tasks.)

Once children with food allergy have been identified, keeping good records for these children is vital. Each child's enrolment record should contain an individualised *allergy management plan* that includes detailed information on the following:

- ✔ The child's specific allergies.

- ✔ Emergency contact details.

- ✔ A *risk minimisation plan* that outlines the situations or ways that the child could be accidentally exposed to known allergens while at school or child care (for example, in art class, or during class parties and excursions) and practical strategies to minimise those risks. The plan should also cover who's responsible for implementing these strategies. (See the following section for more on risk minimisation plans.)

- ✔ A *medical emergency action plan* completed and signed by the child's doctor that outlines what to do if the child has an allergic reaction, what medications have been prescribed for the child and when to use them. (Examples include the ASCIA personal emergency action plan — see Chapter 11 for more information on emergency action plans.)

As well as keeping a copy of the medical emergency action plan in the child's enrolment record, a copy should be kept in the child's emergency medical kit with any allergy medications.

The allergy management plan should be developed jointly with the families of children with food allergies. All staff at your school or child care should be aware of who the children with food allergies are, and be familiar with each child's allergy management plan. The development of an allergy management plan for each child with food allergy is a vital step in providing a safe and supportive environment for children with food allergies while they're at school or child care.

Each child's allergy management plan should be reviewed at least annually, and at the time of enrolment or diagnosis of food allergy.

What schools and childcare centres are responsible for

When developing a procedure for managing food allergies in schools, delineating responsibilities that are to be carried out by your school or child care and those that are to be carried out by parents and families is helpful.

The responsibilities of schools and childcare services may include the following:

- Developing an allergy and anaphylaxis management policy with information on what staff can do to provide a safer environment for children with food allergies while these children are at school or child care.

- Providing allergy and anaphylaxis management training for staff that includes training in the use of adrenaline auto-injector devices. This training should preferably be updated on a regular basis.

- Identifying children with food allergies enrolled in the school or childcare service.

- Creating an allergy management plan for each child.

- Ensuring that parents provide an emergency medical kit for their child that contains the child's medications together with the emergency action plan, to be kept while their child is at the school or child care (if a child has been prescribed an adrenaline auto-injector).

- Conducting regular checks of each child's adrenaline auto-injector to ensure that the device hasn't reached its expiry date.

- Ensuring that all staff know where the emergency medical kits are kept for each child with food allergy.

- Writing an emergency response plan that describes exactly what to do in the event that a child has an allergic reaction. This should include information on where the child's allergy medications are kept, the actions staff should take when they become aware that a child is having an allergic reaction, and which staff are responsible for the various actions.

- Implementing a communication strategy for parents/guardians and staff, and encouraging ongoing communication between parents/guardians and staff regarding the current status of the child's allergies, the allergy and anaphylaxis management policy and its implementation.

Developing a risk minimisation plan for children with food allergies

As part of each child's individualised allergy management plan (see preceding section), you need to develop an individual risk minimisation plan that helps the child avoid known food allergens. This risk minimisation plan should

- ✔ Identify the situations when a child may be accidentally exposed to food allergens while at school or child care
- ✔ Offer practical strategies to minimise the risks of accidental exposure, and outline who's responsible for implementing these risk minimisation strategies

We look at these points in the following sections.

When you're developing a risk minimisation plan, you should work together with the family of the child with food allergies. You must review the plan at least annually, and at any time a change occurs in the child's medical condition.

Identifying high-risk situations for food-allergic kids

When you're developing a risk minimisation plan for a child with food allergy, you need to identify all the possible risk situations for that particular child in relation to the child's specific allergy and activities.

High-risk situations may include art and craft classes, cooking lessons, science experiments, sports days, class parties, or school excursions or camps.

These high-risk situations may then be compounded by certain factors, including the following:

- ✔ **The type of food allergen the child is allergic to.** For example, peanut and tree nuts are more likely to cause severe reactions.
- ✔ **The age of the student.** Children aged between 10 and 18 years are at a higher risk of suffering a fatal allergic reaction.
- ✔ **The severity of the allergy.** This is especially important if the child has had a severe reaction and/or anaphylaxis in the past.
- ✔ **Whether the child has asthma.** Poorly controlled asthma is a strong risk factor for anaphylaxis and death from anaphylaxis.

Children who have allergy to peanut or tree nuts, have suffered an anaphylaxis reaction previously, have asthma and/or are aged 10 years or older are at a higher risk for having a severe allergic reaction (anaphylaxis) or fatal reactions due to anaphylaxis, and carefully planning risk minimisation strategies for these higher risk children is crucial.

Offering practical strategies for minimising risks

Your school or child care can put in place general strategies that can reduce the risk of children accidentally eating a food they're allergic to while at school or child care. Some examples of these strategies include the following:

✔ Children with food allergies should only eat food that has been specifically prepared for them.

✔ Children with food allergies shouldn't trade or share food, food utensils or food containers.

✔ All children must wash their hands before and after eating.

✔ All children need to be closely supervised at meal and snack times and should eat their food in specified areas. Ideally, children shouldn't 'wander around' with food.

✔ Parents should be encouraged to provide a 'safe' treat box for their child that's clearly labelled with their child's name.

✔ If food is being prepared by the child care or school, staff should be instructed about how to prevent cross-contamination of food allergens when food is being prepared, handled or served. For example, food preparation areas and utensils should be cleaned appropriately. (Refer to Chapter 7 for more on cross-contamination of foods during food preparation and serving.)

✔ Tables, high chairs and bench tops should be washed down after eating.

✔ Children with food allergies should be more carefully supervised on special occasions such as excursions or family days.

✔ Using food containers, boxes and packaging that contained common allergens (such as egg, cow's milk, peanut, tree nuts) in craft classes, cooking lessons and science experiments should be avoided, depending on the food allergies that particular children have in the classes.

✔ Staff should discuss the use of foods in activities with the child's parents to comply with the agreed risk minimisation plan for that child.

✔ Staff should use non-food rewards, such as stickers, for all children.

Some additional strategies are specific to the childcare setting, and include the following:

✔ When toddlers are together, ensuring a highly allergic child doesn't sit at the same table when others are eating food or drink containing their food allergen may be appropriate. However, children with food allergies shouldn't be separated from all children — they should be socially included in all activities.

✔ If babies and toddlers who are allergic to cow's milk are present, holding babies when they're drinking normal cow's milk formula is advisable, to avoid accidental spilling of milk.

✔ Some parents may choose to provide all the food for their child rather than have the service prepare the food, so discussing this with parents may be appropriate.

The child's risk minimisation plan should also identify the staff responsible for implementing the risk minimisation strategies, because this may not always be the same person.

Getting started with your risk management plan

When you're writing your risk management plan, you need to think about the situations when a child in your care might be exposed to her food allergen. You can assess the risk for accidental exposure during the child's usual routine, and make plans for special circumstances such as class parties, sports days, camps, incursions or excursions.

Discussing various scenarios with other staff and the child's parents may be helpful — you can then establish strategies to minimise risk for each of the scenarios.

For example, you might consider the scenario of a cooking class that Eliza, a 15 year old with peanut allergy and asthma, is attending next week and identify this as a possible risk to Eliza. You can then think of some practical strategies to avoid exposing Eliza to peanut during the class, and discuss these plans with Eliza's parents.

Next, you can work through each of the different classes and activities that Eliza is involved with during the school term, identify situations that might result in Eliza coming into contact with peanut, and plan various strategies to minimise the risk of her having accidental exposure to peanut.

See the section 'Preparing the classroom', later in this chapter, for advice on specific high-risk situations such as art and craft classes, and class parties. See the section 'Taking Allergies on Holiday: School Trips', later in this chapter, for information relating to school excursions and camps. Also, you can find a sample management plan on the website of the Victorian Government's Department of Education and Early Childhood Development; go to www.education.vic.gov.au/healthwellbeing/health/anaphy laxisschools.htm and find the Sample Anaphylaxis Management Plan.

Training staff in anaphylaxis management

As a staff member at a school or childcare centre, you have a duty of care to the children you look after. This includes managing an allergic reaction in a child, if that should happen while the child is with you.

Because of this duty of care entrusted to schools and childcare services, all staff — including volunteers, casual relief teachers, canteen staff and administrative staff — should be familiar with the common causes of food allergy, the signs and symptoms of allergic reactions (including anaphylaxis) and the management of these. As well, all staff should understand their role in the school's or child care's first aid emergency response procedures.

All school and childcare staff members benefit greatly from completing a course in allergy and anaphylaxis management. The courses are also very valuable in helping schools and childcare services provide a safe and supportive environment for children with food allergies.

Several courses are available in Australia and New Zealand, specifically developed for staff in schools and children's services. Options including the following:

- ✔ Australian Quality Training Framework (AQTF) accredited courses delivered by various registered training organisations throughout Australia.

- ✔ Courses that are delivered by specialist allergy services at teaching hospitals (such as those offered by the Royal Children's Hospital Melbourne).

- ✔ An online course developed by the Australasian Society of Clinical Allergy and Immunology (ASCIA). (This course is available for school and childcare staff members throughout Australia and New Zealand.)

These courses teach you about

- Common causes of food allergy and food anaphylaxis

- Not-so-common causes of allergy and anaphylaxis

- Recognising an allergic reaction

- Distinguishing mild to moderate reactions from life-threatening anaphylaxis

- Managing an allergic reaction or anaphylaxis in an emergency

- Minimising the risks of children being accidentally exposed to their food allergen while they're in the care of their school or childcare service

In many Australian states and in New Zealand, dedicated government funding is available to assist with training staff in schools and, in some cases, children's services, where an enrolled child has been identified as being at risk of anaphylaxis. In most Australian states, independent schools are required to cover the costs of training. (Of course, directing more funding towards training would be wonderful, and could increase uptake from schools and children's services.) In Victoria and Western Australia, legislation has been passed mandating that all schools and children's services have an anaphylaxis policy in place and that staff are trained in anaphylaxis management.

Arranging first aid rooms

If a child has been prescribed an adrenaline auto-injector, you must ask the parents to provide the auto-injector together with an emergency medical kit for when their child is at school or child care (refer to Chapter 7 for information on who might need an adrenaline auto-injector).

The *emergency medical kit* should be an insulated container — for example, an insulated lunch pack — containing the child's

- **Current adrenaline auto-injector device.** Most children are prescribed two adrenaline auto-injectors and can leave one of these at school in their emergency medical kit.

- **Medical emergency action plan.** This has information on how to treat an allergic reaction — in case the child has a reaction and the parents or guardian can't be contacted. It also has emergency contact details for the child's parents and doctor.

- **Antihistamines**. If this medication has been prescribed, it may also be included in the kit.

Your school or child care may choose to provide the kit container, but parents must provide everything else that should be contained in their child's emergency medical kit.

The emergency medical kit containing the adrenaline auto-injector should be clearly labelled with the child's name, and stored away from direct heat in a central location that's known to all staff, including relief staff. The storage site should be easily accessible to adults (not locked) but somewhere that children can't easily get to. The adrenaline auto-injector should be kept at a stable room temperature (not in the refrigerator or freezer — which is why the medication needs to be kept in an insulated bag).

For some children (for example, children in secondary school, or children who have experienced severe reactions that developed within seconds of being exposed to their allergen), having their adrenaline auto-injector with them in class or in a bumbag when they are playing outside may be appropriate.

All children who have been prescribed an adrenaline auto-injector must have an emergency medical kit at their school or child care.

Your school or child care may consider purchasing an unassigned adrenaline auto-injector device that can be used as a back-up, particularly if no central, easily accessible location is available in your school or child care. The dosage of a back-up adrenaline auto-injector in kindergarten and pre-school centres (or for any child under 20 kilograms) should be 0.15 milligram of adrenaline, because most children in these centres weigh less than 20 kilograms. For schools and before or after school care services, the dose should be 0.3 milligram of adrenaline, because most children at school weigh more than 20 kilograms. This back-up device should be clearly labelled as not being assigned to any individual child. (***Note:*** The product information supplied with the EpiPen recommends the EpiPen Jr for children up to 30 kilograms and the standard EpiPen for children 30 kilograms or heavier, which contradicts the ASCIA guidelines; however, we recommend following the ASCIA guidelines.)

A dedicated staff member, such as a school nurse, first aid coordinator or other person in charge of anaphylaxis management at the school or child care, should be responsible for regularly checking the expiry dates on all adrenaline auto-injector devices (for example, at the start and end of each term) and should send a written reminder to parents to replace the device at least one month before the expiry date. In the case of EpiPens, this person should also check whether the adrenaline is cloudy or discoloured and, if it is, notify the parents in writing to replace the device.

The manufacturers of the adrenaline auto-injector devices only guarantee the effectiveness of the adrenaline auto-injector to the end of the nominated expiry month.

A lead role for first aid coordinators and school nurses

First aid coordinators or school nurses can take a lead role in supporting school and childcare staff to implement strategies for the prevention and management of food allergy and anaphylaxis.

Their responsibilities may include

✔ Keeping an up-to-date register of enrolled children with food allergy.

✔ Making sure that the child's emergency contact details are up to date.

✔ Checking that the adrenaline auto-injectors are in date and not cloudy or discoloured (in the case of the EpiPen) at the beginning and end of each term.

✔ Informing parents a month before their child's adrenaline auto-injector expires, and notifying them that the adrenaline auto-injector needs to be replaced. This should be in writing.

✔ Making sure that the emergency medication kits (which contain the children's adrenaline auto-injectors) are stored correctly (at room temperature and away from light) in an unlocked, easily accessible place, and that each kit is appropriately labelled.

✔ Providing or arranging support for children and staff following an incident when a child has an allergic reaction while at school or child care.

✔ Working with other staff to conduct regular reviews of prevention and management strategies.

✔ Working with other staff to develop strategies to raise awareness about food allergies and anaphylaxis among children, staff and the parent community.

EpiClub is a free service that sends a reminder to owners of EpiPen adrenaline auto-injectors (by email, SMS or standard mail) prior to the expiry date of their EpiPen. Schools can also access this service — simply register with EpiClub at www.epiclub.com.au.

If a child's adrenaline auto-injector (and emergency medical kit) is removed from its usual place of storage — for example, for a school camp or excursion — the auto-injector and kit should be signed out, and signed back in when it's returned to its usual place. Some families choose to take their child's adrenaline auto-injector home with them each night. In this case, they still need to sign the device in and out each time it's taken from or brought back to school or child care.

Responding to an emergency

Your school or child care must have in place an emergency response plan that outlines the steps that need to be taken when a child has an allergic reaction while in your care, and who's responsible for each of the steps.

Specifically, the emergency response plan should describe

- ✔ Who stays with the child to offer reassurance and monitor the child for signs of an allergic reaction.
- ✔ How to get help and who does this.
- ✔ Who retrieves the child's emergency medication kit and from where (exact location of the kit to be provided).
- ✔ Who administers the child's emergency medication, including the adrenaline auto-injector (if required).
- ✔ Who records the time that medication is administered and what that medication was.
- ✔ Who calls the ambulance and how communication between the ambulance officer and staff member with the child is achieved.
- ✔ Who notifies the parents that their child has had an allergic reaction and outlines the management that has been provided.

If all of these emergency response steps are planned and pre-assigned, confusion and error is less likely to occur in the event of a child having an allergic reaction.

The emergency response plan should be practised on a regular basis — preferably once each term — and any new, casual, relief or volunteer staff must be made aware of the emergency response plan when they commence work.

Your school or childcare centre is responsible for ensuring that a clearly outlined emergency response plan is in place for each possible situation where a child might have an allergic reaction, and that all staff members are familiar with the plan and their role within it.

The emergency response plan should be tailored to the different situations when a child might have an allergic reaction. For example, you need to have a specific emergency response plan for the schoolyard, another for the classroom or first aid centre, and a different one again for school camps or excursions.

Schoolyard procedures

If the allergic reaction occurs in the schoolyard, an example of an emergency response plan for this setting could be as follows:

1. **Ask the child to lie down and stay still.**

   Don't ask the child to move to a different location (for example, school office or first aid room). If the child is having difficulty breathing, you can sit the child up slightly while still keeping the legs flat.

2. **Have the yard duty teacher send two children to the first aid room or school office to notify the school nurse or office staff; have another child alert the second teacher on yard duty.**

3. **Ask the office staff or school nurse to bring the child's medication kit and the mobile phone.**

   The medication kit should contain adrenaline auto-injector, antihistamine and emergency action plan.

4. **Follow procedures on the emergency response plan. Administer the adrenaline auto-injector if the child develops signs of anaphylaxis, according to the child's emergency action plan details.**

5. **Call for the ambulance, if adrenaline is administered.**

   Remain on the phone with ambulance officer and follow any directions provided.

6. **Have another adult meet the ambulance.**

7. **If the child is breathing well, lay the child down with feet elevated; if not breathing well, keep the child sitting down.**

8. **When situation is under control, call parents/carer, or child's doctor if guardians aren't contactable.**

Park and excursion procedures

When teachers are taking children off the school premises, they must take the medication kits and emergency response plans for any children present with food allergy.

If an allergic reaction occurs while on excursion, an example of an emergency response plan for this setting could be as follows:

1. **Ask the child to lie down and stay still.**

   Don't move the child to a different location. If the child is having difficulty breathing, you can sit the child up slightly while still keeping the legs flat.

2. **Have a second adult or teacher bring the child's adrenaline auto-injector and emergency action plan.**

3. **Follow procedures on the child's emergency action plan.**

   Administer the adrenaline auto-injector if symptoms of anaphylaxis develop (as outlined in emergency response plan).

4. **Have a second adult call the ambulance, if adrenaline is administered.**

   This adult remains on the phone with ambulance officer and follows any directions provided.

5. **If child is breathing well, lay the child down with feet elevated; if not breathing well, keep the child sitting down.**

6. **When situation is under control, call parents/carer, or child's doctor if guardians aren't contactable.**

First aid centre procedures

Sometimes the child with allergy presents at the first aid centre with symptoms of an allergic reaction. An example emergency response plan for this setting could be as follows:

1. **Sit the child in one of the first aid centre chairs or lay the child down on the bed (if the centre has one).**

2. **Have the first aid officer or school nurse get the appropriate medication kit and the mobile phone.**

   The medication kit should contain the child's adrenaline auto-injector, antihistamine and emergency action plan.

3. **Follow procedures outlined in the child's emergency action plan.**

   Administer adrenaline auto-injector, if symptoms of anaphylaxis develop (as outlined in emergency response plan).

4. **Call for the ambulance, if adrenaline is administered.**

   Remain on the phone with the ambulance officer and follow any directions provided.

5. **Have a second adult meet the ambulance.**

6. **If child is breathing well, lay the child down with feet elevated; if not breathing well, keep the child sitting down.**

7. **When situation is under control, call parents/carer, or child's doctor if guardians aren't contactable.**

Taking steps after an allergic reaction

When a child has an allergic reaction at school or child care, the experience can be very traumatic for the child, the child's family, staff members who responded, and other children and staff who witnessed the reaction, especially if the reaction is severe (anaphylaxis) and emergency medication has to be administered. While younger children in child care may be less aware of what had happened, students in schools can be emotionally affected when another child has an allergic reaction, particularly teenagers. In such situations, children and staff may benefit from counselling after the event, and this counselling could be provided by the school nurse, school psychologist or other available school counsellors.

After an allergic reaction, your school or child care should also review its management processes to determine if any issues are evident that contributed to the situation, or if any processes could be improved to better prevent a similar incident occurring in the future.

As well, the staff member responsible for managing the emergency medication kits should ensure that the child's adrenaline auto-injector (if used) is replaced by the parents before the child returns to school or child care. The parents should also be advised to take their child to a doctor for review of their food allergy, including a review (and possible updating) of the child's emergency action plan.

Communicating Food Allergy Policies

A *communication plan* outlines how your school or childcare centre discusses with parents and staff the allergy and anaphylaxis policy, and how parents and staff are informed about risk minimisation plans and emergency procedures in relation to a child with food allergies enrolled at the school or childcare centre. It also outlines how parents can communicate new information about their child's food allergy to the school, including who parents should contact.

Having a clearly outlined communication plan in relation to allergy and anaphylaxis management procedures at your school or child care makes it easier for staff and parents to share important information about children with food allergies, and avoid breakdowns in communication that could result in a child having an allergic reaction while at school or child care. The school or childcare centre, together with the child's parents, are jointly responsible for correctly identifying all enrolled children with food allergies — your school or child care must seek out information about whether a child enrolled in your service has food allergies and, at the same time, parents must inform the school if their child is diagnosed with a food allergy.

In the following sections, we cover how to talk to staff and families of children with allergies, as well as other students and families who don't have children with food allergy.

Talking to staff

When talking about allergy management with other staff, discussions must cover the following:

- ✔ Causes, symptoms and treatment of allergic reactions, including anaphylaxis

- ✔ Identities of students at risk of allergic reactions and anaphylaxis

- ✔ Preventative strategies in place

- ✔ The school's first aid and emergency response procedures

- ✔ The staff's role in responding to an allergic reaction

- ✔ Where medications such as adrenaline auto-injectors are kept

All of the topics outlined in the preceding list should be covered in your allergy policy documents. Refer to the section 'Setting allergy policies', earlier in this chapter, for further advice.

Some ways to hold allergy-related discussions with staff include allocating time, such as at staff meetings, to discuss, practise and review the school's management strategies for students with food allergy, and keeping copies of the student's emergency action plan in canteens, classrooms and staff rooms.

Ensuring procedures are in place for informing new staff (including canteen staff, volunteers or casual relief staff) of students with food allergy is particularly important, as is letting these staff know about the steps required for prevention and emergency response. A designated staff member, such as the daily organiser or school operations manager, should be responsible for this briefing.

Speaking to families of children with food allergies

Parents are often very anxious about sending their child with food allergies to school or child care, especially if it's the first time their child will be away from their care. Parents can have greater confidence in the school or child care if they have the opportunity to discuss their child's health concerns with you (their child's teacher or carer) and other staff, and have a good understanding of the policies and procedures that your school or child care has put in place to help provide a safe and supportive environment for their child.

In particular, parents' anxiety can be considerably reduced if they can communicate openly and work cooperatively with the school or child care in planning the management of their child's food allergy. Parents are often reassured to know that their child's school or child care is committed to raising awareness among staff members, students and the school community regarding food allergies and anaphylaxis, and to providing their staff members with training in allergy and anaphylaxis management.

Providing parents with a copy of your school's or child care's allergy and anaphylaxis management policy, which includes a clear communication plan for parents of children with food allergies, can help to achieve an open line of communication between staff and families of children with food allergy.

The allergy policy document (refer to 'Setting allergy policies', earlier in this chapter) should provide information on how parents can communicate any new information to staff caring for their child. Ideally, it also identifies the staff member at your school or child care who's responsible for communicating with parents on matters related to allergy and anaphylaxis management. This way, parents know who they should contact and can become familiar with that person — so providing any new information regarding their child's food allergies to the school or child care as soon as possible is easier.

Staff caring for children with food allergies should also maintain regular communication with parents regarding any newly identified situations when their child might be exposed to an allergen, so that an appropriate risk minimisation plan can be developed together with the parents. If your class is planning to go on an excursion next week, for example, you should notify the parents of children with food allergies in your class in order to develop a specific risk minimisation plan for this situation for each child.

What parents need to do

Parents of children with food allergies can help the school or childcare centre care for their child with food allergy by taking responsibility for keeping staff informed about their child's allergy condition. For example, you can:

✔ Inform the school or childcare service that your child has a food allergy at the time your child is enrolled or when the diagnosis of food allergy is made by your child's doctor.

✔ Work together with staff to develop a risk minimisation plan that is specific for your child.

✔ Provide the school or childcare service with your child's up-to-date personal emergency action plan (see Chapter 11 for more details) that has been prepared and signed by your child's doctor. (This plan provides important information about the medications prescribed for your child and when to use them.)

✔ Provide staff with an emergency medical kit for your child that contains the adrenaline auto-injector, if your child has been prescribed one, as well as any other allergy medications that have been prescribed and your child's personal emergency action plan.

✔ Regularly check the expiry date of your child's adrenaline auto-injector device.

✔ Offer information and answer any questions that staff may have regarding your child's allergies.

✔ Let staff know as soon as any changes to your child's allergy status occur and provide a new emergency action plan that has been updated with these changes.

Explaining allergies to other kids

Children with food allergy also need to feel supported by other children at their school or child care. You can help other children learn about food allergy and anaphylaxis and understand how children with food allergies are affected by their health problem.

Some ways to increase awareness of food allergy and anaphylaxis among children are to display fact sheets or posters in your classroom, hallways and the canteen. A range of story books about food allergy for toddlers and school-aged children are also available (check out Anaphylaxis Australia's range at www.allergyfacts.org.au/links/online-store), which you can share with children in your class or child care.

You can talk about food allergies during class and offer a few simple key messages to children in your class, such as the following:

✔ Always take food allergies seriously — severe allergies are no joke

✔ Be respectful of another child's adrenaline auto-injector

✔ Don't pressure your friends to eat food that they're allergic to

✔ Don't share your food with friends who have food allergies

✔ If you see someone become sick, get help immediately

✔ Know what your friends are allergic to

✔ Wash your hands after eating

Some parents may not want their child's identity or the fact that their child has food allergies shared with the wider school community. Similarly, some children with food allergy may not want to be singled out or seen to be treated differently. Discuss with each child and their parents what they feel works best for them and whether parents agree to have their child's name, photograph and relevant treatment details displayed in staff areas, canteens or other common areas.

Bullying is a problem that can affect all children, and children with food allergy are no exception. Children may tease children with food allergies, try to trick them into eating a food or threaten them with the food the children are allergic to — for example, taunt them with a peanut butter sandwich. If you're told about or discover this sort of behaviour, your school is likely to have general strategies in place for dealing with bullying situations and these can be followed. However, you can also tailor your reaction to this specific situation, as follows:

✔ Talk to the child performing the bullying and explain to that child that an allergic reaction, especially anaphylaxis, is extremely serious and possibly life-threatening.

✔ Emphasise to the child that any behaviour that attempts to harm a child who has food allergy with a food allergen is treated as a serious and dangerous incident, and managed accordingly.

✔ Remind the child about ways children with food allergies can be helped. (Hopefully, by this stage, the child will be sufficiently remorseful to take note of this information.)

In Chapter 10, we provide some information for kids with food allergy about dealing with peer pressure and bullying. In Chapter 14, we outline some key lessons that parents can teach their kids with food allergy.

'Be a MATE' program

MATE (Make Allergy Treatment Easier) is a program that explains to children how they can help support their friend with food allergy — or, in other words, how to 'be a MATE' to their friend with food allergy. The program is offered by Anaphylaxis Australia, a support group that raises awareness of food allergy and anaphylaxis through education and support. (The MATE program was originally developed by the Food Allergy and Anaphylaxis Network (FAAN) in the USA, and has been adapted by Anaphylaxis Australia for use in Australia.)

Everybody can be a **MATE** by following five easy steps:

✔ Always take food allergies seriously

✔ Don't share food

✔ Wash hands after eating

✔ Ask friends what they're allergic to

✔ Get help immediately if a schoolmate has a reaction

If you would like more information on the Be a MATE program, look on the Anaphylaxis Australia website: `www.allergyfacts.org.au`.

Helping parents understand other children's allergies

If a child with food allergies is enrolled in your school or child care, let all the parents know about the situation, and that plans are in place to prevent that child being exposed to the food allergen. Also make parents aware that situations may arise when other parents are asked to assist the school or childcare service in providing a safer environment for the child with food allergy.

Many parents may not understand why the school or child care taking some responsibility in managing another child's allergy problem is important, so also provide some general information to other parents about food allergy and the potentially serious nature of anaphylaxis, some practical strategies the school has put in place to minimise the chances of children being exposed to their food allergens, as well as ways in which other parents can help.

You can download posters, fact sheets and brochures from a variety of reliable websites, including the Department of Education and Early Childhood Development Student Wellbeing website, `www.education.vic.gov.au/healthwellbeing/health/anaphylaxis.htm`, or from the Australasian Society of Clinical Allergy and Immunology website,

www.allergy.org.au. (See Chapter 17 for more information on useful
websites.) These resources can be used to promote greater awareness of
food allergies and anaphylaxis in the school community.

Dealing with Food in Schools

You can implement a number of practical strategies to minimise the risk of a
child being exposed to food allergens while at school — including in-school
and out-of-school settings.

Times that you need to prepare for include the following:

- Classroom activities
- In canteens or during lunch or snack times
- In the yard, before and after school, and during breaks
- Special events such as sport days or class parties
- Excursions and camps

We look at the situations within the school grounds in the following
sections, and excursions and camps later in the chapter, in the section
'Taking Allergies on Holiday: School Trips'.

Preparing the classroom

Children spend the majority of their time while at school in a classroom
and many different class activities are carried out here. Class teachers or
staff in childcare centres must be fully aware of the children in their care
with food allergy, the foods they're allergic to, and the information in their
allergy management plan. This plan includes the child's risk management
plan and medical emergency action plan. (Refer to the section 'Keeping
health records', earlier in this chapter, for more on individualised allergy
management plans, and to 'Developing a risk minimisation plan for children
with food allergies'.)

Because casual relief teachers or volunteer staff may often help in
classrooms or childcare centres, and children may also move to different
rooms during the day, you should help all teachers and childcare staff
remember the children who have food allergies by having a copy of the
student's medical emergency action plan displayed in the classroom.

Some parents or children with food allergies may not wish to have their emergency action plans on display, and so be identified in this way, so you need to meet with parents to determine if they agree with this.

In your role as teacher or childcare worker, you can help children under your care improve their understanding of food allergies and anaphylaxis. Within the classroom, you can talk with children about what food allergy, or anaphylaxis, is, the common foods that children are allergic to, and how children can help their friends with food allergies to manage their allergies while at school or child care. You can also discuss how to 'be a MATE' to children with food allergies (refer to the sidebar '"Be a MATE" program').

If the children in your care are old enough, you should discuss with them the school's emergency response plan for when a child has an allergic reaction. Cover what they can do when they see someone becoming sick from food, including where to go and who to inform.

If a severe allergic reaction occurs, many schools instruct children to find a teacher immediately and notify that teacher of what has happened, and to then follow any further instructions from the teacher. A child can be asked to help notify other teachers or staff, to help get a mobile phone or perform other actions that form part of the school or childcare emergency response plan. You can explain to the children in your care that their help is very important in such emergency situations.

In the following sections, we look at some specific challenges that classroom activities can present when caring for children with food allergy.

Art classes and activities

Art classes and activities are a great opportunity to reuse old food boxes and containers, and parents often help out by sending in old containers. However, if children in your care with food allergies are participating in these classes and activities, you have to be careful to avoid accidental exposure to allergens.

Here are some strategies for avoiding allergic reactions in art classes or activities:

✔ Talk about allergies before the class or activity, including how small amounts of food allergens can make children with food allergies really sick.

✔ Inform other parents about children with food allergies and ask them not to send in food containers that held allergen-containing foods.

✔ Invite parents of children with allergies to offer additional suggestions for how to manage the situation — for example, they may offer to bring in special supplies for their child to work with. Or they may come up with a different approach you hadn't thought of.

✔ Screen the boxes and containers before the class and remove any containers that have held products containing relevant allergens.

✔ Pay particular attention to the boxes and containers on the table where children with food allergies are working.

✔ Discuss the risk minimisation plan in place for children with food allergies with other staff — they may have other thoughts or suggestions that can be useful to implement.

Small amounts of some food allergens, such as peanuts, remain in containers even after washing, and can cause severe reactions. Be particularly cautious about food containers that were used to store products containing peanuts.

In some childcare centres, art teachers visit the centre on a particular day each week, doing various activities with children in different rooms through the day. As with all casual teachers, ensure any visiting art teachers are aware of children with food allergies and their allergy management plans. (Refer to the section 'Talking to staff', earlier in this chapter, for more.)

Food treats

Many teachers and childcare workers use treats to reward children when they have achieved something important or been especially well behaved.

If you have a child with food allergies in your class or childcare room, avoid using food treats where possible. If you do choose to use food treats, make sure you offer treats that don't contain any of the allergens that children in your care are allergic to, in case children share their treat with someone who has food allergies.

Instead of food treats, we encourage teachers to use non-food rewards, such as stickers or stamps, for all children, as a way to help reduce the risk of an allergic reaction. And non-food treats are the healthier option for all children!

Sometimes, such as during class parties or birthdays, food treats may be unavoidable. For these situations, ask the parents of children with food allergies to provide a treat box for their child that contains special food treats that their child can have. These treats can be offered to their child at appropriate times — meaning the child can have a treat and still feel included in the celebrations.

Special food treats for a child with food allergies should be kept in a treat box that's clearly labelled with the child's name and only used for that child.

Setting up canteens and kitchens

Ideally, children at school with food allergy should only eat foods that they have brought to school from home. However, this may not be possible at all times, or children may want a treat or to be able to do what their friends can do.

Eating meals that are made by a person other than a child's parents are a common cause of a child accidentally eating a problem food and having an unexpected allergic reaction. So schools and childcare centres need to take extra care when offering food to children when under their care. You (or the person responsible for allergy and anaphylaxis management at your school or child care) should also meet with the parents of the child with food allergy to discuss what foods are suitable for their child.

All staff working in the canteen, including volunteers, should be informed about the children who have food allergy, any prevention (risk minimisation) strategies that are in place for that child, and the information in their medical emergency action plans.

Banning food allergens in schools and childcare centres is generally not recommended because this can provide a false sense of security that the school or child care offers an allergen-free environment, which just can't be guaranteed. (See the sidebar 'Banning food in schools' for the recommendations of Australasian Society of Clinical Immunology and Allergy (ASCIA)). Instead, a 'no sharing' approach is recommended for food, utensils and food containers.

Some schools or childcare centres may decide not to stock peanut and tree nut (such as hazelnut, cashew, almond) products, including nut spreads, in their canteens to lessen the chances of a child accidentally eating one of these allergens in foods prepared by the school or child care — although, in the case of schools, other children may continue to bring along their own foods (including peanut and tree nut products). Canteens can provide a range of healthy meals and foods that don't include peanut or other nut products.

Younger children in child care can't be responsible for discerning the safety of the food they're about to eat, so childcare staff must be responsible for making sure the children are only served food that doesn't contain their food allergen.

When a child with food allergy enters school, you can then begin teaching the child about how to manage their allergy. This includes education about how to avoid accidentally eating a food allergen.

Banning food in schools

Medical experts and food allergy support groups don't recommend food bans. The Australasian Society of Clinical Immunology and Allergy (ASCIA), Australia's peak professional society of allergy specialists, and Anaphylaxis Australia Inc (AAI) both advise against banning of allergenic foods in schools.

Food bans create a false sense of security for children with food allergy and are difficult to guarantee in the school setting. Risk minimisation strategies, such as hand washing and not sharing food, are far more effective ways to reduce the risk of children with food allergy being exposed to a food allergen.

Moreover, implementing food bans can cause unnecessary anxiety for both parents and children with food allergy because the bans suggest that casual contact with a food allergen could cause a serious allergic reaction — whereas no evidence exists that casual contact with a food allergen can cause serious allergic reactions or anaphylaxis.

Skin contact with allergens may cause localised hives and swelling but doesn't cause anaphylaxis. Severe reactions such as anaphylaxis require eating the food or having the food touch the mucous membranes such as on the inside of the mouth. Refer to Chapter 7 for more on avoiding food allergens.

Teach children with food allergy that they must always ask whether the food they're allergic to is in a food before they eat it — if they can't be 100 per cent sure the food doesn't contain their food allergen, they must not eat that food.

Canteen staff should be careful to avoid cross-contamination of foods with food allergens when preparing, handling, displaying or serving food. Such contamination is called *cross-contact* with food allergens and can commonly occur when staff are preparing or serving food. For example, a tiny amount of peanut butter left on a knife and used to make another meal may be enough to cause a severe reaction in someone with food allergy who's at risk of anaphylaxis. So staff need to follow good food handling practices, and use clean equipment and utensils, when working with different foods. (Refer to Chapter 7 for more information on cross-contact and how to avoid cross-contamination when preparing and serving food.) Making sure that all tables and surfaces where food is prepared, served or eaten are wiped down regularly is also good practice.

Ask children to sit quietly during meal times (snack time or lunch time) to avoid the possibility of a child with food allergy accidentally being exposed to a food allergen. However, keep in mind that accidental skin contact with a food allergen that causes a severe allergic reaction (anaphylaxis) is extremely unlikely — such contact usually only results in localised hives or swelling. Physically isolating a child with food allergy from other children during meal times isn't recommended — although in childcare and primary school settings with toddlers and younger children, having nut-free tables or nut-free zones may be appropriate.

Being prepared in the schoolyard

If a child with food allergies is enrolled in your school or child care, an emergency response plan should be in place that all staff are familiar with. This emergency response plan must outline what to do in the event that a child suffers an allergic reaction in specific situations, and who is responsible for the various actions.

Allergic reactions that happen in the schoolyard may not only be due to foods — reactions to insect stings can also occur when children are playing outdoors. The management and emergency response to allergic reactions is the same whether they are to a food or to an insect sting.

Schools and childcare centres always have staff members on yard duty when children are playing outdoors, and this staff member on duty should carry a communication device to notify the general office or first aid team if a child has an allergic reaction in the playground. We cover the key elements of an emergency response plan in the section 'Responding to an emergency', earlier in this chapter.

Holding functions at school

Occasions when special events or functions are held for children while they're at school or child care, such as sporting events, class parties and so on, pose an increased risk for a child with food allergies being accidentally exposed to a food allergen because staff are usually less able to closely supervise children. Reviewing each child's allergy management plan and ensuring you've developed a situation-specific risk minimisation plan and a site-specific emergency response plan for that child is, therefore, important. (We discuss risk minimisation and emergency response plans in the sections 'Developing a risk minimisation plan for children with food allergies' and 'Responding to an emergency', earlier in this chapter.)

In some cases, you may decide to provide an alternative food menu for the child with food allergy at school functions, or you may ask the parents to provide a meal for their child. If a child is allergic to peanut or tree nuts, you may decide to exclude any nut products from the menu provided to other children. However, if the child is allergic to egg or milk, excluding such foods is more difficult, and usually not recommended.

Taking Allergies on Holiday: School Trips

Field trips and excursions are part of a child's normal activities in schools and childcare centres. These trips are lots of fun for children, teachers and staff, as well as parents. However, they also carry an increased risk for children with food allergy because such children are more likely to accidentally come into contact with their food allergen, and they're away from the usual school or childcare environment so the usual procedures aren't automatically in place.

For example, the emergency medical kits aren't in their usual storage place, the emergency action plans aren't readily visible, and the emergency response plan is specific to the setting of the field trip rather than the usual response plans in place at school or child care. All of these changes can increase the chances of accidents or errors happening and staff members must take extra care to prepare and plan for these activities.

Staff members who have received training in allergy and anaphylaxis management must be in attendance on the field trip or excursion, and be fully aware of the children with food allergies who are participating in the activities.

In the following sections, we look at field trips and school camps.

Taking a trip

Some important things to remember when planning a field trip, excursion or other activity outside of the school or child care are the following:

- ✔ You must develop an individualised allergy management plan for each child with food allergy participating in the trip; this plan should include risk management and the child's medical emergency action plan. Develop the plan in consultation with the child's parents or carers and be sure to take into account the risk situations specific to the excursion or field trip. (For example, you may discuss an alternative food menu with the parents or request that the parents send a meal with their child.)

- ✔ Parents of a child with food allergies may wish to accompany their child on field trips or excursions to help manage their child's food allergies. Discuss this with the parents and the child as a potential strategy for supporting the child with food allergies.

✔ Always take the child's emergency medication kit on all field trips or excursions. Keep the kit in a central, readily accessible location that's known to all staff, and away from direct sunlight in a cool place (but not refrigerated).

✔ Take a mobile phone (or other communication device such as a satellite phone if not being able to pick up a mobile phone signal is possible) on all field trips or excursions.

✔ Be sure that all staff present on the field trip or excursion are aware of any children with food allergy participating in the field trip or excursion, and what they're allergic to.

✔ Put appropriate risk minimisation strategies in place while the children are being transported.

Planning for camps

If you're preparing for camp and children with food allergies are participating in the camp, you need to plan very carefully, well in advance, in order to provide a safe and supportive environment for children with food allergies while they're under your care at the camp. If the camp involves teenagers, planning with the utmost care is especially crucial.

Camps are extremely high-risk situations for children with food allergies. In the past ten years in Australia, two tragic deaths in teenagers have occurred on school camp due to food allergy. In both cases, the children knew that they were allergic to peanut, but were inadvertently exposed to the allergen and subsequently succumbed. These very sad events highlight that camps are a time of very high risk for children with food allergies, but also that teenagers in particular are a high-risk group.

Staff who have been trained in the recognition and emergency management of allergy and anaphylaxis should be present during the camp and accompany the children with food allergies during camp activities. You should ensure that the child's emergency medication kit is taken with them on the camp. As well, several mobile phones (or other communication devices, such as a satellite phone if no mobile phone coverage is possible) should be taken along on the camp to ensure that staff on the camp can maintain communication with the school, emergency medical support facilities and families.

What parents can do to plan for a school camp

If you're a parent about to send your child off on school camp, here are some guidelines on what you can do to help staff taking care of your child:

✔ Communicate with the school (particularly the camp coordinator) well in advance of the camp to discuss your child's food allergies and the school's allergy and anaphylaxis policy. Check that the school has an emergency response plan that has been developed specifically for the camp location and discuss the risk minimisation strategies that will be put in place for your child while on camp.

✔ Provide the school with written information about your child's food allergies and any other medical conditions such as asthma, including an up-to-date personalised emergency action plan for allergic reactions (or an emergency action plan for anaphylaxis if your child has been prescribed an adrenaline auto-injector) and asthma action plan (if required).

✔ Meet with the camp operators to discuss how they usually manage food allergies and whether camp staff have been trained in recognition and management of allergic reactions and the use of adrenaline auto-injectors.

✔ Meet with the camp chefs and/or cooks to discuss whether they have knowledge of the special attention required when preparing meals for children with food allergies and for your child's food allergies.

You may also wish to explore whether you could supply meals and snacks for your child to bring on camp.

✔ Make an appointment with your doctor to review your child's food allergies. Your doctor can update your child's emergency action plan, check that the adrenaline auto-injector (if prescribed) is appropriate for your child's weight and not expired, provide any additional medications or documentation your child may need for the camp. If your child has asthma, your doctor can also check that the asthma is under control and can update the asthma action plan.

✔ Prepare your child's emergency medical kit. Check that this is clearly labelled and contains up-to-date medications, including an adrenaline auto-injector (if prescribed) and an up-to-date emergency action plan that contains contact details and clear instructions on when to administer your child's medications (and the correct dose) should an allergic reaction occur.

✔ Talk to your child and remind him about some simple ways he can manage his food allergy while on camp — for example, avoiding sharing food and drinks, washing hands before eating (if possible), always checking with staff that the meal doesn't contain the problem food before eating. Also remind your child that if he can't be sure that the food is safe, he shouldn't eat it, and to always get help immediately if he feels unwell — he shouldn't 'wait and see'.

The important things to remember when preparing for a camp, in addition to the advice covered in the preceding section, include the following:

✔ If the camp is run by an independent organisation, the school should notify the camp organisers in advance that a child with food allergies is attending the camp and provide details of the foods the child is allergic to.

✔ The camp should avoid stocking peanut or tree nut products, including nut spreads, because these foods are more likely to cause severe allergic reactions (anaphylaxis). Products that 'may contain traces' of nuts may be served, but shouldn't be served to children known to be allergic to nuts who wouldn't normally be allowed to eat food that 'may contain traces' of nuts when at home. (Refer to Chapter 8 for more information about reading ingredient labels.)

✔ For younger children, the child's emergency medication kit should be kept with the school first aid kit. For older children, particularly adolescents, letting them carry their own adrenaline auto-injector while they're on camp may be appropriate. The school may wish to purchase additional unassigned adrenaline auto-injectors that can be kept in the school's first aid kit, which can be used as back-up devices.

✔ Staff still have a duty of care to students even if students have been allowed to carry their own adrenaline auto-injectors.

✔ Staff must be aware of local emergency services in the area and how to access them. The school should liaise with these emergency services before the camp.

✔ Cooking or art and craft classes and games must not involve the use of known allergens for children with food allergies.

Chapter 10

Educating Food Allergic Kids

· ·

In This Chapter

▶ Understanding your food allergies and allergic reactions

▶ Explaining your allergies to other people

▶ Managing peer pressure and bullying

▶ Learning when and how to take your medications

▶ Gaining more independence as a teenager

· ·

*W*e've written this chapter specifically for kids with food allergy — normal, healthy kids who just happen to need to avoid some foods in their diet. Some kids with food allergy are so good at avoiding their problem food that they rarely have any accidental ingestion reactions and, other than having to choose what they eat carefully, live a perfectly normal life. Hopefully, with the information in this chapter, you can be one of these kids.

Managing your food allergy isn't rocket science — and you shouldn't feel embarrassed or ashamed because you are food allergic. Everyone has a choice about what they eat — your choice can just make a great deal of difference to your health and safety.

In this chapter, we give you the tools to enable you to live a normal life and successfully control your food allergy — rather than allow your food allergy to control you. We talk about how to read your symptoms to know if you're having a small (mild) or big (severe) allergic reaction, how to tell your friends about your food allergy, and how to deal with bullying and peer pressure that may come about because of your food allergy needs.

If you're a teenager, we've written a special section at the end of the chapter just for you.

Learning to Manage Your Allergies

The fact that you're reading this chapter means you want to find out more about managing your food allergy — and that's a great start. You need to know the difference between an allergic reaction that doesn't require treatment and anaphylaxis (where treatment with an adrenaline auto-injector could save your life). In the following sections, we look at the difference between reactions, along with what you should do in each situation.

Knowing the difference between a mild reaction and anaphylaxis

A mild or moderate allergic reaction is one that involves the skin and/or gut. Skin symptoms include *hives* (itchy lumps like mosquito bites), a swollen face (around the eyes or mouth), eczema flare or redness and flushing. Gut reactions include vomiting, abdominal pain and diarrhoea. These symptoms usually occur within minutes of ingestion (except for diarrhoea, which can take a few hours to develop) and, although you can temporarily look like the Michelin Man (big and puffy!), none of these symptoms are life-threatening. What they might be, though, are early symptoms of a more severe reaction yet to come. So if you have these symptoms you need to remain calm but vigilant, and locate your adrenaline auto-injector if you have one.

Severe reactions equate to *anaphylaxis* and include involvement of the airways, breathing and circulation. Symptoms include coughing, wheezing, noisy or difficulty breathing, hoarse voice or collapse. Treatment with adrenaline (via an auto-injector) is required if you have anaphylaxis, and the medication helps open up your airways and helps your heart beat harder and faster to improve your breathing and circulation.

Skin and gut symptoms can occur without going on to develop a severe reaction. On the other hand, sometimes anaphylaxis can occur without signs of skin or gut reactions — but these are uncommon and often need to be distinguished from an asthma attack, which can be treated with ventolin.

Note: If you'd like more information about allergic reactions, refer to Chapters 4 and 5. We talk about adrenaline auto-injectors in more detail in Chapter 11.

What to do if you're having an allergic reaction

If you're having an allergic reaction, stay calm and follow the steps outlined in your emergency action plan (see Chapter 11 for more on these).

Alert those around you — never wait and watch — and let them know exactly what you're experiencing. Also feel confident to tell people around you what you think your reaction and situation mean. For example, you may say, 'I think I've eaten some peanut, but I'm not sure; I don't have any symptoms yet'. Or 'I've just eaten some peanut and I have an itchy throat. Can you please help me find my adrenaline auto-injector? I don't need to administer it yet but if I have any problems with coughing or breathing, I will need to administer it and an ambulance should be called immediately'.

Should you use an adrenaline auto-injector or call an ambulance?

Many kids worry that they won't know when to use their adrenaline auto-injector — or even that they may know they need to use it but be too scared to actually use it on themselves.

Knowing the important signs that indicate you're developing anaphylaxis as part of an allergic reaction help you to have more confidence in knowing when adrenaline needs to be administered. If you have any problems with your breathing, a feeling that your throat is closing over or that you might collapse, you should administer your adrenaline auto-injector.

We recommend that if you're not really sure about whether to use your adrenaline auto-injector, you should go ahead and use it. The potential benefits (your episode of life-threatening anaphylaxis is stopped in its tracks) are enormous while the downside is virtually non-existent. If you give yourself a dose of adrenaline when it wasn't really necessary, the main side effect is probably just a headache and a racing heart rate.

If you have fired off your adrenaline auto-injector, always call an ambulance — a second-phase late anaphylactic reaction can occur in up to 15 per cent of cases. You need to go to hospital for a four- to six-hour observation period in case this happens. The hospital staff will monitor your airway and breathing and let you know when the episode has safely resolved.

Telling People about Your Allergies

The desire to tell others about yourself varies greatly from one person to the next. Some are keen to tell the world intimate details about themselves on Facebook while others are uncomfortable with telling people even the smallest amount of information about themselves. These sorts of differences reflect the full range of humanity and different personality types and are usually quite unrelated to what sort of health you have.

But in the case of food allergy, being overly private or secretive about the risk some foods pose to your health is just not an option. One way to think about it is this: If something unfortunate that could have been prevented happened to my friend, would I have preferred to know? You need to empower your friends and those responsible for your care to do something to help you if you were to have an allergic reaction to a food. In the next sections, we discuss who needs to know about your allergies and how to broach the subject.

Deciding who to tell

Making a decision about who to tell about your food allergies varies from person to person. But when it comes to telling those charged with your care, not telling them isn't an option — the reality is that telling your teacher or supervising adult about your allergies, and what to do in the case of a severe allergic reaction, could save your life.

Other people to consider telling you have food allergies include friends and buddies, your extended family and others involved in outside school activities.

Passing on the most important information to your friends

People charged with your care, such as teachers, need to know a lot about your food allergies and how to deal with them, including the foods you're allergic to, strategies in place to avoid these foods, and how to deal with an allergic reaction if one occurs. (Chapter 9 goes into much more detail about the responsibilities of teachers and staff at schools and childcare centres.)

When it comes to passing on information about your allergies to others such as friends, the difficulty becomes what should you actually tell them. Do you stick with the bare essentials or do you convey the full shebang? And what are the bare essentials anyway? How do you tell your friends about things without either scaring them or making them too relaxed about the risks?

A lot depends on your own attitude to your food allergy. At the very least, however, you should let your friends know that you won't risk eating food that might contain your problem allergen — not even as a dare.

We also recommend that you explain how severe food allergy reactions are very serious and can even be life-threatening. Many of your close friends are likely to feel quite comfortable being told how to specifically help you if you have an episode of anaphylaxis, which may include showing them how to use your adrenaline auto-injector with your demonstrator device, or letting them fire an expired shot of adrenaline into an orange. Most importantly, if your friends have been shown how to use your adrenaline auto-injector, they need to know when the device should be administered.

When you're telling others about your food allergy — including your friends and perhaps your friends' parents — here's a list of the information you may need to pass on:

- ✔ You have a food allergy that could result in a severe reaction called anaphylaxis.

- ✔ You need to avoid a certain food or foods (specify what food/s).

- ✔ You could have a mild/moderate or a severe allergic reaction within minutes if you accidentally eat this food.

- ✔ Mild/moderate symptoms involve rashes, a swollen face or tummy upsets and usually resolve without treatment.

- ✔ Severe reactions (anaphylaxis) cause difficulty with breathing or collapse and require treatment with adrenaline and an ambulance to be called immediately.

Most people are naturally curious about food allergy and your friends are unlikely to be an exception. After all, everyone needs to eat and food allergy is only a recent phenomenon. In the sidebar 'Questions your friends may ask you about your allergies', we give you some tips for answering common questions you might receive.

Questions your friends may ask you about your allergies

Here we provide some common questions your friends might have once you let them know about your food allergy — and we even give you some sample answers. (You can use the answers as part of a school project if you wish!)

Question: What is a food allergy?

Answer: When the person eats food containing the protein *allergen* (the bit the person is allergic to), the immune system releases massive amounts of chemicals (*histamines* and others), triggering symptoms that can affect the person's skin, tummy, breathing and/or circulation.

Question: What are the most common food allergies?

Answer: Peanut, tree nut, egg, cow's milk, soy, wheat, fish and shellfish account for around 90 per cent of food allergies.

Question: Is food allergy becoming more common or is it just that more people are aware?

Answer: Both — cases of diagnosed food allergy and anaphylaxis (the most severe type of reaction) are on the rise but this is more in developed countries than in developing countries, suggesting that the rise is due to factors associated with a 'modern' lifestyle. (What those factors are we just don't know.)

Question: Do kids grow out of food allergy?

Answer: Yes, they do — 80 per cent outgrow egg and cow's milk allergy but only 20 per cent outgrow nut allergy.

Question: Are all food allergy reactions the same?

Answer: Allergic reactions aren't always the same — they can range from mild to severe and can differ depending on how much of the food I've eaten. The more I eat, the more likely the reaction is to be severe. But I shouldn't try even a small amount of the food because the severity of a reaction can be unpredictable. A mild or moderate reaction involves reactions of the skin and gut. So skin rashes, such as hives, or vomiting and diarrhoea aren't severe reactions but they can precede symptoms of anaphylaxis (the most severe reaction). So if I have any type of allergic reaction, I need to be on red alert to watch for signs of anaphylaxis.

Question: What is anaphylaxis?

Answer: Anaphylaxis is the most severe form of an allergic reaction, involving breathing and/or circulation. The condition is potentially life-threatening and treatment is an injection of adrenaline into the muscle (an adrenaline auto-injector is called an EpiPen or Anapen, depending on the brand). Symptoms associated with anaphylaxis include coughing, wheezing like an asthma attack, hoarse voice, difficulty breathing or noisy breathing or collapse.

Question: What should your friend do to help you deal with food allergies?

Answer:

- Always take food allergies seriously.

- Don't share food with friends who have food allergies.

- Wash hands after eating.

- Know what your friends are allergic to.

- Get help immediately if a schoolmate with food allergy becomes sick.

Question: What should your friend do if you have an allergic reaction to a food?

Answer:

- Run fast and tell the teacher.

- Tell another friend to stay with me (I shouldn't be made to walk to the office or sick bay; I need to sit or lie down where I am).

- Help keep other children out of the teachers' way who are helping me.

- Be prepared to help the teachers if they need it.

Dealing With Peer Pressure and Bullying because of Your Food Allergies

Peer pressure is part of the landscape for any normal adolescent and, unfortunately, many children have to contend with some form of bullying. However, bullying children with food allergy — which can occur at schools but also other venues such as sporting clubs — can take on new meaning if the behaviour potentially causes a life-threatening event.

If you have feelings of either negative peer pressure or bullying because of your allergies, act early and seek help from your parents and teachers.

All adults have been through adolescence and, although they may choose to forget some of the less pleasant memories, they're likely to have felt teased or even bullied at some stage while growing up. This means adults in your life, such as parents and teachers, are likely to react with sympathy if you let them know you've experienced bullying, and be able to come up with strategies to combat it.

If you're having problems with people teasing or bullying you about your allergies, turn to a trusted adult (a parent or guardian, or teacher or coach) for guidance. Schools take bullying seriously, especially if the behaviour involves children with allergies and is potentially dangerous, such as threatening or taunting children with foods they're allergic to.

Kids often tease others who are different. Helping to explain differences can be the best way to make kids with food allergy feel less different.

Adults can help with a bullying situation by taking the lead with explaining your food allergy to other children. So ask your parents to talk to the adult in charge about whether this adult can talk about your food allergy in more detail to the class or sports club, including describing what causes your allergy and how it has to be managed.

When your teacher or your coach tells the class or the team that your food allergy needs to be taken seriously and that this can be really straightforward, others are much more likely to help you. Just make sure your teacher or coach has the right information — plenty of information is available for parents on the ASCIA website (www.allergy.org.au) and this can also be used by teachers and coaches. Anaphylaxis Australia also has some very helpful information for parents and schools (check out the website at www.allergyfacts.org.au).

Taking Your Medications

Food allergy is really not such a bother if you don't accidentally ingest a problem food. Essentially, unlike other illnesses such as diabetes, you don't need to take any regular medication. That means some kids can get pretty relaxed about the whole deal. But while not worrying too much about your food allergies is good, being too relaxed doesn't help if it increases your risk of having an accidental ingestion and allergic reaction — and, more importantly, if it means you don't know how to treat yourself if you're having an episode of anaphylaxis.

In the following sections we talk about how and when to take your medication.

Learning how to take your medication

Kids with food allergy should be shown how and when to use an adrenaline auto-injector from around the age of ten years — although the exact age also depends on how you and your parents feel about the matter (no hard and fast rule can be applied about this).

Your allergist can demonstrate to you how and when to use your auto-injector, and provide you with a training device that doesn't contain a needle and that you can use to practice without risk. You can also use the training device to show others how to use an auto-injector.

Practising at least once with a live adrenaline auto-injector is a great way to give you more confidence about using the device. If you have an expired auto-injector, get some practice by injecting it into an orange. Nothing is like activating a real auto-injector for focusing your attention.

We have a colleague in Sweden who insists that his adolescent patients fire a live adrenaline auto-injector into their own thigh while seeing him for an appointment! Quite astounding, really, and not something we recommend — although this allergist claims the practice improves compliance with adrenaline auto-injectors dramatically!

You should be shown where on your thigh the auto-injector should be administered (the upper outer thigh). Your parents can help you know how to store your adrenaline auto-injector and check whether it has expired or become inactive.

Adrenaline auto-injectors can be administered through clothing. Once administered to someone showing symptoms of a severe allergic reaction (anaphylaxis), an ambulance should always be called. Adrenaline auto-injectors shouldn't be stored in fridges and care should be taken not to leave them in hot sunlight.

For more about adrenaline auto-injectors, see Chapter 11.

Taking your medication with you

If you've been prescribed an adrenaline auto-injector, you need to carry it with you at all times — or at least during any situation that might involve eating.

You've been prescribed an adrenaline auto-injector because you are at increased risk of anaphylaxis and it will ensure that treatment is at hand if an accidental food allergen ingestion reaction occurs. However, if you don't have your auto-injector with you, and you don't know when or how to use it, you have no protection whatsoever. It's a bit like wearing a safety belt. You only really appreciate the use of the safety belt if you're in an accident — just like how your adrenaline auto-injector could save your life in the event of a serious allergic reaction.

No Epi, no eatie!

In the United States, they have a little saying: 'No Epi, no eatie'. This means, if you don't have your EpiPen (or other adrenaline auto-injector) with you, you shouldn't be eating out.

This saying is a good one to remember, since the unexpected reactions in unexpected places are the ones most likely to be unsafe — and the ones most likely to require adrenaline.

Earning Your Independence: Going Out as a Teenager with Food Allergy

By the time most kids with food allergy get to the teenage years, they've been living with a food allergy for years. Funnily enough, while parents' levels of anxiety can go up around this time, teenagers themselves often become more relaxed about the whole issue of food allergy.

Our studies show teenagers are less likely to tell their teachers or their friends that they have a food allergy and suggest that they may be more willing to take risks. Don't put yourself at unnecessary risk and remember that good, clear communication to others about your food allergy is key for your health and safety.

Becoming a teenager is a time of great change and you need to continue to accommodate the fact that you have special dietary needs, and develop strategies for new situations such as eating out and staying over at friends' houses.

Understanding that teenagers have special needs

The needs of teenagers with food allergy are different from younger children — you're less likely to be directly supervised by a parent and you're more likely to be in situations of uncertainty with regards to food allergy risks. Growing up is all about taking responsibility and that's easier for some than for others.

Even though fewer teenagers have food allergies than do younger kids, teenagers and young adults represent the largest group of people who've died from an anaphylactic reaction to food. And if that's not sobering enough, no-one really knows why that is.

The figures could be because peanut allergy is the most common food allergy in teenagers and is more serious or because teenagers take greater risks and are unsupervised. Perhaps you can't remember a previous episode of an allergic reaction and so you've become a bit slack about how strict you should be with regards to food avoidance. Perhaps your circle of friends is widening and you're being allowed to go to different venues.

In addition to managing your food allergy, if you have asthma, you need to make sure that your asthma is well controlled. Uncontrolled asthma is the biggest risk factor for a bad outcome following anaphylaxis.

Whatever the reason for the higher rates of death for teenagers with food allergies, allergists take the care of teenagers very seriously. However, teenagers sometimes don't go back to see their allergist because nothing may have changed during the late childhood years, which can create some problems.

Make sure you have a check up with an allergist at the end of your primary school years and before you start secondary school — particularly if you haven't seen an allergist for a few years. Then you can find out whether your food allergy is still a problem (you may have unexpectedly outgrown it) and how you yourself should manage your food allergy if it has persisted.

Knowing the risks: Going to restaurants and staying over with friends

Ensure that when going out to restaurants or when staying with friends you give staff or your friend's family plenty of warning about your dietary requirements. Not only does doing so make their lives easier but being organised enough to forewarn them about your special needs shows your respect and courtesy.

Always call ahead to a restaurant before turning up to dine there. That enables you to find out whether the restaurant has things on the menu that you can safely eat without feeling like you're missing out and, more importantly, lets the restaurant prepare for you if they don't have a sufficiently diverse menu to suit your needs. Most chefs are up for the challenge — but if you don't forewarn them, you don't give them the opportunity to succeed in meeting your needs.

The same applies if you're going to a friend's house for a meal or a stay-over. If you let your friend's parents know what they need to prepare, your stay is likely to be a lot less complicated for your friend's parents and a lot safer for you. If you don't feel comfortable doing this — because the stay is short or you're part of a larger group — you may consider taking your own food with you.

Talking to your doctor

Now that you're a teenager, you might start to feel that you'd prefer to talk to your doctor on your own. This is not only reasonable but perfectly appropriate. Everyone is different so you might want to try solo appointments earlier than some and later than others.

Some teenagers may also want to see their allergist on their own sometimes and, at other times, want Mum or Dad to be present. You may find you go through a bit of a transition phase — so you may like to chat to your allergist on your own first and then your parent can join you for the latter part of the appointment.

The important thing is that, as you grow up, you need to take charge of your own health and safety. And you need to remember that the adults in your life want that for you too.

Chapter 11

Emergency Action Plans

In This Chapter

▶ Discovering why all children with food allergy need an individual emergency action plan

▶ Understanding how the emergency action plan helps you manage an allergic reaction

▶ Learning how to use antihistamines and an adrenaline auto-injector

▶ Being aware of what your child's doctor needs to know

▶ Knowing where to find extra support

An important part of managing your child's food allergy is being familiar with what happens during an allergic reaction and what to do when your child is having one; this knowledge allows you to act quickly and with confidence.

An emergency action plan is a vital tool for caring for your child with food allergy. An emergency action plan helps to identify your child to others as having a food allergy, meaning special care must be taken to ensure your child avoids a food allergen. The plan also has essential specific information about what foods your child is allergic to, and who to contact in the event that your child has an allergic reaction. Most importantly, the plan has vital information to help you and other people caring for your child to recognise an allergic reaction and provide first aid management in an emergency, until medical assistance can be sought.

In this chapter, we discuss emergency action plans, including what they are and how they can help you to be prepared for an allergic reaction. We also provide details on how to recognise an allergic reaction and what you can do to manage the reaction. We cover the different adrenaline auto-injectors and how to use them, so that you can act quickly if your child needs to be treated with adrenaline, and we also detail which information you need to give your child's doctor after the allergic reaction, so that the doctor can provide the best medical care for your child. And, if you need some additional support, we show you where you can find it.

Being Prepared for an Allergic Reaction

Because no cure for food allergies is yet available, management is centred on avoiding the food allergen. Unfortunately, this is not an easy task and most children with food allergy accidentally eat the food they're allergic to at some stage, despite everyone's best efforts (refer to Chapter 7 for more on avoiding food allergens).

The times when accidental exposures are most likely to happen are when children are out and about, away from home and eating food that has been prepared by someone else other than their parents. You may be with your child at a friend's house, at the park having a picnic or at a restaurant when your child accidentally eats something that she didn't know contained the food she's allergic to. When this happens, your child is likely to have an allergic reaction, and both you and your child need to be prepared and know what to do.

The best way to be prepared for an emergency is for your child to have an up-to-date personal emergency action plan, provided by your child's doctor, and for you and your child to be very familiar with the information contained in this plan. All children who have a food allergy should carry their emergency action plan, together with their allergy medicines, with them at all times. Anyone who is with the child can then read the plan and help treat the allergic reaction, even if that person isn't familiar with what to do.

In the following sections, we discuss what details are included in an emergency action plan.

Writing the emergency plan

Personal emergency action plans should always be completed by your child's doctor, so that the plan contains accurate information about which foods your child is allergic to, as well as the doctor's contact information.

Children who have been prescribed an adrenaline auto-injector are given a more detailed emergency action plan that includes information on how to use the medication. Your child's doctor must update your child's emergency action plan every year and go through the information contained in the action plan with you (and your child, if old enough).

Your child should carry his personalised emergency action plan with him at all times, together with his allergy medicines. The plan should also include the specific foods your child is allergic to. This list of foods needs to be as accurate as possible, so that no confusion can occur about what your child is allergic to and what he can tolerate.

Mimi has often heard people say things like, 'Jack's mum says he can't eat any nuts, but he often eats Nutella and the other day I saw him eating almonds and nothing happened ... I think she's just an over-anxious mum; I wouldn't be too concerned about the nuts'. Having a careless and possibly dangerous attitude can happen when emergency action plans aren't accurate. If your child has a nut allergy, the specific nuts that cause allergic reactions in your child should be included in the personalised emergency action plan.

Another reason for your child's emergency action plan to be as accurate as possible when listing the specific allergens is that researchers' understanding of allergic reactions has developed over recent years. In the past, allergy specialists may have recommended avoidance of all nuts if someone was just allergic to one of the nuts, in the mistaken belief that avoiding a food could prevent you developing an allergy to that food.

We now know that this isn't correct — avoiding a food doesn't prevent you from developing an allergy to that food (refer to Chapter 3 for more information about preventing food allergies). These days, allergy specialists try very hard to work out exactly what your child's allergic to and then recommend avoiding only those foods that are known, or likely (based on allergy testing), to be allergens for your child, and to continue eating all other foods.

Describing the symptoms of an allergic reaction

The most valuable information in your child's emergency action plan is the description of the symptoms that can develop when someone's having an allergic reaction, and the instructions on what to do in this situation.

All emergency action plans (whether plans for allergic reactions, anaphylaxis, or general purpose emergency plans) note the various symptoms of an allergic reaction and describe the symptoms that can develop when someone is having a mild to moderate reaction or severe reaction (anaphylaxis — refer to Chapter 4 for more on immediate allergic reactions).

Having this information clearly presented and readily available is vital for someone who doesn't know about allergic reactions. Even people who are already familiar with how to manage allergic reactions can refer to the emergency action plan and feel more confident about what they need to do.

The instructions on the emergency action plan are very simple to follow and help a person manage an allergic reaction with a step-by-step approach.

In the section 'Managing an Allergic Reaction When a Doctor Isn't Around', later in this chapter, we go through the signs and symptoms of an allergic reaction, so that you can readily distinguish between mild/moderate and severe (anaphylaxis) allergic reactions, and be comfortable knowing what to do in each of these situations.

Personal emergency action plans cover the specific allergies that your child has, and how to treat an allergic reaction if one develops. If your child has an adrenaline auto-injector (used for treating anaphylaxis), they will have a more detailed plan that includes instructions for when and how to administer the medication.

Listing important phone numbers

All emergency action plans have a dedicated space to put a photo of the child for whom the plan is being developed, as well as contact details for an emergency contact person. Plans also include a dedicated space to add the contact details of your child's doctor and a section for the doctor to complete to show that the plan has been developed together with that doctor.

All of these contact details are extremely important so that the parent (or relevant emergency contact person) can be informed should a child experience an allergic reaction, and the child's doctor can also be contacted should anyone need further advice from the doctor.

Your child's emergency action plan should be updated each year, preferably at the start of the school (or childcare) year, or as any new information emerges regarding the allergies that your child has. To show that the emergency action plan is current and accurate, the doctor must include contact details and the date when the plan was created.

Managing an Allergic Reaction When a Doctor Isn't Around

Allergic reactions can happen, despite your best efforts (and the efforts of others who look after your child). For example, your child may be invited to go on a picnic with her friend's family. The parents are aware of your child's peanut allergy, and you've shown them a few times how to use her adrenaline auto-injector. They've made sure to pack food that doesn't contain peanuts but, as a special treat, decide to buy the children ice-creams. Your child develops hives on her face and starts to cough — her ice-cream must have been cross-contaminated with peanut and she's having an allergic reaction. In this situation, it's vital that the parents have your child's medicine bag and her emergency action plan to refer to.

One in twelve children has a food allergy, so many people may find themselves in a situation similar to this at some time. Your child with food allergies isn't always with you, so keeping his emergency action plan and allergy medicines with him at all times helps to keep him safe.

If you're a parent but you don't have a child with food allergy, or if you're a school teacher or childcare worker, you're still highly likely to be caring for a child with food allergy at some time, so being at least familiar with what an emergency action plan is and the information it contains is worthwhile.

Recognising the symptoms of allergic reactions

The symptoms of an immediate allergic reaction are discussed in detail in Chapter 4. But here's a brief reminder of the symptoms of an allergic reaction:

✓ **A mild to moderate immediate allergic reaction** involves some or all of the following symptoms:

- Hives (these look like welts or mosquito bites and are usually on the face but can also be all over the body)

- Swelling of the lips, eyes or whole face

- Vomiting and abdominal pain or cramps

The symptoms of a mild to moderate allergic reaction generally involve the skin and the gut. These symptoms are very frightening, especially if they develop rapidly right in front of your eyes, but they're not dangerous (life-threatening) and go away either by themselves or (more quickly) with antihistamine medication.

✓ **A severe immediate allergic reaction (anaphylaxis)** occurs when the person develops any symptoms affecting the airway or the circulation. The person may have some or all of these symptoms:

- A hoarse voice (due to the voice box becoming swollen)

- Coughing (due to the airway becoming irritated)

- Noisy breathing (either a wheeze, like in asthma, or a stridor, like in croup) if the airway starts to narrow

• Fainting/collapse (due to the circulation becoming affected) — younger children and toddlers may just go pale and floppy

Anaphylaxis is a severe allergic reaction that involves the breathing or circulation. Any reaction that involves these systems of the body can be life-threatening because we need to be able to breathe and to supply oxygen to the brain and heart in order to stay alive.

✔ Younger infants and children may not faint or collapse and can just look pale and floppy when their circulation is affected. This is an important sign to look out for because it indicates a very serious allergic reaction that requires emergency treatment.

Allergic reactions to insect stings are different to food allergic reactions

In insect sting reactions, the development of vomiting or abdominal pain is often a sign that the reaction might quickly progress to a severe reaction involving the circulation. So, if someone who is allergic to bees has been stung by a bee and starts to vomit or complain of abdominal pain, this is a sign that the person's likely to progress to a severe reaction involving the circulation and that emergency action is required.

The situation with allergic reactions to foods is quite different. Vomiting and abdominal pain are very common symptoms that develop because the food is in the intestines. Most allergic reactions to foods involve some vomiting, abdominal pain or diarrhoea, and these symptoms indicate a mild or moderate reaction.

Severe allergic reactions to foods most commonly involve the airway with hoarse voice, noisy breathing, difficulty swallowing or talking, or difficulty breathing; much less commonly, the circulation is affected.

The ASCIA emergency action plans (covered in the section 'Accessing Additional Support') have been developed for all people with allergies, not just children with food allergy. So people with allergy to insect stings (for example, bees or wasps) also use the emergency action plans.

Because the symptoms of vomiting and abdominal pain mean something different in insect sting allergic reactions, the emergency action plans include a note to highlight this.

Acting in an emergency

When you've ascertained that your child (or a child in your care) is having an allergic reaction (refer to the preceding section), your first action should be to find and reread (or read) your child's emergency action plan, because this action plan tells you exactly what to do to help.

You must not leave your child alone when they develop signs of an allergic reaction. You must stay with your child and follow the instructions on the emergency action plan. If needed, send a second person for your child's medicine or to call for help.

If your child develops hives, swelling, vomiting and/or abdominal cramps, you know she's having a mild to moderate allergic reaction and can refer to her emergency action plan for instructions on what to do.

If your child hasn't been prescribed an adrenaline auto-injector, she has what's called an *emergency action plan for allergic reactions* (see Figure 11-1).

The emergency actions you need to take for children with allergic reactions are as follows:

1. **Stay with the child and call for help.**

2. **Ask the child to lie down straightaway — do not move the child.**

3. **Continue to watch out for any further symptoms that might indicate a severe allergic reaction (anaphylaxis).**

4. **Give any medications that are listed on the emergency action plan.**

5. **If the child develops any signs of anaphylaxis, call the ambulance.**

6. **Arrange to call the child's parent or emergency contact (if not present). Don't leave the child alone.**

If your child has been prescribed an adrenaline auto-injector, he has an emergency action plan for anaphylaxis that's specific for the prescribed device (see Figures 11-2 to 11-4). The key difference in the emergency action plans for anaphylaxis as compared to the plan for allergic reactions is that people following the plan are told to locate the child's adrenaline auto-injector as soon as they ascertain that the child is having an allergic reaction and to treat the anaphylaxis using the adrenaline auto-injector if the child develops symptoms of anaphylaxis. (See the section 'Using Emergency Medications' later in this chapter for more on using adrenaline auto-injectors.) These actions are completed *before* they attempt to contact parents or emergency contact (if applicable — that is, if you're not present at the time).

ascia
australasian society of clinical immunology and allergy inc.
www.allergy.org.au

ACTION PLAN FOR
Allergic Reactions

Name: _____

Date of birth: _____

Photo

Confirmed allergens:
_____
_____
_____
_____

Family/emergency contact name(s):
_____

Work Ph: _____
Home Ph: _____
Mobile Ph: _____

Plan prepared by:
Dr _____
_____
Signed _____
Date _____

Note: The ASCIA Action Plan for Allergic Reactions is for people with mild to moderate allergies, who need to avoid certain allergens. For people with severe allergies (and at risk of anaphylaxis) there are ASCIA Action Plans for Anaphylaxis, which include adrenaline autoinjector instructions.

© ASCIA 2011. This plan was developed by ASCIA

MILD TO MODERATE ALLERGIC REACTION

- swelling of lips, face, eyes
- hives or welts
- tingling mouth
- abdominal pain, vomiting (these are signs of a severe allergic reaction to <u>insects</u>)

ACTION

- **For insect allergy, flick out sting if visible. Do not remove ticks**
- Stay with person and call for help
- Give medications (if prescribed) ....
  dose: ....
- Contact family/emergency contact

▼ **Watch for <u>any one</u> of the following signs of Anaphylaxis**

ANAPHYLAXIS (SEVERE ALLERGIC REACTION)

- difficult/noisy breathing
- swelling of tongue
- swelling/tightness in throat
- difficulty talking and/or hoarse voice
- wheeze or persistent cough
- persistent dizziness or collapse
- pale and floppy (young children)

ACTION

1 **Lay person flat, do not stand or walk. If breathing is difficult, allow to sit**
2 **Phone ambulance - 000 (AU), 111 (NZ), 112 (mobile)**
3 **Contact family/emergency contact**

Additional information _____
_____
_____

Figure 11-1:
Personal emergency action plan for allergic reactions.

ascia

australasian society of clinical immunology and allergy inc.
www.allergy.org.au

ACTION PLAN FOR

Anaphylaxis

for use with EpiPen® or EpiPen® Jr adrenaline autoinjectors

Name: _____

Date of birth: _____

Photo

Confirmed allergens: _____
_____
_____

Family/emergency contact name(s): _____
_____
_____

Work Ph: _____

Home Ph: _____

Mobile Ph: _____

Plan prepared by:
Dr _____
_____

Signed _____

Date _____

MILD TO MODERATE ALLERGIC REACTION

- swelling of lips, face, eyes
- hives or welts
- tingling mouth
- abdominal pain, vomiting (these are signs of a severe allergic reaction to <u>insects</u>)

ACTION

- **For insect allergy, flick out sting if visible. Do not remove ticks**
- Stay with person and call for help
- Give medications (if prescribed) ....
  dose: ....
- Locate EpiPen® or EpiPen® Jr
- Contact family/emergency contact

▼ **Watch for <u>any one</u> of the following signs of Anaphylaxis**

ANAPHYLAXIS (SEVERE ALLERGIC REACTION)

- difficult/noisy breathing
- swelling of tongue
- swelling/tightness in throat
- difficulty talking and/or hoarse voice
- wheeze or persistent cough
- persistent dizziness or collapse
- pale and floppy (young children)

ACTION

1 **Lay person flat, do not stand or walk. If breathing is difficult allow to sit**
2 **Give EpiPen® or EpiPen® Jr**
3 **Phone ambulance - 000 (AU), 111 (NZ), 112 (mobile)**
4 **Contact family/emergency contact**
5 **Further adrenaline doses may be given if no response after 5 minutes (if another adrenaline autoinjector is available)**

If in doubt, give EpiPen® or EpiPen® Jr

EpiPen® Jr is generally prescribed for children aged 1-5 years.
*Medical observation in hospital for at least 4 hours is recommended after anaphylaxis.

Additional information _____
_____

How to give EpiPen® or EpiPen® Jr

1 Form fist around EpiPen® and PULL OFF GREY SAFETY CAP.

2 PLACE BLACK END against outer mid-thigh (with or without clothing).

3 PUSH DOWN HARD until a click is heard or felt and hold in place for 10 seconds.

4 REMOVE EpiPen® and DO NOT touch needle. Massage injection site for 10 seconds.

© ASCIA 2011. This plan was developed by ASCIA

Figure 11-2: Personal emergency action plan for anaphylaxis when original version EpiPen has been prescribed.

ascia

australasian society of clinical immunology and allergy

www.allergy.org.au

ACTION PLAN FOR Anaphylaxis

for use with EpiPen® or Epipen® Jr adrenaline autoinjectors (with blue safety release and orange needle end)

Name:

Date of birth:

Photo

Confirmed allergens:

Family/emergency contact name(s):

Work Ph:

Home Ph:

Mobile Ph:

Plan prepared by:

Dr

Signed

Date:

How to give EpiPen® or EpiPen® Jr

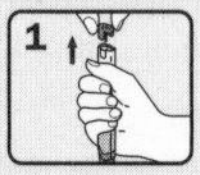

Form fist around EpiPen® and PULL OFF BLUE SAFETY RELEASE.

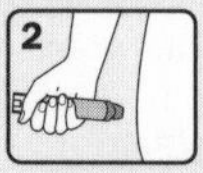

PLACE ORANGE END against outer mid-thigh (with or without clothing).

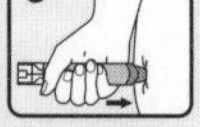

PUSH DOWN HARD until a click is heard or felt and hold in place for 10 seconds.

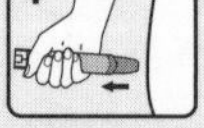

REMOVE EpiPen®. Massage injection site for 10 seconds.

MILD TO MODERATE ALLERGIC REACTION

- swelling of lips, face, eyes
- hives or welts
- tingling mouth
- abdominal pain, vomiting (these are signs of a severe allergic reaction to insects)

ACTION

- **For insect allergy, flick out sting if visible. Do not remove ticks**
- Stay with person and call for help
- Give medications (if prescribed) ....
  Dose: ....
- Locate EpiPen® or EpiPen® Jr
- Contact family/emergency contact

Watch for any one of the following signs of Anaphylaxis

ANAPHYLAXIS (SEVERE ALLERGIC REACTION)

- difficult/noisy breathing
- swelling of tongue
- swelling/tightness in throat
- difficulty talking and/or hoarse voice
- wheeze or persistent cough
- persistent dizziness or collapse
- pale and floppy (young children)

ACTION

1. **Lay person flat, do not stand or walk. If breathing is difficult allow to sit**
2. **Give EpiPen® or EpiPen® Jr**
3. **Phone ambulance*- 000 (AU), 111 (NZ), 112 (mobile)**
4. **Contact family/emergency contact**
5. **Further adrenaline doses may be given if no response after 5 minutes (if another adrenaline autoinjector is available)**

If in doubt, give EpiPen® or EpiPen® Jr

EpiPen® Jr is generally prescribed for children aged 1-5 years.

*Medical observation in hospital for at least 4 hours is recommended after anaphylaxis.

Additional information

Figure 11-3: Personal emergency action plan for anaphylaxis when new-look EpiPen has been prescribed.

ascia
australasian society of clinical immunology and allergy inc.
www.allergy.org.au

ACTION PLAN FOR
Anaphylaxis

for use with Anapen® or Anapen® Jr adrenaline autoinjectors

MILD TO MODERATE ALLERGIC REACTION

- swelling of lips, face, eyes
- hives or welts
- tingling mouth
- abdominal pain, vomiting (these are signs of a severe allergic reaction to <u>insects</u>)

ACTION

- **For insect allergy, flick out sting if visible. Do not remove ticks**
- Stay with person and call for help
- Give medications (if prescribed) ....
  dose: ....
- Locate Anapen® or Anapen® Jr
- Contact family/emergency contact

Watch for <u>any one</u> of the following signs of Anaphylaxis

ANAPHYLAXIS (SEVERE ALLERGIC REACTION)

- difficult/noisy breathing
- swelling of tongue
- swelling/tightness in throat
- difficulty talking and/or hoarse voice
- wheeze or persistent cough
- persistent dizziness or collapse
- pale and floppy (young children)

ACTION

1 Lay person flat, do not stand or walk. If breathing is difficult allow to sit
2 Give Anapen® or Anapen® Jr
3 Phone ambulance - 000 (AU), 111 (NZ), 112 (mobile)
4 Contact family/emergency contact
5 Further adrenaline doses may be given if no response after 5 minutes (if another adrenaline autoinjector is available)

If in doubt, give Anapen® or Anapen® Jr

Anapen® Jr is generally prescribed for children aged 1-5 years.
*Medical observation in hospital for at least 4 hours is recommended after anaphylaxis.

Additional information _____

_____

Name: _____

Date of birth: _____

Photo

Confirmed allergens:

_____

_____

_____

Family/emergency contact name(s):

_____

Work Ph:

Home Ph:

Mobile Ph:

Plan prepared by:

Dr

_____

Signed

Date

How to give Anapen® or Anapen® Jr

1 PULL OFF BLACK NEEDLE SHIELD.

2 PULL OFF GREY SAFETY CAP from red button.

3 PLACE NEEDLE END FIRMLY against outer mid-thigh at 90° angle (with or without clothing).

4 10 seconds PRESS RED BUTTON so it clicks and hold for 10 seconds. REMOVE Anapen® and DO NOT touch needle. Massage injection site for 10 seconds.

© ASCIA 2011. This plan was developed by ASCIA

Figure 11-4: Personal emergency action plan for anaphylaxis when Anapen has been prescribed.

Emergency instructions for children prescribed an adrenaline auto-injector are as follows:

1. **Stay with the child and call for help**.

2. **Ask the child to lie down straightaway — don't move the child**.

3. **Locate the child's adrenaline auto-injector**.

4. **Continue to watch out for any further symptoms that might indicate a severe allergic reaction (anaphylaxis)**.

5. **If signs of anaphylaxis develop, give the child their EpiPen or Anapen (following the instructions on the side of the device, or in the emergency plan)**.

6. **Call an ambulance**.

   Symptoms can recur in around 10 to 16 per cent of children who have an anaphylaxis, so once you have used the EpiPen or Anapen, you must call an ambulance and have the child taken to hospital for further observation.

7. **Call the child's parent or guardian (if applicable — but don't leave the child alone)**.

8. **Give a second dose of the EpiPen or Anapen if the child shows no response to the first treatment and a second adrenaline auto-injector is available**.

If the child is having an allergic reaction, stay with the child and follow the instructions outlined in the personalised emergency action plan. The actions you follow depend on whether the child's having a mild/moderate or a severe allergic reaction, and whether the child has been prescribed an adrenaline auto-injector.

Using Emergency Medications

Emergency action plans outline the emergency management of an allergic reaction, and this may include giving medications to the child having the allergic reaction. The medications that can help treat the symptoms of an immediate allergic reaction are antihistamines and adrenaline.

Antihistamines can treat hives and swelling, which are symptoms of a mild to moderate allergic reaction. But antihistamines aren't effective for the treatment of anaphylaxis, which involves the airway and circulation. Adrenaline is the best treatment for life-threatening symptoms that develop because of changes in the airway and circulation, and these dangerous symptoms usually improve almost immediately after adrenaline is given.

The following sections give more information about antihistamines and adrenaline (including the different types of auto-injectors available).

Antihistamines

All emergency action plans have a space for the child's doctor to leave instructions regarding medicines (including the correct dose) to be given to the child when having a mild to moderate allergic reaction.

Some doctors use this space to provide instructions to give the child an antihistamine if the child develops symptoms of a mild to moderate allergic reaction, because antihistamines can help with symptoms of hives and swelling.

However, other doctors feel that including information about antihistamines isn't helpful because antihistamines aren't effective in the emergency management of a severe allergic reaction — they don't prevent or reverse the severe symptoms of anaphylaxis (breathing and circulation problems). These doctors believe that when a child is having an allergic reaction, carers must focus on watching out for the development of symptoms of a severe allergic reaction (anaphylaxis), rather than worrying about treating symptoms that aren't dangerous or life-threatening.

We agree with the second opinion — that, because antihistamines aren't effective in the emergency management of a severe allergic reaction, the most important thing is to watch out for symptoms of these severe reactions. We recommend that you stay with your child and look out for symptoms of anaphylaxis so that these can be treated immediately, rather than having to worry about giving other medications that aren't essential. The symptoms of hives and swelling resolve on their own even if they're not treated (they're not life-threatening), and you can always give your child some antihistamine medication once you're sure the reaction has stabilised and isn't progressing to a severe allergic reaction (anaphylaxis).

Whenever Mimi provides an emergency action plan for a child with food allergy, she usually leaves the space where medications can be entered empty, and covers it over using a thick black marker. She explains why to her patient (if the patient is old enough) and the parents, and they're always comfortable with her explanation.

If an antihistamine is included in the emergency action plan, it should be a newer-generation, less-sedating antihistamine such as Claratyne, Zyrtec, Telfast or Aerius, as these don't cause drowsiness. The older, first-generation antihistamines commonly cause drowsiness and this can be confusing in the situation of anaphylaxis — because drowsiness can be a sign of severe allergic reaction (anaphylaxis) when the circulation is affected. The correct dose of antihistamine must be written on the personalised emergency action plan, so it's very clear to anyone using the plan.

Adrenaline

Adrenaline is a natural hormone produced by the adrenal gland (which sits above the kidneys). The hormone is released during the 'fight or flight response', such as just before you run a race or sit an exam. Adrenaline causes the airways to widen, which improves your breathing; it also makes the heart pump harder and faster, and constricts the small blood vessels, which helps to raise the blood pressure. During anaphylaxis the airways constrict and the blood pressure can drop due to leaking of fluid out of the blood vessels, so these effects of adrenaline are exactly what are needed to treat the life-threatening symptoms of anaphylaxis.

Adrenaline auto-injectors are self-injectable devices that have been designed to deliver a single pre-measured dose of adrenaline. Several different types of devices are available — EpiPen, the new-look EpiPen and Anapen — and each has a different mechanism of action. Adrenaline auto-injectors are injected into the muscle in the upper outer thigh, because this leads to a rapid uptake of adrenaline into the blood and because the blood level of adrenaline is sustained for a longer period than when given into the fat tissue (known as a *subcutaneous injection*).

Knowing not just when to use an adrenaline auto-injector but how

A number of years ago Katie had a friend who had been carrying an EpiPen for her child for the previous five years because he had peanut allergy and was deemed at high risk for anaphylaxis. Katie suggested to her friend that activating an expired EpiPen in to an orange was a good idea if she had never done so before. (Katie made the mistake of assuming that her friend had been educated by her doctor at each of the annual visits about how to use an EpiPen.)

A few minutes after the telephone call, Katie's friend rang back urgently to say that she had activated the EpiPen but that it had discharged into her finger. Katie suggested her friend go to the nearest emergency room to assess whether there was any damage to her hand. (Luckily, her hand was fine.)

The lesson for Katie was never to assume that someone who has been carrying an EpiPen has been properly trained. She often uses this story to illustrate to her own patients that carrying an EpiPen without knowing how and when to use the device is akin to carrying a safety blanket with a great big hole in the middle of it.

The reason adrenaline needs to be injected into the thigh muscle is because the blood supply to this muscle is protected and continues even when a person is in circulatory shock, whereas the blood supply to the subcutaneous tissues (mostly fat) is rapidly shut down when the circulation is affected during anaphylaxis.

Once adrenaline has been given to someone who is having a severe allergic reaction, you must call an ambulance because, in some cases, the allergic symptoms can return and a second dose of adrenaline may be required.

Mimi's research has shown that everyone (including doctors) needs to be shown how to use an adrenaline auto-injector. When doctors who had not been trained in the use of an EpiPen were asked to administer an EpiPen trainer, only one-third used it correctly, even after reading the instructions. And believe it or not, around ten per cent were close to injecting their thumbs! So although the steps to use adrenaline auto-injectors seem very straightforward, it's important that your doctor spends time showing you (and your child, if they are old enough) how to use your child's adrenaline auto-injector and that this training is repeated at least every year.

EpiPens

Two types of EpiPens are in use in Australia. The original EpiPen was redesigned to offer improved features, resulting in the new-look EpiPen, which has been available in Australia since June 2011.

Note: Because the shelf life of the EpiPen is up to 18 months, and stocks of the original EpiPen were available for a period of time after the new-look EpiPen was introduced, both versions of the EpiPen are likely to still be in use into 2013. So we've included information on the original EpiPen in this book.

Both the original and the new-look EpiPen are operated by a spring-activated mechanism. An original EpiPen has a grey safety cap, and a black sheath at the needle end, as well as a window that shows the contents of the device.

The new-look EpiPen provides several advantages, as follows:

- **The colour scheme has been revised so that the safety cap is blue and the needle sheath is orange**. This increases the colour contrast, so users are less likely to confuse the ends.

- **The safety cap has been changed to a flip-cap mechanism**. This means the safety cap can be flipped up with one hand, rather than having to be removed completely using two hands.

✔ **The needle sheath covers the needle after activation.** This means users face no risk of a needle stick injury.

✔ **The shape has been modified to an ellipse.** This shape fits within the hand more ergonomically than the original cylindrical shape.

EpiPens are available in two doses: 0.15 milligrams (which is recommended for children between 10 kilograms and 20 kilograms; this version is called the EpiPen Junior) and 0.3 milligrams (which is recommended for children and adults 20 kilograms or heavier, known as the EpiPen).

These devices are available on authorised prescription (meaning that EpiPens can be prescribed by allergists, paediatricians, respiratory physicians, emergency physicians; other doctors can only prescribe the EpiPen following phone consultation with one of the authorised prescribing doctors) for children identified as being at increased risk for having an anaphylaxis (severe allergic reaction). A GP is also able to prescribe an EpiPen on authorised prescription if the GP has administered adrenaline to a patient for the treatment of anaphylaxis, or consulted with one of the preceding specialists after having assessed the patient.

Each authorised prescription for the EpiPen provides two devices for each patient. In children, this is so they can carry one of the devices with their emergency action plan at all times, and also leave one at school or at child care. For adults, this allows the patient to carry two devices with them at all times so that a second dose can be administered if required. (Studies suggest that a second dose of adrenaline is required in around 15 per cent of anaphylaxis reactions.)

To use the original EpiPen, follow these instructions (also see Figure 11-5 for an illustrated version):

1. **Place all fingers around the barrel of the EpiPen and remove the grey safety cap.**

2. **Place the black needle end against the upper outer thigh.**

3. **Push hard to activate the device and hold for 10 seconds while the medication is delivered.**

   After use, you must place the device back in its container to prevent needle stick injuries.

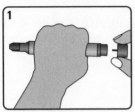 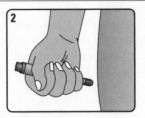 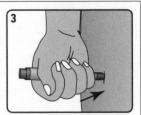

Figure 11-5:
Using an original EpiPen.

Place all fingers around the barrel of the EpiPen and remove the grey safety cap.

Place the black needle end against the upper outer thigh.

Push hard to activate the device and hold for 10 seconds.

To use the new-look EpiPen, follow these instructions (also see Figure 11-6 for an illustrated version):

1. **Place all fingers around the barrel of the EpiPen and remove the blue safety cap.**

2. **Place the orange needle end against the upper outer thigh.**

3. **Push hard to activate the device and hold for 10 seconds while the medication is delivered.**

   The device automatically sheaths the needle once it's fired, removing the risk of a needle stick injury.

 If the contents of your child's EpiPen are cloudy or discoloured, the device should be discarded because this suggests the adrenaline medication within the device may be contaminated or has degraded.

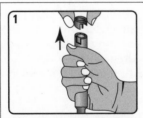  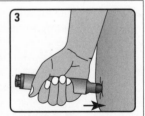

Figure 11-6:
Using a new-look EpiPen.

Place all fingers around the barrel of the EpiPen and remove the blue safety cap.

Place the orange needle end against the upper outer thigh.

Push hard to activate the device and hold for 10 seconds.

Anapens

The Anapen became available in Australia in 2010. The device delivers a single dose of adrenaline by a syringe plunger mechanism, which is different to the mechanism in place in the EpiPen (refer to the preceding section for more information about how to administer EpiPens).

The Anapen was originally available in two doses: 0.15 milligrams (for children weighing between 10 kilograms and 20 kilograms; the Anapen Junior) and 0.3 milligrams (for children and adults weighing 20 kilograms or heavier; the Anapen 0.3mg). In September 2011, an additional 0.5-milligram dose Anapen was introduced in Australia, for adults weighing 50 kilograms or heavier.

Using a 0.5-milligram dose of adrenaline for adults makes sense, because many adults weigh significantly more than 50 kilograms. (A doctor usually prescribes 0.01 milligrams of intramuscular adrenaline per kilogram.) However, your doctor may decide not to change your child over to the 0.5 milligram Anapen even if over 50 kilograms, because experts are still uncertain whether a higher dose is important for the emergency management of anaphylaxis, and it may be confusing to change your child's device from an EpiPen to an Anapen while in the midst of adolescence. Prior to the availability of the 0.5-milligram dose of adrenaline, the highest dose of adrenaline that could be delivered by an adrenaline auto-injector was 0.3 milligrams and, despite this, a second dose of 0.3 milligram adrenaline was only required in approximately 15 per cent of cases of anaphylaxis. The 0.3 milligram dose may also be more appropriate for people with heart conditions who may not tolerate the higher 0.5 milligram dose.

The Anapen is available on authorised prescription (meaning that it can be prescribed by allergists, paediatricians, respiratory physicians, emergency physicians; other doctors can only prescribe the Anapen following phone consultation with one of the authorised prescribing doctors) for children identified as being at increased risk for having anaphylaxis (severe allergic reaction). A GP is also able to prescribe an Anapen on authorised prescription if the GP has administered adrenaline to a patient for the treatment of anaphylaxis, or consulted with one of the above specialists after having assessed the patient.

As per EpiPens, each authorised prescription for the Anapen provides two devices for each patient. (See preceding section for the reasons behind this.)

To use the Anapen, follow these instructions (also see Figure 11-7 for an illustrated version):

1. **Remove the black needle sheath**.

2. **Remove the grey safety cap**.

3. **Place the black needle end firmly against the upper outer thigh**.

4. **Push the red activation button at the top of the device and hold for 10 seconds while the medication is delivered**.

   After use, you must replace the black needle sheath to prevent needle stick injuries.

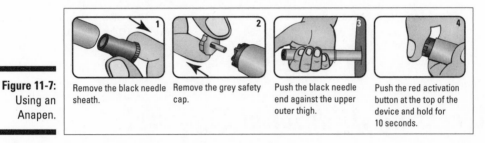

Figure 11-7:
Using an
Anapen.

| Remove the black needle sheath. | Remove the grey safety cap. | Push the black needle end against the upper outer thigh. | Push the red activation button at the top of the device and hold for 10 seconds. |

Telling Medical Staff What They Need to Know

In order for the personal emergency action plan to be useful, it must be accurate, with up-to-date information on the specific food allergies that your child has. In addition, your child's doctor needs to go over the information contained in the emergency action plan with you (and your child, if old enough), so that you and your child can be reminded of the symptoms of an allergic reaction and how to provide emergency management for an allergic reaction. This also aids you in teaching other people who might be responsible for caring for your child when you're not around, such as nannies or babysitters, friends and other family members.

Your child's doctor needs to know a number of things to keep your child's emergency action plan up to date and to help the doctor manage your child's food allergy.

The most important information you need to tell your child's doctor relates to asthma — you must let the doctor know if your child has had any asthma symptoms (such as coughing, wheezing, difficulty breathing or wheezing with exercise), because asthma that's not controlled is the strongest risk factor for a person with food allergy having anaphylaxis, and also for someone with food allergy having a fatal anaphylaxis. Your child's doctor can review your child's asthma status and recommend appropriate medications. In addition, if your child's asthma isn't well controlled and your child doesn't already have a prescribed adrenaline auto-injector, your doctor may decide now is the time to prescribe one.

Other information your doctor needs to know includes whether your child has accidentally eaten a food he's allergic to and suffered an allergic reaction as a result, or whether your child has had an allergic reaction due to another food that you didn't know he was allergic to. Your doctor also reviews your child's diet with you to be sure that she's getting all the nutrients she needs, and may refer you to a dietitian to help with managing your child's diet. Of course, if you have any concerns at all, these should also be discussed with your child's doctor.

Accessing Additional Support

The Australasian Society of Clinical Immunology and Allergy (ASCIA) has developed a range of emergency action plans that can be used to support people with food allergies; these can be accessed at www.allergy.org.au.

A number of emergency action plans are available, as follows:

- **Personal emergency action plans for allergic reactions**: These plans are designed to be used for children who don't have an adrenaline auto-injector.

- **Personal emergency action plan for anaphylaxis**: These plans are for children who've been prescribed an adrenaline auto-injector by their doctor, and a specific plan is available for each of the different adrenaline auto-injector devices.

- **General purpose emergency action plans**: These plans are usually presented as posters, or included in first aid kits.

All of the different emergency action plans have general information to help people recognise an allergic reaction and act quickly in managing the reaction. In addition, personal emergency action plans also have a place where your child's doctor can list the foods that your child is allergic to and a place to put your child's photo and emergency contact information.

Part IV
Looking To the Future with Allergies

Glenn Lumsden

'My dad had allergies as a kid, but now he's just generally intolerant.'

In this part ...

As your doctor is likely to have told you, most children outgrow their allergies — but, of course, this also means some children don't grow out of their food allergies. Chances are, you want to find out more about what's in store for your child. Articles often appear in the paper or segments are aired on television or the radio that talk about possible new treatments for food allergy, but how effective are they really and when are they likely to be available to treat your child?

In this part, we discuss the natural history of food allergies and explain the likely course of the different food allergies. We explore the latest research into finding a cure for food allergies and explain the ways that these treatments may work. Although there are no cures for food allergy available yet, don't be disheartened — some promising research findings have started to appear, which may lead to new treatments in the not-too-distant future.

Chapter 12

Growing Out of Food Allergies

· ·

In This Chapter

▶ Understanding the likelihood of outgrowing a food allergy, and how allergists assess for tolerance

▶ Considering the reintroduction of problem foods in the home

▶ Knowing what's involved in a hospital-based food challenge

▶ Continuing to avoid your child's problem food

· ·

Developing tolerance to foods is the Holy Grail for those with food allergy and their carers — as well as allergy specialists and researchers. The type of food allergy, the age of your child and the level of allergen-specific IgE (detected by allergy tests) are all important factors for helping decide whether or not your child is likely to develop tolerance. Keeping in touch with your allergist is not only important for working out whether tolerance has or is likely to happen, but also enables you to keep up with the latest developments in this hot area of medical research.

In this chapter, we look at the likelihood of growing out of certain allergies, reintroducing problem foods to check whether tolerance has developed, and monitoring your child's allergies over time.

Knowing What to Expect Over Time from Your Child's Allergies

Some food allergies are more likely to be lifelong than others. For instance, only one in five children outgrow either a peanut or tree nut allergy by age five, and only one in ten people outgrow their fish and shellfish allergies. The onset of fish and shellfish allergies is also more likely to occur in adulthood (especially shellfish allergy).

On the flip side, the most common childhood food allergies — egg and cow's milk allergy — have a fantastic prognosis, with historical data showing more than 80 per cent of children with these allergies outgrow the allergy during childhood. Other common childhood food allergies — such as wheat and soy allergy — also tend to resolve during childhood.

Note: More recent data suggests that fewer children are outgrowing their food allergies than originally believed, with some studies from the United States suggesting that 50 per cent of children still have their allergies to egg or cow's milk at age 16 years. Whether these recent findings are because food allergies are becoming more persistent or because doctors are becoming more likely to ask about persistent food allergies is still not clear.

No-one knows why some food allergies are more likely than others to persist but experts do know allergens in egg and cow's milk become less allergenic when cooked or baked, while the same isn't true for the allergens in nuts, fish and shellfish. In fact, the reverse may be the case for peanut allergens, where dry roasting appears to increase the potency of peanut allergens. (Refer to Chapter 2 for more on the way cooking can change allergens.) Whether this is more than just an interesting observation is yet to be seen.

In the following sections, we look at how doctors monitor for the development of tolerance to a problem food, and which groups of children with food allergies are more like to develop tolerance to their problem food.

Testing for the development of tolerance

Children who are diagnosed with food allergy require regular follow-up appointments with their doctor (GP or paediatrician) every 12 months (refer to Chapter 7 for more on managing your child's food allergy). These follow-up visits are vital to review how well your child is managing to avoid the food allergen, the nutritional adequacy of your child's diet, how you can recognise and treat an allergic reaction, and your child's asthma control.

Your doctor should update your child's emergency action plan each year, and may review the status of your child's food allergy (by doing skin prick tests or arranging a blood test to measure the level of food-specific IgE antibodies) to monitor whether your child is outgrowing an allergy (developing tolerance). How often your child's doctor arranges for allergy testing to monitor for the development of tolerance can vary depending on the type of allergy your child has, the age of your child, and your doctor's preference, but most doctors perform testing every 12 to 18 months for the first few years after diagnosis, because the chances of growing out of food allergy are greatest before the age of five years.

Your doctor is likely to follow your child's IgE antibody levels, either through repeat skin prick tests (SPT) or through blood tests that check for food-specific IgE antibodies (refer to Chapter 6 for more on these tests). If the SPT wheal size or level of allergen-specific IgE antibody falls with time, your child is more likely to be developing tolerance to that food.

Reasonable evidence exists from our own studies that (at least for peanut) the direction of change in SPT wheal size between one and four years of age is the best predictor of tolerance development. If the wheal size falls over that period, tolerance development is likely. If it remains elevated or even rises, this suggests persistence of allergy.

Unfortunately, predictions based on SPT wheal size variation can be a somewhat self-fulfilling prophecy, because children with large wheal sizes are not generally offered oral food challenges (see the section 'Predicting who might grow out of food allergies', later in this chapter, for more on this). No-one has studied children with food allergies to understand whether a persistently elevated SPT is as good at predicting persistent food allergy as it is at predicting the initial diagnosis of allergy to that food.

Grasping possible reasons behind different rates of allergy resolution

Unfortunately, we don't yet know how to predict which children are likely to grow out of their food allergy. Although we know that nut, fish and shellfish allergies tend to persist while egg, milk, wheat and soy allergies tend to resolve, we don't understand why this is the case. We also don't yet understand the reasons for some children not outgrowing their egg or milk allergy when most children do, or the reasons some children with nut allergies grow out of their allergy when most children don't.

In the case of egg and milk allergy, some evidence is emerging that children who can tolerate egg or cow's milk in baked goods are more likely to outgrow their allergy at a younger age. This is suggested to be due to the fact that the child's immune system is being exposed to low doses of allergen — so, essentially, the immune system is being made to tolerate the food (see Chapter 13 for the difference between desensitisation and tolerance).

Another possibility is that those children who can tolerate egg or cow's milk in baked goods have a different, milder, type of allergy to those who can't — in other words, children who are allergic to proteins in the egg or milk that are broken down by heating or cooking have the type of allergy that generally resolves, whereas children who are allergic to proteins that aren't broken down with cooking have the type of allergy that usually persists.

So, we don't yet know for sure whether the better prognosis among those who can tolerate egg or cow's milk in baked goods is due to a different, milder, type of food allergy or because regular intake of the food is actually inducing tolerance. Importantly, initial studies of *oral immunotherapy* (which involves feeding the problem food to children with food allergy) haven't found an ability to induce tolerance, which suggests that the latter reason may be more correct. A number of further studies using oral immunotherapy are in progress — see Chapter 13 for more.

A very real risk exists of anaphylaxis occurring in oral immunotherapy studies, with up to 10 per cent of children participating in such studies experiencing some evidence of allergic reaction involving the airway, usually when the dose is being increased, but also during maintenance dosing. The emergence of oral immunotherapy studies has the potential to cause some confusion in the community and it can't be stated strongly enough that oral immunotherapy protocols are still highly experimental and this treatment approach should only be attempted under strict medical supervision as part of a research study.

Predicting who might grow out of food allergies

Children with cow's milk and egg allergy are more likely to outgrow their food allergy than those with nut and shellfish allergy. Children whose SPT wheal sizes or blood levels of food-specific IgE antibodies fall over time are also more likely to develop tolerance to their problem food. And large SPT wheal size or high levels of the food-specific IgE antibody in the blood test appear to predict a lower likelihood of growing out of that allergy.

However, one reason for a poorer prognosis in those children with larger wheal sizes or higher food-specific IgE antibodies may be to do with the fact that doctors don't recommend that these children undergo a food challenge to assess whether they have developed tolerance to their problem food. This is because they know that the larger the wheal size, the more likely the child is to react to a food — which is a somewhat circular argument!

Although the size of the SPT wheal and the level of food-specific IgE can predict the likelihood of food allergy as compared to sensitisation, they don't predict the severity of the allergic reaction.

Importantly, the link between the SPT wheal size or level of food-specific IgE and likelihood of clinical allergy has only been examined by studies looking at these tests for the initial diagnosis of a food allergy (as compared to tolerance). So far, no studies have assessed whether the size of a SPT wheal (or level of food-specific IgE antibodies) is useful for assessing the persistence of food allergy or the development of tolerance. So if the SPT wheal size stays high, your doctor usually won't test to see whether your child has developed tolerance. This means that the data becomes self-fulfilling. Those children with persistently large SPT wheals are believed to have persistent food allergy — because doctors usually don't test these children with a food challenge to see whether or not this is the case.

Luckily, studies are in progress to address this deficit. But, in the meantime, if your child's SPT wheal size remains large, your child should continue to avoid the food because your child is likely to be still allergic to that food. If your child's food-specific IgE antibody levels fall to very low, your child may have outgrown the food allergy, and should be reviewed by an allergist to determine whether or not a food challenge can be performed to assess this — your child's GP or paediatrician can make a referral. If the SPT wheal or food-specific IgE fall to a negative result, your child is very likely to have outgrown the allergy, and your doctor may recommend for you to introduce the food without your child needing to have a hospital-based food challenge. (See the following section about reintroducing foods at home.)

Younger children have a better prognosis for resolution of food allergy than older children or adults, for reasons that aren't yet known.

Safely Reintroducing Problem Foods at Home

Various factors can influence the decision about whether or not a problem food should be reintroduced into your child's diet at home. Primarily, these factors are the following:

✔ Whether your child's current SPT wheal size or food-specific IgE antibody level is negative or positive

✔ Anecdotal evidence supporting development of tolerance (for example, your child — accidentally or intentionally — ate the problem food and no symptoms of allergic reaction occurred)

✔ Imminent commencement at primary school when your child has not eaten the food previously

✔ Whether or not your child has an IgE mediated (immediate) food allergy (refer to Chapter 4 for an explanation of IgE mediated food allergies)

If your child has a history of an immediate reaction to a food and a positive IgE-antibody test, you should not reintroduce a problem food at home. This should only be done as part of a food challenge under the strict supervision of your doctor, usually in a hospital setting. This is because of the potential risk of inducing anaphylaxis if your child hasn't outgrown the allergy.

Knowing when you're safe to try problem foods at home

Introducing problem foods at home should only be undertaken after consultation with your child's doctor.

You're safe to introduce problem foods at home in the following circumstances:

✔ When SPTs or food-specific IgE antibody levels are negative. (This indicator can be used provided your child hasn't had a recent reaction that would suggest the test is wrong.)

✔ If your child has a food intolerance or delayed (non-IgE mediated or mixed IgE/non-IgE mediated) food allergy.

You're not safe to introduce problem foods at home in the following circumstances:

✔ If SPTs or blood food-specific IgE tests remain positive. (In exceptional circumstances, your doctor may approve trying foods at home but usually a hospital challenge is required.)

✔ If your child has a history of *food-protein-induced enterocolitis syndrome* (FPIES, which is associated with profuse vomiting approximately two to four hours after eating an introduced food — refer to Chapter 5), as there is a chance that the vomiting can be severe enough to affect the blood pressure.

Introducing problem foods at home

When introducing a problem food in the home, make sure you're sensibly prepared for any unexpected allergic reactions by doing the following:

✔ If your child has an adrenaline auto-injector, locate it.

✔ Give the dose of problem food during daylight hours — not at night just before bed — so that you can observe any unexpected evolving reaction.

✔ Give one dose of food each day, starting with a small amount of the food then trying a little more each day, and watch for any signs of allergic reaction over the next one to two hours. These include (but are not limited to) skin rash (such as hives or eczema flare), swollen face, vomiting, diarrhoea and/or anaphylaxis (coughing, wheezing or difficulty breathing, becoming pale and floppy or collapse).

If your child develops anaphylaxis after a dose of problem food during a home introduction, administer the adrenaline auto-injector and call an ambulance. (Refer to Chapters 7 and 11 for how to treat allergic reactions).

Our directions in the following sections for introducing problem foods are split into two categories: Children with a history of IgE mediated food allergies, and those with a history of delayed (non-IgE mediated or mixed IgE/non-IgE mediated) food allergies.

For children with a history of IgE mediated food allergies

Here are our recommendations for the steps to introduce problem foods for children with a history of IgE mediated, or immediate, food allergies.

When introducing solid problem foods, turn the food into a paste or use a lightly cooked version of the food — for example, peanut butter for a peanut allergy or lightly cooked scrambled egg for an egg allergy.

Food should be introduced in the following amounts:

Day 1: A smear of food inside your child's lip

Day 2: One-eighth of a teaspoon

Day 3: A quarter of a teaspoon

Day 4: Half a teaspoon

Day 5: One teaspoon

Day 6: Two teaspoons

Day 7 and beyond: Continue doubling the dose each day until a full serve is tolerated. Continue giving a full serve daily for the next week.

For administering fluids (such as cow's milk or soy milk), you might find using a syringe easier, because this gives you an accurate dose.

Here are our dosage recommendations for introducing fluids:

Day 1: 1 millilitre

Day 2: 5 millilitres

Day 3: 10 millilitres

Day 4: 20 millilitres

Day 5: 40 millilitres

Day 6 and beyond: Continue doubling the dose each day until a full serve is tolerated. Continue giving a full serve daily for the next week.

For children with a history of delayed (non-IgE or mixed IgE/non-IgE mediated) food allergies

For introducing solid foods to children with a history of delayed food allergies, we recommend you follow the guidelines in the previous section.

For introducing fluids (such as cow's milk or soy milk) to children with a history of delayed food allergies, we recommend you mix the liquid food you are testing into a currently tolerated formula, to improve compliance. Here are our dosage recommendations:

Day 1: 10 millilitres

Day 2: 20 millilitres

Day 3: 50 millilitres

Day 4: 100 millilitres

Day 5: 200 millilitres

Day 6 and beyond: Continue doubling the dose each day until a full serve is tolerated. Continue giving a full serve daily for the next week.

Monitoring your child's allergies

Sometimes parents are keen to confirm whether their child has developed tolerance — because of either a need to travel, or a transition point of independence (such as entering primary or high school, or becoming an adult and leaving home).

The main ways to monitor your child's allergy are through following the size of the SPT wheal or food-specific IgE antibody level on a blood test. (Chapter 6 discusses these tests in more detail.)

We recently published data showing that the best predictor for remission of peanut allergy is a falling SPT wheal size between the age of one and four years. We also showed that the higher the initial wheal size, the less likely your child is to develop eventual tolerance. So follow-up testing in the first five years of life is important. On the other hand, recent studies suggest that children are outgrowing their egg and cow's milk allergies more slowly than was previously thought, so after the age of five years, testing can be spaced out to every 18 to 24 months.

Another incidental way that you may discover your child has developed tolerance to a food is through the absence of a reaction following accidental ingestion. If this happens, discuss the scenario with your doctor. Your doctor can then take a history to assess whether the absence of a reaction is due either to an insufficient dose of the allergen in the food ingested or to tolerance development (if they have eaten a decent amount of the food). Your doctor can confirm whether the likelihood of tolerance development is high by performing a SPT or food-specific IgE blood test and checking whether the SPT wheal size or food-specific IgE level has dropped.

If your child has recently ingested a decent amount of the problem food and experienced no associated reaction and the SPT or food-specific IgE test is negative, your doctor is very likely to suggest you carefully introduce the food to your child at home. If the history is equivocal or the SPT (or food-specific IgE test) remains elevated despite history of possible tolerance, a hospital-based food challenge is most likely be recommended to maximise safety. A hospital-based food challenge may also be recommended if no accidental ingestions have occurred and the SPT or food-specific IgE test remains unchanged over an extended time period.

Confronting Your Child's Allergies with Hospital-Based Food Challenges

During a hospital-based oral food challenge, your child is exposed to increasing amounts of an allergen (such as peanut butter), over a two- to three-hour period. Usually, the challenge starts with a small smear inside your child's lip and finishes when the total amount offered reaches approximately a standard serve of the food. Your child is normally expected to stay in the challenge clinic for one to two hours after the final dose is given, so that the staff can monitor for any reaction.

Some children have an allergic reaction during the oral food challenge. The risk of anaphylaxis during a controlled food challenge is low — some allergists estimate that less than 1 in 100 children presenting to challenge clinics with food allergies develop anaphylaxis. Despite this, full precautionary measures should always be in place in each oral food challenge setting, including availability of a resuscitation trolley just in case your child develops anaphylaxis. If your child develops anaphylaxis, your child requires treatment with adrenaline and observation in hospital for four to six hours after the event. The Australasian Society of Clinical Immunology and Allergy (ASCIA) recommends that oral food challenges should only take place in a fully supervised setting with appropriate resuscitation facilities.

Your child is discharged from hospital once all airway and circulatory symptoms have settled. However, some signs or symptoms such as hives (itchy lumps on the skin) may not have fully resolved before discharge and a risk of a return of some allergic symptoms in the next 24 hours also exists.

Signs and symptoms to watch for after discharge include the following:

- **Gastrointestinal problems:**
  - Diarrhoea
  - General stomach upset or pain, or colic
  - Vomiting or nausea
- **Skin reactions:**
  - Eczema or other rashes
  - Hives (welts which look like mosquito bites)
- **Breathing or circulatory problems:**
  - Wheezing or noisy breathing
  - Coughing
  - Difficulty breathing
  - Hoarse voice
  - Pale colour and floppiness

If gastrointestinal or skin reactions occur, you should seek medical attention at either your local doctor or at the emergency department of a hospital. If any signs or symptoms suggesting anaphylaxis occur, such as those involving the breathing or circulatory compromise, you should administer your child's adrenaline auto-injector (if your child has one) and immediately call an ambulance for emergency assistance.

Those children who have passed their oral food challenge (that is, have completed the challenge without reaction — a negative challenge) are asked to continue to have some of this food each day for at least the next week. If children are able to take the food without any reactions, they have outgrown their food allergy — or, explained a different way, they have developed tolerance to their problem food.

The likelihood of an allergic reaction developing while continuing the food challenge at home (after having tolerated the first day of the challenge in hospital) is very low. However, you should give the challenge food at a time when you can observe your child for a few hours after the food has been eaten in case such an unlikely event does occur.

If no reaction occurs during the next week as the food is continued at home, it's a good idea for your child to have some of the food approximately once each week for the next one to two months to ensure the diagnosis of tolerance is consolidated.

Being Careful With Allergen Avoidance: Trace Amounts in Foods

We cover the significant confusion that remains about precautionary labelling in Chapter 8. What's worth noting here is that just because your child tolerates foods that 'may contain traces of' your child's problem food, this doesn't mean your child is tolerant to that food.

Because precautionary labelling is voluntary, the declaration 'may contain traces of' may or may not indicate presence of allergen and, conversely, foods that don't declare such precautionary labelling are just as likely to contain trace levels of allergen. Therefore, evidence that your child can eat foods that may contain traces of a problem food isn't evidence that your child has been exposed to the problem allergen in significant amounts nor is it evidence that your child is now tolerant to that allergen.

Also, some children with food allergy can tolerate very small doses of the food and will only have an allergic reaction after eating larger amounts of their problem food. Nevertheless, allergists believe that all children with food allergy should completely avoid their problem food and that strict avoidance remains critical to your child's safety, because the threshold for eliciting a reaction in a person with food allergy can change with time.

Chapter 13

Treating Allergies in the Future

- -

In This Chapter

▶ Knowing the difference between desensitisation and tolerance

▶ Looking into allergen-specific immunotherapy

▶ Learning about oral immunotherapy as a possible approach to treating food allergies

▶ Considering immunotherapy with modified allergens

▶ Discovering what other theories have been explored

- -

*B*ecause no long-term cure yet exists for food allergies, the approach to managing your child's food allergy relies on supportive measures, such as helping your child to avoid the food allergen, reducing the chances of your child accidentally eating the food allergen and minimising the risks for your child should an allergic reaction actually occur (by knowing how to recognise and treat allergic reactions). (The management of food allergy is discussed in detail in Part III.)

However, this management approach to treating food allergies is fraught with difficulties, because your child is likely to accidentally eat her food allergen at some time and, when this happens, the possibility exists that your child will have a severe allergic reaction (anaphylaxis) that's life-threatening. So with the current approach to management of food allergies, you and your child must constantly pay attention to what foods are on offer and whether the foods contain your child's food allergens.

This continuing responsibility and worry affects your child's and your family's quality of life — studies have shown that the quality of life of a child with food allergy is affected to a similar degree as that of a child with diabetes, and that the family's quality of life is affected to a similar degree as that of a family with a child suffering from arthritis. The only way to improve the lives of children with food allergies and their families is to find a way to cure food allergies (in other words, make them go away), so that children and families can be relieved of the ongoing burden and anxiety of managing food allergies.

The recent increase in food allergies in Australia has mostly affected children under the age of five years, and allergies to peanut, tree nut, fish and shellfish have increased by the greatest amount (refer to Chapter 2 for more information on rising rates of food allergy). Although children usually grow out of their allergies to milk, egg, wheat and soy (refer to Chapter 12), allergies to peanut, tree nuts, fish or shellfish generally aren't outgrown and instead remain with children into adult life. This means that not only is the number of children with food allergies increasing, but a higher proportion of children with food allergy suffer from those very allergies that usually persist into adult life. In light of all of this, many researchers are working hard to find a long-term cure for food allergies.

Most people are excited by the future, because it holds the promise of new and undiscovered treasures that they can only dream about. In this chapter, we tell you about exciting research being carried out by experts to find a curative treatment for food allergy. Many of these experimental treatments are still in the very early stages of being studied and may or may not turn out to be effective for treating people with food allergies. But some treatments, such as oral immunotherapy and sublingual immunotherapy, are already being tested in clinical trials in people with food allergies, and results will soon reveal whether these are effective.

Distinguishing between Tolerance and Desensitisation

Two types of treatments for specific allergies are available: One that induces tolerance to an allergen (for example, immunotherapy for treating bee venom or pollen allergy), and another that only induces desensitisation to an allergen (for example, desensitisation for penicillin allergy). We look at the difference in the following sections.

Tolerance to allergens

Tolerance is when the immune response of a person with allergy is reprogrammed away from an allergic response towards a tolerance response, and his immune system no longer recognises the allergen as harmful — the person is able to tolerate the allergen without developing an allergic reaction to it.

This type of reprogramming of the immune system can already be achieved using allergen-specific immunotherapy for the treatment of insect venom allergies and allergies to airborne allergens (see the section 'Investigating Immunotherapy', later in this chapter). Using bee venom immunotherapy, more than 95 per cent of people with severe allergies to bee stings can be cured of their specific bee venom allergy, and no longer have an allergic reaction if they're stung by a bee.

However, allergen-specific immunotherapy has only been successfully applied to induce tolerance in the treatment of allergies to insect venoms and various inhaled allergens, such as pollen, house dust mite and some pet danders. Researchers haven't been able to induce tolerance using immunotherapy in the treatment of other specific allergies, such as drug allergy, food allergy, latex allergy and so on.

Desensitisation to allergens

Desensitisation is when a person can be exposed to her allergen without reacting to it while she continues on a specific treatment, but once that person stops the treatment, she's no longer protected and again reacts to the allergen — the person is still allergic to the allergen and the immune system hasn't been reprogrammed. Desensitisation simply allows a person to take the allergen without having an allergic reaction for a short time while receiving the desensitisation treatment.

Desensitisation is used for the management of drug allergies and allows people who are allergic to a medication to receive that medication while on the desensitisation treatment.

 Desensitisation treatment doesn't provide long-lasting protection against having an allergic reaction because it doesn't cure the underlying allergy. When desensitisation treatment is stopped, the risk of having a serious allergic reaction to the allergen returns. This means the treatment is usually only used when a person needs a life-saving medication — for example, allergen desensitisation is used if someone needs to have an antibiotic or a cancer treatment that he's allergic to.

 If you take the situation of your child's food allergy, the ultimate goal is to find a curative treatment that can induce long-lasting tolerance — a treatment that can make your child's food allergy go away forever. Desensitisation isn't a long-term solution to food allergies, because once the desensitisation treatment is over, the allergic reactions come back.

Investigating Immunotherapy

Although no cures exist for most of the allergic conditions, such as asthma, eczema, hay fever, food allergy and drug allergy, allergists do have a curative treatment for specific allergies to insect venoms such as bee, wasp or hornet venoms, known as *allergen-specific immunotherapy*. A person with asthma or hay fever can also be cured of a specific pollen or house dust mite allergy, which can help to control the asthma or hay fever symptoms — although the person continues to have hay fever and asthma.

Allergen-specific immunotherapy usually involves regular injections of the allergen into the fatty tissue in the arm, starting at very low doses of allergen and increasing the amount of allergen until the highest maintenance dose is reached. This maintenance dose is then injected every month for a total of three (pollen immunotherapy) to five (insect venom immunotherapy) years.

Immunotherapy treatment for non-food allergies

For many decades, treating allergies to bee, wasp or hornet stings has been possible using allergen-specific immunotherapy, and the majority of people who are allergic to these insects can be cured of their allergy after treatment for five years. More recently, Australian researchers have also developed allergen-specific immunotherapy to treat allergies to Jumper Jack Ants, an ant species that is unique to Australia and mainly found in the southern states — including Tasmania, South Australia, Victoria, and southern parts of New South Wales and Western Australia.

Allergen-specific immunotherapy has also been used to treat specific allergies to pollen, house dust mite or pet danders in people with hay fever and in some people with asthma, as a way of improving their hay fever and asthma symptoms. (In people with hay fever or asthma who have allergies to inhaled allergens, their symptoms are triggered whenever they're exposed to these allergens.)

So, if you have severe hay fever that's triggered by pollens or house dust mite and your symptoms can't be controlled using standard medications (topical corticosteroids and anti-histamines) together with allergen-avoidance strategies, allergen-specific immunotherapy can be used to improve your hay fever symptoms by curing you of your specific allergies to pollen or house dust mite.

Similarly, allergists may offer allergen-specific immunotherapy to some patients with asthma (immunotherapy isn't recommended for people with severe asthma due to the increased likelihood of the immunotherapy causing anaphylaxis) as a way of improving asthma symptoms when standard medication (inhaled corticosteroid and bronchodilator) together with allergen-avoidance strategies have failed to control asthma symptoms.

In both situations, however, the underlying condition of hay fever or asthma hasn't been cured; the allergen-specific immunotherapy has only cured the person's specific allergies to pollen, house dust mite or pet danders.

The way that allergen-specific immunotherapy works is that the therapy reprograms a person's immune response to an allergen, so that the immune system no longer sees the allergen as harmful and doesn't generate an allergic response to the allergen; in other words, the therapy induces 'tolerance' to the allergen (refer to the section 'Tolerance of allergens', earlier in this chapter, for more about what this means). The result is that the person is no longer allergic to the allergen and can be said to be cured of that specific allergy.

Immunotherapy isn't yet available for the treatment of food allergies. However, research studies evaluating the use of sublingual and oral immunotherapy are providing interesting results, as we discuss in the sections 'Trying immunotherapy for food allergies' and 'Eating Your Way Out of Allergies: Oral Immunotherapy', later in this chapter.

Administering immunotherapy

Traditionally, immunotherapy has been injected into the fatty tissue in the arm — in what's known as *subcutaneous immunotherapy* (SCIT). This is the type of allergen-specific immunotherapy that's used for the treatment of insect venom allergies.

In the last 10 to 15 years, allergists have looked at delivering allergen-specific immunotherapy as drops or tablets under the tongue — in what's known as *sublingual immunotherapy* (SLIT). In sublingual immunotherapy, the allergen is made up as drops or a dissolvable tablet that's kept under the tongue for two to five minutes and then swallowed or expelled. This approach is more acceptable to many people because it doesn't require an injection, and has a lower chance of causing severe allergic reactions during treatment — although children can find holding the drops or tablets under their tongues for the full two to five minutes difficult.

Researchers have shown that prolonged injection of high doses of allergen is needed to reprogram a person's immune response to the allergen and induce tolerance to that allergen. However, highly allergic people and people with severe asthma can react to the immunotherapy, making it difficult for them to reach the high maintenance doses necessary to achieve beneficial effects with subcutaneous immunotherapy. Delivering the allergen extract by sublingual immunotherapy reduces the chances of severe allergic reactions to the immunotherapy, most likely because much less of the allergen extract reaches the blood circulation, whereas higher amounts of the allergen can enter the circulation when it is injected into the tissues.

Sublingual immunotherapy is effective for the treatment of hay fever in adults, but it has not yet been shown to be consistently effective in children, so researchers are continuing to test its use in this setting. Sublingual immunotherapy is not used for the treatment of insect venom allergies.

The allergen extracts used for immunotherapy treatment are purified extracts made from the crude substance that causes allergy (such as insect venoms, pollen grains, house dust mites or pet danders), meaning that they contain a mixture of proteins, including the relevant allergens that are contained in the substance in question. So, for example, the bee venom extract used for bee venom immunotherapy contains a collection of proteins purified from bee venom that includes the specific allergens a person with bee allergy is allergic to. These allergens in the immunotherapy are the same allergens that can bind to IgE antibodies and cause allergy, so the immunotherapy itself can cause allergic reactions, including anaphylaxis, during treatment. This is why subcutaneous immunotherapy treatments are started by injecting very low doses and then increasing the dose very gradually to the higher maintenance dose.

Trying immunotherapy for food allergies

Because subcutaneous immunotherapy has been very effective for the treatment of insect venom allergy and allergies to inhaled allergens (see the preceding section), researchers have attempted to apply such an approach for the treatment of food allergy.

Studies of subcutaneous immunotherapy were initiated more than 20 years ago, using purified peanut extract as a treatment for peanut allergy in adults; however, the first trial caused an unexpected death, due to a treatment allocation error, and a later study caused a very high rate of anaphylaxis, so this approach was abandoned.

To avoid inducing severe allergic reactions with subcutaneous immunotherapy, researchers have investigated the use of sublingual immunotherapy for the treatment of food allergy. Two randomised controlled trials have evaluated sublingual immunotherapy for the treatment of food allergy (hazelnut and peach allergy), which both showed that the majority of people treated with sublingual immunotherapy were desensitised to their allergen; however, the researchers didn't test to see if the sublingual immunotherapy had induced tolerance. (Refer to the section 'Distinguishing between Tolerance and Desensitisation', earlier in this chapter, for the difference between the two.) A third randomised placebo-controlled trial is underway to evaluate sublingual immunotherapy for the treatment of peanut allergy, and will assess for development of tolerance. So far, the results show that sublingual immunotherapy can desensitise patients with peanut allergy and can induce changes in the immune response to peanut, suggesting that using sublingual immunotherapy to induce tolerance may be possible. Results of this study will be available in a few years.

Interestingly, a case report of sublingual immunotherapy with kiwifruit extract for the treatment of severe kiwifruit allergy in an adult showed that after five years of treatment she had developed long-lasting tolerance (no reaction to an oral food challenge with kiwifruit four months after immunotherapy was stopped).

One possible barrier to using sublingual immunotherapy for the treatment of food allergy in children is that the extract needs to be held under the tongue for at least two to five minutes before it's swallowed or expelled, and children can find this difficult to manage. To address this problem, researchers are looking at the possibility of dissolvable tablets, which can make it easier for children to keep the extract in their mouths without swallowing for the required time. This approach has already been used for pollen and house dust mite sublingual immunotherapy.

Eating Your Way Out Of Allergies: Oral Immunotherapy

In addition to immunotherapy drops or tablets under the tongue or injections (see the preceding sections), researchers have also investigated *oral immunotherapy* for treating food allergies. In oral immunotherapy protocols, the allergen compound is taken orally once daily, starting at a low dose and then increasing the dose gradually to reach a higher maintenance dose. The maintenance dose is then continued for varying amounts of time up to one or two years. The allergen compound is usually the food itself in its natural form or as a dry powder.

Oral immunotherapy was first reported for the treatment of food allergy as early as 1908. Since then many case reports and studies have been completed, including a number of placebo-controlled clinical trials evaluating the effectiveness of oral immunotherapy for the treatment of food allergy in children and adults. However, most of these studies have only assessed for the development of desensitisation, with only a few trials assessing for tolerance. (Refer to the section 'Distinguishing between Tolerance and Desensitisation', earlier in this chapter, for the difference between the two.)

So far, all the oral immunotherapy trials show that most people treated with oral immunotherapy become desensitised, including people with severe allergies (anaphylaxis to cow's milk or peanut). These studies have also showed that oral immunotherapy can induce immune changes that can be associated with tolerance, suggesting that oral immunotherapy may be able to induce tolerance. However, only three studies have assessed for tolerance in children or adults treated with oral immunotherapy, and these have not found a conclusive effect on tolerance. (See the sidebar 'Testing for tolerance after oral immunotherapy' for more on this.)

TECHNICAL STUFF

Testing for tolerance after oral immunotherapy

Three studies have tested for tolerance in children or adults treated with oral immuno-therapy. Only one of these studies included a dummy (or *placebo*) treatment to compare with the oral immunotherapy treatment. A placebo treatment is important in food allergy trials because many children can grow out of their allergies to egg or milk, and some can also grow out of their allergies to peanut. So, to show whether an oral immunotherapy treatment can or can't induce tolerance, half of the study subjects need to be randomly allocated to take the active oral immunotherapy and the other half to take the dummy treatment — this is called a *placebo-controlled randomised clinical trial*. (We explain more about different types of clinical trials in Chapter 3.)

In the only placebo-controlled randomised clinical trial of oral immunotherapy assessing for tolerance, involving children with cow's milk and/or egg allergies, the proportion of children who developed tolerance following treatment with oral immunotherapy or dummy treatment was almost exactly the same (36 per cent of children who received the active oral immunotherapy and 35 per cent of children who received the dummy placebo treatment developed tolerance), suggesting that the oral immunotherapy was no better than the dummy treatment in inducing tolerance.

A study of egg oral immunotherapy similarly showed tolerance in 29 per cent of children

with egg allergy (two out of seven children with egg allergy) after treatment with egg oral immunotherapy. This study didn't include a comparison group that received treatment with a dummy immunotherapy; however, because the percentage of children who developed tolerance was similar to that in the study of cow's milk oral immunotherapy discussed earlier, it is likely that these children had experienced natural resolution of their egg allergy.

The third study of oral immunotherapy that assessed for tolerance looked at peanut allergy and found that tolerance was induced in 17 per cent of study participants. Again, no comparison group that received treatment with a dummy immunotherapy was used in this study, so determining whether the tolerance was produced by the peanut immunotherapy or by the study participants growing out of their allergy is difficult. However, the oral immunotherapy is more likely to have worked in this study, since natural resolution of peanut allergy wouldn't be expected in such a high number of study participants over the short time of the study (12 weeks).

At this time, oral immunotherapy programs that have been tested for the treatment of food allergy do seem to induce desensitisation and also induce some changes in the immune response to allergen; however, this approach hasn't yet been shown to successfully induce tolerance.

Researching ways to induce tolerance

Researchers (including Mimi's own research team) are now investigating ways to improve the ability for oral immunotherapy to induce tolerance (and so reprogram the immune response) by using higher maintenance doses of allergen, treating with oral immunotherapy for a longer period of time (more than one or two years) and/or combining it with an adjuvant.

Because previous studies have shown that existing oral immunotherapy programs can at least modulate immune responses in the direction of tolerance, researchers are hopeful that these changes to the way oral immunotherapy is conducted can improve its ability to induce tolerance. Results of these studies are expected to be available very soon and, if shown to be effective, will provide an exciting new approach to the treatment of food allergies.

Working out if desensitisation is enough

The majority (around 70 to 80 per cent) of people treated with oral immunotherapy develop some degree (either partial or complete) of desensitisation to the allergen and are able to take larger amounts of their allergen while they remain on daily doses of their oral immunotherapy. Because of this, some allergists believe that even if oral immunotherapy fails to induce long-lasting tolerance, the development of desensitisation is still a significant advantage for people with food allergies, and may be a worthwhile outcome.

However, in published oral immunotherapy studies and also Mimi's own ongoing oral immunotherapy study, patients can have unexpected allergic reactions, including anaphylaxis, even while they're taking their daily oral immunotherapy treatments, suggesting that desensitisation may not be a safe option for some children and adults.

Published studies have identified some factors that increase the chances of an allergic reaction while someone is on continuing oral immunotherapy — such as having an infection (particularly if a fever is involved), exercising within a few hours of taking a dose of immunotherapy, or menstruation. However, in Mimi's study, participants sometimes also had unexpected allergic reactions unrelated to any of these triggers, which suggests that further studies are needed before the induction of desensitisation can be recommended in clinical practice as a treatment option for people with food allergy.

Even if accurately identifying triggers for allergic reactions in people who are desensitised and taking daily oral immunotherapy were possible, those people would still be at risk of having an unexpected allergic reaction if they forgot to take their allergen. Unfortunately, this would be a common occurrence since most people find it extremely difficult to always remember to take a daily medication.

The development of desensitisation may not be a safe management approach in some people with food allergy, and further studies are needed to better understand the specific triggers for allergic reactions in people who are desensitised and taking daily oral immunotherapy treatments. For this reason, and because whether oral immunotherapy on its own can induce tolerance remains uncertain, we don't yet recommend the use of oral immunotherapy in clinical practice. Further clinical trials are still needed to more clearly define the effects and safety of oral immunotherapy before the treatment can be applied in the clinical setting.

Learning About Modified Allergens for Use in Immunotherapy

Because subcutaneous immunotherapy using a standard purified food extract caused frequent anaphylaxis (refer to the section 'Trying immunotherapy for food allergies', earlier in this chapter), researchers wondered whether safer alternative allergen preparations containing small protein fragments of the allergens (*peptides*), or modified allergens (*mutated allergens*) that did not cause allergic reactions, could be used in place of the whole food extract — or, more specifically, hypo-allergenic forms of the major proteins that cause the allergy.

The reason researchers are looking at developing peptides and modified allergens for use in immunotherapy is to avoid causing allergic reactions to the treatment. The idea is to use peptides and modified allergens that still contain some parts of the food allergen that can be recognised by the immune system and induce tolerance, but are changed from their original form so they no longer bind to the IgE antibody and, therefore, don't cause allergic reactions. Researchers have developed a number of modified allergens and peptides for use in pollen and pet dander immunotherapy, and some of these preparations are being tested in early clinical trials.

Subcutaneous immunotherapy using purified whole peanut extract resulted in a high rate of severe reactions (refer to the section 'Trying immunotherapy for food allergies', earlier in this chapter, for more).

Because of this, some researchers have explored the development of modified allergens and peptides from peanut, in the hope that this may allow the safe use of subcutaneous immunotherapy for treatment of peanut allergy.

Researchers have identified some potential peptides from peanut and work is now in progress to produce standardised preparations that can be tested for their ability to treat peanut allergy. However, peptide extracts that can be used for testing in human clinical trials won't be ready for a number of years. Researchers have also been testing mutated allergen injected together with a bacterial adjuvant. Based on positive results from animal studies, a phase I study in adults with peanut allergy is underway to confirm safety.

One of the difficulties with peptide immunotherapy for the treatment of peanut allergy is that a number of major peanut allergens are involved in causing peanut allergy and the major peanut allergens that people react to can vary from person to person. So for the immunotherapy extract to induce tolerance to the relevant peanut allergens in different people, the extract needs to contain peptides derived from a range of major peanut allergens that are relevant for the majority of people with peanut allergy. The alternative approach is to identify the major peanut allergens that are relevant in each person with peanut allergy and to tailor an allergenic peptide extract for that person; however, this approach may not be feasible in clinical practice.

Researchers in the European Union are working on developing peptide extracts for the treatment of fish and fruit allergies. Fish and fruit allergies may be better suited to a peptide immunotherapy approach than peanut allergy because, in these conditions, the allergies are caused by a single major allergen: Parvalbumin is the major fish allergen, and lipid transfer protein is the major fruit allergen. This makes the development of an effective peptide extract more feasible, because peptides can be developed from just the one major allergenic protein. Work is in progress to develop effective peptides that can then be tested in human clinical trials.

Exploring Other Treatments

While there are a large number of studies examining oral and sublingual immunotherapy, and results have been promising (see preceding sections), other treatments are also on the horizon — and a number of these experimental treatments are also being investigated in human clinical trials, including Chinese herbal extract FAHF-2 and various adjuvants and bacterial products. We look at these treatments in the following sections.

Food Allergy Herbal Formula

A Chinese herbal preparation called Food Allergy Herbal Formula (FAHF) has been developed by researchers in the United States. The formula is based upon traditional Chinese herbal medicine concepts, and results from initial testing seem to hold some promise.

The first FAHF preparation (FAHF-1) included eleven herbal extracts that were selected for their reported benefits on intestinal symptoms such as vomiting and colic. This preparation was shown to induce clinical tolerance to peanut in a mouse model of peanut allergy and to also divert immune responses away from allergic-type responses towards tolerance-type responses.

The researchers later developed a second herbal formula (FAHF-2). This formula removed two of the herbal extracts, due to the concern of potential toxic effects if they weren't prepared correctly or were used in excessive doses. Testing of FAHF-2 in mice showed similar results to FAHF-1.

Based upon these positive results in animal models, FAHF-2 is being tested in human clinical trials. A Phase I trial has confirmed that FAHF-2 is safe and well tolerated by adults, and further clinical trials are now underway to assess whether it's effective for the treatment of food allergy.

Probiotics

Probiotic bacteria have also been tested for the treatment of food allergy. *Probiotics* are live bacteria, which can provide benefits by improving the balance of intestinal bacteria. Probiotics are generally considered to be safe for use in humans and the most commonly used probiotic bacteria are called *bifidobacteria* and *lactobacilli*.

The beneficial effects of probiotic bacteria are related to their actions on the immune system as well as their ability to promote the growth of other beneficial bacteria in the intestine; both of these effects are thought to promote the development of tolerance and counter allergic responses in the intestine.

Nevertheless, even though probiotic bacteria can be considered together as a class of bacteria that have potent effects on the immune system, the specific immune effects of the different types of probiotic bacteria can vary — for example, while some types of probiotic bacteria are very good at inducing tolerance to allergens, others strongly promote immune responses, including allergic responses, and so can worsen allergic problems rather than improve them.

Some types of probiotic bacteria promote *T helper type 1* immune responses, which are typically generated to fight bacteria and viral infections. Others may even activate *T helper type 2* allergic immune responses — the kind of response the immune system launches when an allergen is ingested.

Because of the varying effects of different kinds of probiotic bacteria, the clinical benefits of any particular probiotic must be assessed individually and carefully.

Studies suggest that some probiotic bacteria (particularly those of the lactobacillus rhamnosus species) may be effective for preventing the development of eczema in babies if these probiotics are given to mothers in the last weeks of pregnancy and to the babies for the first six to 12 months of life. So researchers are also interested in determining whether probiotic bacteria might be useful for the treatment of established food allergy. However, the only randomised controlled trial of a mixture of probiotic bacteria for food allergy didn't find any beneficial effects.

In one study that looked at the effectiveness of probiotics in treating established food allergy, over 100 infants with cow's milk allergy were randomly allocated to receive two probiotic bacteria (lactobacillus casei CRL431 and bifidobacterium lactis Bb-12) or a dummy treatment for 12 months. At the end of the treatment, 81 per cent of infants in the placebo group and 77 per cent of infants in the active probiotic group were desensitised to cow's milk. The researchers didn't assess for tolerance.

Other adjuvants and bacterial products

Other experimental approaches to the treatment of food allergy under investigation are directed at activating T helper type 1 immune responses. These are usually generated to protect against bacteria and can be used to suppress T helper type 2 allergic immune responses. These include bacterial *adjuvants* (a compound with the ability to modulate the immune system; used with an antigen to enhance effects on the immune response to that particular antigen), heat-killed bacteria that have been engineered to express allergenic proteins, engineered DNA sequences that contain allergen sequences, and immunostimulatory DNA sequences, which can be delivered either by injection into the tissues, orally, intranasally or as a suppository.

These treatments are still in early stages of investigation — although heat-killed bacteria that express allergen are being evaluated in Phase I safety trials.

Part V
The Part of Tens

Glenn Lumsden

Antibody Counselling.

In this part ...

This part is all about providing you with some quick lessons, tips and websites — oh, and busting some myths!

In this part, we cover the key lessons you should be passing on to your child with food allergy, provide some helpful tips on replacing common food allergens, and debunk common myths about food allergies. To support you, your child, and other people who care for your child into the future, we also list some useful websites where you can find information on food allergies.

Chapter 14

Ten Key Lessons to Teach Your Kids About Food Allergies

*R*aising children and teenagers who have food allergies can present a real challenge — especially when eating food is an essential part of life. Your child has to be able to deal with unknown situations, sometimes without your supervision. What adds to the challenge is the fact that the lessons you need to teach your child with food allergy change as your child grows older and gains more independence. Although not unique to children with food allergy, transition and change through different stages of life can add an extra degree of difficulty if you have a food allergy to contend with.

In this chapter, we reveal the top ten talking points that you, as a parent, should pass along to help your child successfully handle food allergy in all situations — both physically and emotionally. We also point out special tips for taking developmental changes into account as your child grows through adolescence.

Finding Comfort in Numbers: Many People Have Food Allergies

The good news about the rise in food allergy is that you don't need to feel alone. Between 5 and 10 per cent of kids in Australia have food allergy, meaning literally thousands of families each year find out they have a child with food allergy just like you. And most people now know someone with a food allergy.

Awareness of food allergy has also increased in the community — certainly through stories about food allergy in the media but also because of a concerted effort by doctors and scientists to educate both the medical community and the general population.

All schools and childcare centres in Victoria that have a child at risk of anaphylaxis enrolled are now legally required to ensure that their staff are trained in the recognition and management of anaphylaxis, and personalised anaphylaxis management plans have to be developed for each individual child with an adrenaline auto-injector in a school. Training must be provided through an accredited course or other government-approved course, which ensures appropriate content is covered and adequate skills are taught.

Restaurants have also got on board with being aware of, and catering for, food allergies. Many menus now include nut, dairy and/or gluten-free options.

Decoding Labels and Asking Questions

For families with food allergy, reading labels can be one of the most difficult daily aspects in caring for their child.

The good news is that ingredients that have been added to a food need to be declared on the label if they're one of the top-priority allergy foods — that is, egg, peanut, tree nut, cow's milk, soy, wheat, fish or shellfish (crustacean). What's more, the ingredients need to be written in plain English — rather than a difficult-to-interpret Latin name or as a sub-component of the food. This is great because now even quite young children can recognise the name of the food they should avoid.

In general, children aren't ready to reliably read labels until they're around age 10 or 11 — and, of course, you still need to take your child's reading ability into account when deciding whether your child is ready. But you should be ensuring that your child is at least becoming familiar with decoding labels by the end of primary school, since the time of transition to secondary school is the time when children have to take more responsibility for their lives (including getting to the right class at the right time and ensuring they know what homework they should be doing!). Children at secondary school are also more likely to be in a situation where an adult isn't present and so need to be more self-reliant to ensure they stay safe.

Chapter 8 looks closely at interpreting ingredient labels.

Teaching Your Friends a Thing or Two

Children with food allergy can worry about what their friends are going to think. The most important thing to tell your child with food allergy is that she needs to remember that her friends' prime concern is going to be her safety. True friends really just want to help make your child's life as safe and uncomplicated as possible. However, if you (or your child) haven't told friends about your child's food allergy, you can't really expect them to know what to do to help keep your child safe.

Your child's friends take the lead from your child. So you and your child should make the time to tell friends about food allergy.

How you do this is, of course, completely up to you — but here are some suggestions:

✔ **For close friends:** You may find the conversation easier if you invite the friends over for a play and then explain to them what they need to know. If your child is going to play over at a friend's place or stay for a sleepover, you may wish to first invite the parents (or carers) of the friend over to also get them up to speed.

✔ **For school friends:** Enlist the help of your child's teacher to explain to the class what your child's allergy is, and some of the simple information about food allergy and the warning signs of anaphylaxis. (Refer to Chapter 9 for how staff in schools and childcare centres can help manage your child's food allergy).

If your child's teacher doesn't know anything about how to prevent or manage a food allergy reaction, we would encourage you to also educate the teacher in a similar way to your child's friends' parents. (Keep in mind that many staff in Australian and New Zealand schools have been trained in appropriate management of food allergy in a school setting and in Victoria all schools that have a child with food allergy enrolled must, by law, provide training for the majority of their staff.)

Friends usually want to know answers to the following questions:

- ✔ What is food allergy and what foods is your child allergic to?
- ✔ What sort of reactions are going to occur if your child eats that food?
- ✔ What sort of things does the friend need to do to keep your child safe?
- ✔ What should the friend do if your child has an accidental ingestion?
- ✔ What should the friend do if your child has an allergic reaction?

In general, getting your child used to telling friends while still in primary school is much easier. Younger children are perhaps a little less sceptical and certainly don't have the same peer-pressure issues that adolescents can have.

Helping your adolescent child work out who to tell, as well as how and what to tell, is really important. Sometimes, you can help by coaching your child about exactly what he should tell his friends at school. You should also give your child some tools to help deal with an uncertain peer-pressure situation. Empowering your child with statements such as 'What I eat is my choice' can be very helpful in a group setting where, in addition to friends, others who are unaware of your child's food allergy status may also be present. This kind of empowerment is even more important when no adults are at hand who can help your child deal with a difficult situation.

Providing your child with the communication tools to express his needs and choices can be useful for all types of peer-pressure settings, including situations where alcohol and recreational drugs may be offered.

Sitting at the Cleanest Table

One way to keep your allergic child safe is to make sure that she doesn't accidentally ingest the allergen she's allergic to, which can happen at dirty tables.

When it comes to touching food that has been left or smeared on tables, common sense should prevail. Your child should be aware that she won't necessarily get an allergic reaction if she touches her problem food accidentally and then washes her hands. (Some children may get a contact reaction such as a skin rash if they touch food, but such contact is very unlikely to result in anything more.)

Your child doesn't need to worry that some microscopic contamination of a food may be on a table or place of contact. However, if your child then licks the food off her hand or is unaware that she has come in contact with the food and it somehow contaminates something else that goes into her mouth, then she is at risk of a more serious allergic reaction.

The simple rule is this: If your child can feel a food residue on his skin (for example, peanut butter if allergic to peanut, or breadcrumbs if allergic to wheat), he should wash his hands immediately or use a wet wipe to wipe off the residue.

Water and soap is an effective way to either wipe down the bench before sitting (being careful not to touch the offending food if possible) or to wash hands and skin after accidental contact has occurred.

Eating Off a Plate or Napkin

Kids with food allergies don't need to have their own eating utensils and can use the school or caterer's utensils, but these should be properly washed in hot soapy water to avoid cross-contamination.

Refer to Chapter 7 for more on cross-contamination and Chapter 8 for advice about setting up your home for food-allergic kids.

Steering Clear of Sloppy Eaters

In general, your child needs to ingest the problem allergen in order to get a serious food allergy reaction. Children are unlikely to be at risk of reacting to a food just by sitting close to people who are eating the food that they're allergic to.

This is why the Australian Society of Clinical Immunologists and Allergists doesn't recommend food banning at school. Educating school-aged allergic children not to share food is the best way to keep them safe.

The exception to this rule are pre-schoolers. ASCIA advises that food banning may be appropriate in some areas within kindergartens and pre-school childcare centres (such as rooms that look after a child with food allergy) because toddlers are notoriously sloppy eaters (and naturally curious) and the risk of accidental ingestion by children with food allergies is much higher. However, a more general food ban for the entire kindergarten or pre-school childcare centre isn't recommended.

Avoiding Lunch Room Food Swaps and Food Fights

Food trading at school seems to be a time-honoured tradition and, although some parents may be horrified to hear this, is quite common. Some teachers turn a blind eye to it while others even condone it with the belief that lunch box food swapping might sharpen trading skills — a great asset for children wanting to be stock brokers!

The difficulty is that a child who has a food allergy really shouldn't engage in food trading due to the unknown risks involved with eating someone else's food — meaning that child may be isolated or marginalised. Again, it comes back to teaching your child not to share food. But asking your child about food swapping is worthwhile — check whether it occurs at her school and, if it does, how she feels about it. If she's feeling left out, a quiet word to the teacher might be in order.

As for food fights: Most schools now have a no-tolerance policy. Although some kids may think they're just having fun, food fights really aren't acceptable for all sorts of reasons apart from the risks for food allergic children.

For some students, the last day of secondary school has evolved into a highly ritualised event called 'muck-up day', and 'egging' or throwing raw eggs as missiles at other children in the playground frequently occurs on such days. Again, the practice of egging can be dangerous for all sorts of reasons, not just because of the risks to egg-allergic children.

Luckily, teachers have cracked down (no pun intended) on the egging that can occur during muck-up day, but teachers and parents do need to remain vigilant to preventing this type of silly and dangerous behaviour.

Stocking up on Healthy, Yet Yummy, Snacks

Providing your child with healthy, allergen-free snacks to take to school or child care is important. The snacks can then be given when classroom food sharing occurs at times of celebration such as birthdays or special occasions such as Christmas or Easter. You can also provide a packaged product, such as allergen-free sweets or chocolate, that can be on hand for any unexpected occasions — since your teacher may not always know when another child might be bringing in a celebratory cake, for example.

Some parents of children with coeliac disease provide a tasty gluten-free cake recipe for the class at the start of the year. You can try this tactic for your child with food allergy, too, but keep in mind that not every parent in a class may wish to comply with this request.

Asking for Help Immediately When Feeling Funny

One of the most important things your child needs to know is when and how to get help if he thinks he's having a food allergy reaction. Waiting until it's too late to do something about possible symptoms is pointless — and dangerous.

Children with food allergies should be told that

- ✔ They should ask for help from the nearest adult if they're concerned that they might be having any symptoms, no matter how mild.

- ✔ Asking for help when they're starting to feel funny won't necessarily activate any intervention but rather enables an informed plan to be discussed and activated as necessary.

- ✔ They should take an active role in assessing the risk of the situation.

- ✔ A rash or vomiting in itself isn't a sign of anaphylaxis but may be one of the early signs.

Emphasis should be given to explaining that any symptoms involving the airway, breathing or the circulation, such as coughing, wheezing, shortness of breath, feeling faint or an impending sense of collapse, should activate concerns about anaphylaxis, administration of adrenaline and calling an ambulance. Refer to Chapter 7 for information about treating allergic reactions, and Chapter 11 for details about emergency action plans.

Foster an awareness in your child of the early signs and symptoms of an immediate reaction. Teach your child the following three important points:

- ✔ Symptoms may differ with each reaction — so your child needs to be aware of all of the potential symptoms, as described in Chapter 2.

✔ Symptoms usually occur right after eating the food but can occur up to one to two hours later.

✔ Your child should seek help immediately in the case of any of these early warning signs:

- Itchiness in or around the mouth

- Rash

- Vomiting

- Tightness in the throat or any difficulty breathing

- An impending sense of doom — even if your child's not sure that she has accidentally eaten an allergen, because it's better to be safe than sorry

Carrying an Emergency Action Plan

That your child understands that he should always carry his emergency action plan and his adrenaline auto-injector (if he has been prescribed one) is absolutely critical. Emergency action plans are available on the ASCIA website (www.allergy.org.au) and should be filled out in consultation with your child's doctor. Several different types of allergy plans are available, depending on whether your child carries an adrenaline auto-injector and, if so, which brand (refer to Chapter 11 for more information on emergency action plans).

Chapter 15

Ten (Well, Almost!) Common Food Replacements

*T*he first step to managing your child's food allergies is to help her avoid her food allergens (read more on managing food allergies in Chapter 7). This can be a challenging task for you and other people who care for your child because the most common food allergens are prominent ingredients in foods from almost all cultures. Egg, milk and wheat are especially difficult to avoid in Western diets, because they're staples in this kind of diet. Nuts are also difficult to avoid simply because they're common ingredients in snack foods, cakes and biscuits.

In this chapter, we provide some tips on how to replace the common food allergens in your child's diet and in cooking.

Replacing Egg in Cooking

Egg allergy is the commonest food allergy in children. Children with egg allergy react to allergens contained within the egg white, but the yolk can often be contaminated with some egg white so if your child has egg allergy, your child needs to avoid both the egg yolk and the egg white. Chapter 4 covers egg allergy in more detail.

The proteins in other bird eggs are similar to the proteins in hen's eggs, so all eggs (for example, duck or quail egg) should be avoided by children with egg allergy.

Avoiding egg in the diet can be difficult because it's a very common ingredient in many foods that children eat. Eggs are used in baking to bind ingredients together or to aerate the ingredients allowing a light texture. However, you can use several options to replace egg when you're baking:

- **Commercially available egg replacer:** Options include Orgran Egg Replacer, which is a powder made from potato starch, tapioca flour and vegetable gums. This product can be purchased from online allergy stores, health food stores and some supermarkets.

- **Home-made egg replacers:** These can be made out of water and baking powder, or gelatine, vegetable or fruit, as follows (each recipe replacing one egg):

  - 1 teaspoon baking powder, 1 tablespoon water, 1 tablespoon vinegar
  - 1½ tablespoons water, 1½ tablespoons oil, 1 teaspoon baking powder
  - ⅓ cup water and 2 teaspoons gelatine — dissolve gelatine in warm water
  - ¼ cup mashed potato or pumpkin
  - ½ cup mashed banana or puree apple

Egg substitutes can't be used to replace egg if you have egg allergy — these are made of egg whites and are used for people with high cholesterol (who aren't allergic to egg but wish to avoid egg yolk, which contains cholesterol). If your child is allergic to egg, your child must avoid egg substitutes — you can recognise egg substitutes on ingredient labels because the label clearly lists egg as an ingredient.

Children with egg allergy don't usually have to avoid egg lecithin or egg emulsifier. Egg lecithin and egg emulsifier are made from the fat component of the egg and the chance of an allergic reaction to these ingredients is very unlikely.

Finding Alternatives to Cow's Milk Formula for Babies

Cow's milk allergy is one of the most common food allergies in children. In the first year of life, breast milk or formula milk is the predominant source of nutrition for a baby and most formula milks are made from cow's milk.

So, if your baby has cow's milk allergy and is under one year of age, you need to choose the right replacement that still provides an adequate source of nutrition.

A good way to manage cow's milk allergy is to breastfeed your baby. Although small amounts of milk allergen can cross over into your breast milk, most babies don't react to such small amounts of milk allergen and you can continue to take cow's milk and cow's milk products in your diet. Some babies with delayed forms of allergy to cow's milk do react to the small amounts of cow's milk allergen in breast milk and you may need to avoid cow's milk and cow's milk products in your diet while you're still breastfeeding. Your child's doctor can advise you on this.

Some mothers and babies are unable to breastfeed, and need an alternative milk formula that doesn't contain cow's milk allergens. The formula that's suitable for your baby depends on the type of cow's milk allergy and how old your baby is.

If your baby has an IgE mediated allergy and is

- ✔ Under six months of age, current recommendations advise to use an *extensively hydrolysed formula* (eHF; a special low-allergy cow's milk formula) as a replacement to standard cow's milk formula.

- ✔ Older than six months, you can use soy formula.

- ✔ Also allergic to soy milk, your doctor prescribes an eHF for your baby.

- ✔ Unable to tolerate eHF, your doctor prescribes a different formula called an *elemental formula*. Around 5–10 per cent of infants who are allergic to cow's milk can't tolerate eHF (because they react to the small amounts of cow's milk allergen that remain in eHF) and need an elemental formula. Elemental formulas are made of single amino acids (the building blocks of proteins) and don't contain any cow's milk or soy proteins.

If your baby has a delayed form of cow's milk allergy, the type of formula that's suitable as a replacement for cow's milk formula depends upon the type of delayed allergy your baby has and whether your baby is growing nicely.

For babies who

- ✔ Have poor growth due to a cow's milk allergy and babies with the non-IgE mediated conditions (food protein induced enterocolitis (FPIES) or food protein induced procto-colitis), the appropriate replacement is eHF.

- ✔ Have eosinophilic oesophagitis, one of the mixed IgE/non-IgE mediated forms of cow's milk allergy, an elemental formula is recommended.

✔ Are older than six months, with milder forms of delayed cow's milk allergy that cause tummy pain and diarrhoea, eczema or colic, and who are growing well, soy formula can be offered.

Your doctor can also advise you on the best formula replacement for your baby.

Partially hydrolysed cow's milk formulas (pHF), also known as hypoallergenic HA cow's milk formulas (available without prescriptions) aren't suitable for babies with cow's milk allergy because they contain some cow's milk allergens that can cause allergic reactions. pHF (HA formulas) may be effective for the prevention of allergic disease in babies at high risk of developing an allergic disease (those with a first-degree relative who has one of the allergic diseases, such as asthma or hay fever), and can be recommended for high-risk babies if the mother is unable to breastfeed in the first four to six months (refer to Chapter 3 for more on prevention of food allergy). However, evidence is now emerging that pHFs are ineffective in the prevention of food allergies and eczema.

Goat's milk, sheep's milk and other animal milks are very similar to cow's milk and usually cause allergic reactions in babies with cow's milk allergy, so formulas made from these milks aren't a suitable alternative for babies with cow's milk allergy. Non-formula milks, such as whole soy milk and cereal-based drinks, aren't suitable for babies under one year of age.

Swapping Out Cow's Milk for Older Children

Cow's milk and cow's milk products such as cheese or yoghurt are important sources of protein, fat, calcium and vitamin A and D. Like egg, cow's milk is a common part of the diet and can be difficult to avoid.

If your child is older than one year of age and is no longer on formula, you can replace cow's milk products with soy versions, including soy milk, soy yoghurt, soy cheese, soy ice cream and soy cream. Milk-free butters and margarines (such as Nuttelex and Becel) are widely available, as are other milk options, including cereal milks such as rice milk or oat milk.

All of these products are available at the supermarket — just make sure you choose products that are fortified with calcium because this means that calcium has been added to the soy or cereal milk product to match the levels contained in cow's milk.

Some soy cheeses contain *casein*, which is a cow's milk protein, so you need to check the ingredient list and avoid these brands. Also, some soy yoghurts use cow's milk in the starter culture so most children who are highly allergic to cow's milk may still react to these.

A2 milk is cow's milk that doesn't contain A1 beta casein, but still contains all of the other proteins in cow's milk, so most children with cow's milk allergy aren't able to drink this product.

Cow's milk and cow's milk products are the main source of calcium in your child's diet, so you need to ensure that your child's calcium intake is adequate if you've taken cow's milk out of the diet. A person's calcium needs change depending on age. If your child's calcium intake is lower than the daily recommended amount for her age, your doctor or pharmacist can recommend a calcium supplement, available at supermarkets and pharmacies.

Replacing Nuts

Two types of nuts can cause allergies: Peanuts and tree nuts.

Peanut is a legume and grows in the ground. Peanut allergy affects 1 to 2 per cent of children. Tree nuts are nuts that grow on trees, such as cashews, hazelnuts, almonds, walnuts, pecan nuts, pistachios, brazil nuts, macadamia nuts and pine nuts. The most common tree nut allergy is cashew allergy. Other common tree nut allergies include hazelnut, almond and walnut allergy, but children can be allergic to any of the tree nuts. Peanut and tree nut allergies are more likely to cause a severe allergic reaction (anaphylaxis) than other food allergies, and are the most common cause of a food-induced anaphylaxis.

Children with peanut allergy are more likely (a 20 to 30 per cent chance) to also be allergic to tree nuts. Because of this increased risk for having other nut allergies, your child's doctor may perform allergy tests for the tree nuts. Depending on the results of these tests, the doctor may be able to confirm whether or not your child has an allergy to the tree nuts but, in many cases, the testing may not provide a clear answer and a food challenge is required to clarify whether an allergy is present or not. (Refer to Chapter 6 for more on testing for food allergies.)

Clarifying whether your child has a tree nut allergy may be more important if your family relies on nuts as a staple part of the diet, such as if your family are vegetarian or vegan.

Most children with peanut allergy don't have allergies to the tree nuts and can include the tree nuts in their diet, taking care to avoid any situations that can result in cross-contamination, such as mixed-nut products.

Most of our patients who are allergic to peanut but not the tree nuts can eat cashew butter, almonds, Nutella and other tree nut products, while taking care to avoid mixed nuts and any food that they can't be sure doesn't contain peanut.

Peanut oil is something that can cause confusion. Here's how you can tell the difference between peanut oil options:

- ✔ Refined peanut oils have been highly processed to remove the peanut proteins, so higher quality peanut oils are usually safe for children with peanut allergy.
- ✔ Less-refined oil products, such as cold-pressed peanut oil, still have some peanut proteins remaining, and can cause allergic reactions in some children who are highly allergic to peanut and react to even small amounts of peanut protein.

If your child has a severe allergy to peanut, you may need to avoid peanut oils, but most children with peanut allergy can tolerate peanut oil used in cooking.

A number of foods sound like they may be a nut but aren't. Coconut comes from the seed of the palm tree, nutmeg is from the seed of the drupaceous fruit, and water chestnuts are the edible portion of a plant root; so these are not related to peanut or tree nuts. Although peanut is a legume and comes from the same family as other legumes, beans and pulses such as soy, lentils and peas, children with peanut allergy can eat these other foods safely.

If your child is allergic to peanut or tree nuts and these foods are an important part of your family's diet, you can try some alternatives. For example, if your child is only allergic to peanut and can take the other nuts, a healthy alternative to peanut butter is to try options from the Naturals Nut Spread range, such as almond, brazil and cashew spread, which has a similar appearance and taste to peanut butter.

If your child is allergic to both peanut and the tree nuts, you may consider soy butter or sunflower butter, which also have a similar texture to peanut butter. Snack foods commonly contain nuts, so you need to stock up on nut-free snack alternatives, such fresh or dried fruit, or seek out nut-free snack products such as nut-free chocolate.

Removing Wheat

Wheat is a common staple in most diets around the world. Children with wheat allergy need to avoid all forms of wheat, but they don't usually have to avoid other cereal grains, such as barley, oat or rye, unless they're also allergic to these. Your child's doctor or dietitian can advise you on whether your child with wheat allergy can try these other grains.

People with coeliac disease must avoid all gluten-containing foods, which includes wheat, barley, oat and rye, whereas people with wheat allergy can usually tolerate other grains that contain gluten such as oats and rye. So gluten-free products are safe for your child with wheat allergy, but your child isn't necessarily restricted to these products.

You can use a number of cereal grains to replace wheat if your child is allergic to wheat; these include

- Amaranth
- Arrowroot
- Buckwheat
- Chia
- Chickpea or besan
- Corn (maize)
- Millet
- Rice
- Potato
- Quinoa
- Sago
- Sorghum
- Soy
- Tapioca

All of these grains can be used in place of wheat in cooking and most of these are available as flour.

Some children may also be allergic to multiple grains so make sure you try the different grain replacements individually. Most supermarkets and health food stores offer products made from these alternative grains.

Kamut, spelt, semolina and triticale are types of wheat so aren't suitable replacements for children with wheat allergies.

Some wheat-based ingredients don't contain wheat protein and so don't have to be avoided. Ingredients like glucose, glucose syrup, caramel colour, dextrose and monosodium glutamate are made from wheat but are so highly purified and processed that no wheat proteins are left in the ingredient.

Avoiding Soy

Soybeans and soy products are a common ingredient in Asian diets. Although soybeans are less prominent as a food in the Western diet, soy is commonly used as a flour in commercially prepared processed foods.

If your child has soy allergy, your child needs to avoid all of the different foods that are made from soy. Many low-allergy foods (for milk or wheat allergy) are made from soy and so aren't suitable for your child with soy allergy. If your child is allergic to cow's milk or wheat as well as soy, you may want to get advice from a dietitian to help you manage your child's diet.

Some ingredients are made from soy but don't contain any soy protein and can be tolerated by most children with soy allergy. Soy lecithin and soy oil are made from the fat component of soybeans, and don't usually cause allergic reactions in children with soy allergy. However, more caution may be required if your child has had severe allergic reactions (anaphylaxis) to small amounts of soy because soy oils may contain small amounts of soy protein.

Because of the way soy is used in Western diets and foods, usually a very similar product is available that doesn't contain soy. This means the issue is usually simply avoiding soy rather than trying to find a soy replacement. However, families with a vegetarian or vegan diet (who may use soy products such as tofu and tempeh as a good source of protein), may need a soy replacement. Options include other legumes such as chickpeas, lentils and kidney beans, and mushrooms.

Replacing Milk and Soy

Between 20 and 40 per cent of children with cow's milk allergy also have a soy allergy, and need to avoid both foods (see earlier sections on replacing cow's milk and replacing soy). Babies with delayed forms of allergy to cow's milk (non-IgE or mixed IgE/non-IgE mediated allergy) are more likely to develop an allergy to soy milk than babies with IgE mediated cow's milk allergy, possibly because they're more likely to have inflammation of the gut lining, which can result in a leaky intestinal barrier.

If your baby is on formula and has allergy to cow's milk and soy milk, your doctor can prescribe an extensively hydrolysed formula (eHF).

For older infants and children who are allergic to both cow's milk and soy milk, they may take cereal milks such as rice milk or oat milk. These are available at supermarkets and health food stores — just make sure you choose a brand that has been fortified with calcium, meaning that calcium has been added into the milk, because this helps to maintain your child's calcium intake.

Avoiding foods that contain cow's milk as well as foods that contain soy can result in a very restricted diet and you need to ensure that your child's nutritional needs are still being met. Your child's doctor can refer you to a dietitian who specialises in food allergies to guide with appropriate replacement options and help you plan a diet that provides adequate calories and nutrition for your child.

Keeping Away from Fish

Fish allergy is more common in adults and usually develops during adult life but some children can have allergy to fish. (Children can often have allergy to just one or two types of fish, whereas adults with fish allergy are usually allergic to most other fish.)

The proteins in fish are generally heat stable and aren't destroyed by cooking — although some people can tolerate tinned fish (which has been cooked at very high temperatures) even though they still react to freshly cooked or raw forms of the fish. If your child has fish allergy, your child's doctor may suggest allergy tests to work out if you can still include other fish in your child's diet. If your child is only allergic to one or two types of fish, you can simply replace the problem fish with another fish option. However, if your child is allergic to a number of fish, avoiding all fish is best.

Children who are allergic to fish can have an allergic reaction to vapours coming from the fish while it's cooking, and this can cause serious allergic reactions (anaphylaxis) as the allergen is inhaled, particularly if asthma is poorly controlled. Care should be taken if you're going to a seafood restaurant because vapours from cooking fish are highly likely to be in the air and because of the risk of cross-contamination during food preparation and serving.

Fish is a good source of protein and good fats (omega-3 fatty acids). If your child is allergic to fish, you may offer other healthy sources of protein such as shellfish or tofu, or meat such as chicken. Most children allergic to fish can tolerate shellfish — your doctor can advise you on this.

Sidestepping Shellfish

Shellfish allergy refers to allergies caused by the invertebrate seafoods, such as crustaceans, molluscs, cephalopods and gastropods. (Chapter 4 explains these groups in further detail.)

The proteins that cause allergy to a crustacean are different to the proteins that cause allergy to the molluscs, so being allergic to a crustacean doesn't necessarily mean that you're also allergic to molluscs, although some people can be allergic to both. Similarly, the proteins that cause allergy to shellfish are different to the proteins that cause allergy to fish so having a shellfish allergy doesn't necessarily mean that you're allergic to fish — although some people are allergic to both shellfish and fish.

In general, if your child is allergic to one of the crustaceans, he's likely to also be allergic to other crustaceans in the group, and you should avoid all the crustaceans. However, your child may not be allergic to molluscs and so can still eat these. In reverse, if your child is allergic to a mollusc, she's likely to be allergic to other molluscs in the group and you should avoid all molluscs; however, she may be able to tolerate the crustacean shellfish.

Shellfish are a healthy source of protein, but don't contain any essential nutrients, so can be replaced with any other forms of protein that your child likes. If your child is allergic to the crustacean family of shellfish, you can offer fish, molluscs, or other protein foods such as meat. If your child is allergic to the mollusc family of shellfish, you can replace these with crustacean shellfish, fish or meat.

Chapter 16

Ten Myths about Food Allergies

In some ways, food allergy is a very straightforward condition. If children avoid the food or foods that they're allergic to, they're just normal healthy kids. Certainly, they don't need to take regular medication and, other than be alert to special high-risk situations, they can enjoy all of the regular activities that children without food allergy do.

On the other hand, everyone seems to have an opinion about food allergy and sometimes even allergists seem to offer quite diverse advice. We think the mixture of the readily explained and the complex and confusing is what leads to so many of the myths, misperceptions and, at times, downright-silly falsehoods that surround these increasingly common set of conditions.

In this chapter, we look at the ten more common such issues our patients bring up with us.

Anaphylaxis Can Occur If You Look at a Peanut

An incredible amount of misinformation seems to surround which situations can precipitate a food allergic reaction. Essentially, you need to ingest a food to get a reaction that might be dangerous. Studies have shown that you can't get an allergic reaction from smelling peanut butter.

The only exception to the rule is exposure to highly aerosolised food particles as might occur with cooking foods (particularly fish and shellfish) at high temperatures. In general, the reactions from aerosolised food allergens are likely to be local reactions, such as eye swelling or a runny nose; however, a more serious allergic reaction such as anaphylaxis could occur if the airborne allergen is inhaled in large enough doses (and is more likely with fish and shellfish allergy).

Touching a Food Can Lead to a Severe Reaction

Touching an allergen may cause a local reaction but, quite frankly, unless your child rolls around in a vat of peanut butter, the dose received by skin contact is unlikely to cause anything other than a local skin rash, such as redness or hives, at that point of contact.

Katie was once called by a journalist with a curious question. A school had sent out a statement to the press who were due to visit the school to cover a prime ministerial visit. The statement apparently requested (Katie didn't actually see the media release) that journalists refrain from eating bananas for 12 hours prior to entering the school grounds. Katie reassured the somewhat incredulous journalist that, although uncommon, banana allergy does occur. Because she was not aware of the exact clinical scenario, Katie couldn't comment on whether the request was reasonable or not. However, she did reassure the journalist that most food allergic reactions occur only after ingestion and that a journalist who had eaten a banana and washed her hands prior to setting foot on the school premises was unlikely to endanger a child with food allergy, particularly if kissing was not an anticipated activity.

Drinking Soft Drink Is a Treatment for Anaphylaxis

An old-wives tale (less commonly heard now) says that if a child has a food allergy reaction the best thing to do is to give the child a cola drink. Some old wives tales are not necessarily silly but, in this case, you can have absolutely no doubt that this is just nonsense and potentially extremely dangerous — particularly if the administration of adrenaline is delayed by trialling this theory first. Furthermore, the risk of *aspiration* (through vomiting stomach contents and then inhaling them into the airway) in this scenario is likely to increase dramatically.

Another common urban myth is to make the child vomit to help hasten the resolution of the reaction. This is also a highly dangerous practice, again because the risk of aspiration is increased significantly.

Parents of Kids with Food Allergies Are Overanxious

Until quite recently, a commonly held misconception was that food allergies didn't actually exist. Even today, some grandparents remain somewhat sceptical about the existence of food allergy, since 'Food allergies just weren't around in my day'.

Not only do parents sometimes need to contend with scepticism about whether their child has food allergy but a second problem is that the measures taken to deal with food allergy can seem foreign and the risks exaggerated to the older generation.

To be fair, some parents — clearly a very tiny minority — can overdo how careful they have to be with allergen avoidance. However, the same can be said for almost every potential risk in life. Some people are overanxious, some are underanxious and who's to say what the right level of anxiety is anyway. The most important thing is for parents to feel comfortable with the measures they take to feel in control of the risks that food allergy poses for their child.

Refer to Chapter 8 for information about educating family members about food allergies.

Kids with Food Allergies Want to Be Different or Special

Sure kids who don't want to eat their broccoli might be more than a little misguided when they whine, 'I don't want to eat this; I'm allergic to greens'. But just because some kids use fussy eating habits as a reason not to try new foods doesn't mean that kids with food allergy like to be different.

Certainly, most tell you that they just wish the problem would go away. Others don't know what all the fuss is about and seem to get on with life without making a big deal about the problem. Every kid is different and most kids have aspects of their lives they do and don't like. For kids with food allergy, this is just more obvious than for other problems other kids might face.

Read Chapter 14 to learn about some key lessons to teach your kids about food allergies, and dealing with other people's reactions.

Overusing Antibacterial Handwash Has Caused the Food Allergy Epidemic

No evidence exists that being too clean or hygienic in the home increases the risk of food allergy, or that anti-bacterial handwashes are either good or bad with regards to risk of food allergy.

A current theory, termed the *hygiene hypothesis*, looks at hygiene as one of the factors that may have resulted in the food allergy epidemic. However, this hypothesis relates to the exposure to infections and microbes in early life (as discussed further in Chapter 2) rather than how clean your home environment is. The hygiene hypothesis is probably more related to the overall exposure to good and bad bacteria that occurs over the course of a child's life, particularly during pregnancy and the first years of life, than solely to the exposure to bugs that occurs in the home.

More work needs to be done before we can know for sure what is the cause of the allergy epidemic.

Allergies Happen Because We Bubble-Wrap Our Kids

Some in the community have the perception that children these days are protected from all sorts of risks that those who grew up in the last century were never concerned about.

Sure, the good old days involved fewer health and safety regulations and more freedom to take risks, but anyone with any sense would agree that car seatbelts, bike helmets, pool fences and in-ground or enclosed trampolines have protected a lot of people from unnecessary accidents. Certainly, bubble-wrapping our kids has not been a cause in the rise in food allergy even if these sorts of protective factors developed in parallel to the epidemic.

Increased Use of Preservatives and Chemicals Causes the Rise in Food Allergies

One of the most strongly held beliefs about why food allergies are on the rise is that allergies are linked to the use of preservatives and chemicals in our food chain supply.

A rise in the use of preservatives and chemicals has occurred over the last 30 to 40 years. However, no study has formally investigated this hypothesis. In fact, finding a community that hasn't had any exposure for the whole of their lives to some sort of chemical or preservative would be hard, and so such a study would be difficult to undertake.

You Can't Be Allergic to a Banana!

Some people can be incredulous when you say your child has a food allergy. After grumbling that 'Food allergies never occurred in my day' and 'You must be a clean freak', most people can be brought around to the fact that things like nut allergy really do exist and can actually be life-threatening.

So, if your child has a common food allergy, the battle is halfway won. However, for those with one of the less common types of food allergy, life can get quite awkward. More than 170 different foods have been reported to illicit a food allergy reaction — meaning almost any food you can think of can cause food allergy, including bananas. In fact, banana and latex allergy can sometimes go hand in hand (no pun intended).

Food Allergies Only Affect Kids

While food allergy is far more common in children, food allergies do still affect adults. In our HealthNuts study, we have been surprised how often parents tell us that they've had a reaction to a food that's quite consistent with an IgE mediated food allergy but haven't sought medical attention for the problem because they didn't think it was serious enough.

Most food allergies present early in life, but some IgE mediated food allergies, such as peanut, tree nut, fish and shellfish, can develop later in life as an adult — even when these foods have been previously tolerated.

If you're a parent with symptoms consistent with a food allergy, and with nut or shellfish allergy in particular, you really should see your doctor for further testing. Undiagnosed food allergy in adults can have severe consequences if not properly managed, especially in those with co-existent asthma.

Chapter 17

Ten (Plus Two!) Top Allergy Websites

- -

In This Chapter

▶ Finding reliable medical information and patient hand-outs

▶ Exploring patient support network links

▶ Accessing links to websites covering other allergic diseases

- -

*T*he internet is a treasure-trove of information that seems to be getting more enriched with data and information on an almost minute-by-minute basis. Unfortunately, the internet also provides a safe haven for quacks to set up as experts and misinformation can abound. So the biggest difficulty becomes deciding which websites are ones that you can trust.

In this chapter, we provide the most reliable and evidence-based websites that offer further reading about diagnosing or managing food allergies. We also provide links to support groups.

Note: We have no financial interest in any of the websites listed in this chapter. However, we sit on some of the medical advisory boards of organisations included — for example, Anaphylaxis Australia and AusEEkids — in a pro bono capacity. We are also both full members of the Australasian Society of Clinical Immunology and Allergy (ASCIA), which is the preeminent expert body in Australasia, and also sit on several subcommittees of ASCIA. All of the information presented in this book is in line with ASCIA guidelines and recommendations.

Allergy New Zealand

Allergy New Zealand (www.allergy.org.nz) is a national membership-based, not-for-profit group with the primary role of providing information, education and support to the many thousands of New Zealanders living with allergies, including those at risk of anaphylaxis.

Allergy NZ represents the interests of those suffering from allergy to government, policy makers and the media, and provides information and guidance to the health, education and food sectors, as well as providing support for research. The website offers links to commercial products for allergy sufferers and the *Allergy Today* magazine, and free e-anaphylaxis training and guidelines for those caring for children at risk of anaphylaxis.

Anaphylaxis Australia

Anaphylaxis Australia is a national patient support group that works closely with allergy specialists and the Australasian Society of Clinical Immunology and Allergy to provide accurate and up-to-date information on allergy and anaphylaxis to families with food allergy and the general community. The website (at www.allergyfacts.org.au) provides patient-friendly information designed to help individuals, parents and carers of people living with the risk of anaphylaxis.

Well-researched information is provided about how to care for your child at home, at schools and at school camp. The site also offers details on the Be a MATE program for friends of children with food allergies (refer to Chapter 9 for more).

The three key messages of Anaphylaxis Australia are

- ✓ Awareness
- ✓ Avoidance
- ✓ Action

Anaphylaxis Australia (of which Mimi is on the medical advisory board) has been extremely active in lobbying for the needs of those at risk of anaphylaxis at every level of government and within the medical community, as well as raising awareness in the general community.

Anaphylaxis Australia's website provides coronial inquest findings and recommendations on the tragic deaths that have occurred from anaphylaxis in Australia — these make for very sobering reading about the horror of otherwise healthy individuals dying after accidental ingestion reactions caused anaphylaxis.

ASCIA

The Australasian Society of Clinical Immunology and Allergy (or ASCIA) is the peak professional body of allergy and clinical immunology for Australia and New Zealand. Its members are health professionals or researchers with expertise in allergy and immunology.

The ASCIA website (www.allergy.org.au) is intended for use by the general public and health professionals and is easy to navigate, extremely up to date and evidence based. The site reflects the national standard of care for kids with food allergy and represents the views of the majority of academic allergists in Australasia. On the site, you can access patient information, action plans and care plans for food allergic individuals, as well as details on the most recent infant-feeding guidelines.

More recently, the site has added anaphylaxis and food allergy e-training modules that can be undertaken by anyone, but were developed particularly for those working in schools and childcare facilities, and for health-care professionals.

ASCIA, and its website, supports New Zealanders, too!

Asthma Foundation (Australia and New Zealand)

The Asthma Foundations in Australia (www.asthmaaustralia.org.au) and New Zealand (www.asthmanz.co.nz) are national patient support groups to help people with asthma (and linked conditions, including anaphylaxis) breathe better.

The Asthma Australia website is the overarching Australian website that comprises the individual Asthma Foundations from each state and territory. The site provides patient information, up-to-date research findings, stories of those with asthma and links to related websites.

Asthma Australia manages two programs funded under the Australian Government National Asthma Management Program. The site has a link to the National Strategic Directions document for 2011–2013, which outlines five strategic priority goals including providing education, training and advocacy for people with asthma and linked conditions. Some of the site is under construction as of October 2011.

The New Zealand Asthma Foundation's website offers information on asthma and managing an asthma emergency, as well as tips on creating a healthy home and finding an asthma-friendly school. The site also offers information for New Zealand Maori.

AusEE kids

AusEE Kids (www.ausee.org) is the website for the Australian charity providing support and information to anyone diagnosed with or caring for someone with an eosinophilic gastrointestinal disorder, including eosinophilic oesophagitis (EE or EoE). (Katie is on the medical advisory board for this charity). Eosinophilic oesophagitis is a mixed IgE/non-IgE mediated delayed food allergy.

The site provides patient-support information, including information about allergy-friendly recipes, media and medical journal articles, and books and magazines related to EoE.

Australian Gut Foundation

The Australian Gut Foundation (www.gutfoundation.com) is a not-for-profit organisation dedicated to conducting research and providing public education regarding the treatment and prevention of a range of gastrointestinal diseases and conditions. The site provides links to publications on coeliac disease, and patient information about endoscopic procedures and other gastrointestinal investigations.

Coeliac Australia and Coeliac New Zealand

Coeliac Australia's website (www.coeliac.org.au) is a support-group website that provides information and extensive links to resources for those suffering from coeliac disease. In order to become a member of one of the state-based Coeliac Societies your child requires a letter from a gastroenterologist outlining the histological confirmation of the disease. The website offers links to the *Australian Coeliac* magazine, which has information about patients with coeliac disease and related illnesses, and to the state-based newsletters.

The Coeliac New Zealand website (www.coeliac.org.nz) similarly provides information for those diagnosed with coeliac disease, offering links to education material about the disease and ways to maintain an gluten-free diet, including cookbooks and dining guides (this is a searchable tool for finding restaurants that offer gluten-free menus). The society collaborates with gluten-free manufacturers, medical professionals and supports research into coeliac disease.

Eczema Association of Australasia

The Eczema Association of Australasia provides an educational website (www.eczema.org.au) that offers practical information about living or caring for someone with eczema.

The site provides links to clinical research sites and includes information on how to join studies aimed at preventing eczema and egg allergy.

Food Allergy and Anaphylaxis Network (US)

The Food Allergy and Anaphylaxis Network (or FAAN — www.foodallergy.org) is a US-based, not-for-profit organisation founded in 1991 that aims to raise public awareness, and provide advocacy, education and advance research on behalf of and for all those affected by food allergies and anaphylaxis.

The website is very well linked in to a whole host of interesting sites and includes tips and handouts for food allergy sufferers. The site also offers an e-learning centre that includes some useful YouTube videos on such topics as Living with Food Allergies and Food Allergy Basics.

Food Standards Australia New Zealand

Food Standards Australia New Zealand (FSANZ) is an independent statutory agency established by the *Food Standards Australia New Zealand Act 1991*. FSANZ developed and administers the food standards code for Australia and New Zealand, which lists requirements for foods such as additives, food safety, labelling and genetically modified foods.

The FSANZ website (www.foodstandards.gov.au) is a rich source of consumer information about labelling, food recalls, food complaints and food additives. The site provides a science and education learning centre, access to a wealth of technical reports and policy development, and specific information about both mandatory and precautionary labelling under the food allergies section of the website. (Katie sits on the expert advisory committee for the FSANZ food labelling section.)

Ilhan Food Allergy Foundation

The Ilhan Food Allergy Foundation (www.ilhanfoundation.com.au) is a charitable trust dedicated to improving the lives of people with anaphylaxis and food allergy. The foundation provides funding for research and raises awareness about the issues surrounding these conditions through education of the public.

John Ilhan (of Crazy John's fame) cofounded the Ilhan Food Allergy Foundation with his wife, Patricia, in May 2006 after his daughter was found to have allergy to nuts. John passed away suddenly in October 2007 but his legacy continues through the ongoing involvement in the foundation by his wife. (Katie was appointed to the Board of the Ilhan Food Allergy Foundation in November 2011.)

The website mainly offers information on the foundation's partners and the research programs it has funded, which can provide a good coverage of the kind of research that's happening in Australia. The website also offers useful links to cookbooks and the like.

The Royal Children's Hospital's Information for Parents

The website of The Royal Children's Hospital Department of Allergy and Immunology (where both Katie and Mimi work) has a page with up-to-date patient information sheets on various allergic conditions, including food allergy and anaphylaxis. These patient information sheets explain the different conditions and their management. You can access the web page at www.rch.org.au/allergy. From there, just follow the links to parent information sheets.

The Royal Children's Hospital also provides a comprehensive kids health info (for parents) website that deals with a multitude of health problems; you can visit it at www.rch.org.au/kidsinfo. On this website, you find quality health information on a range of topics, with the information continually being added to. The fact sheets are written for parents and adolescents about medical conditions and hospital services. (To find the factsheet about allergies, click 'Browse by speciality'; the allergy section is found at the top of the list.)

Glossary

adjuvant: a compound with the ability to modulate the immune system; can be added together with an antigen as part of a vaccine or immunotherapy to enhance effects on the immune response to that particular antigen.

adrenaline auto-injector: A device that has been designed to deliver a single pre-measured dose of adrenaline. Available in Australia and New Zealand as an EpiPen or Anapen.

allergen: Component of a food that is recognised by the immune system as harmful. When the immune system sees these components, allergic symptoms are triggered.

allergen-specific IgE antibodies: IgE antibodies that recognise and bind to specific food allergens (such as egg-specific IgE or milk-specific IgE).

allergen-specific IgE blood test: A test which checks the level of allergen-specific IgE in the blood.

allergen-specific immunotherapy: A treatment for specific allergies to insect venom and aeroallergens (such as pollen or house dust mite) that reprograms the immune response to the allergen so the immune system no longer sees the allergen as harmful and the patient is cured of that allergy. The treatment usually involves subcutaneously injecting the allergen into the fatty tissues, starting at very low doses and increasing the amount of allergen until the highest maintenance dose is reached. This maintenance dose is then injected every month for between three (pollen immunotherapy) and five (insect venom immunotherapy) years. Can be *subcutaneous immunotherapy (SCIT)* or *sublingual immunotherapy (SLIT)*. More recently, *oral immunotherapy (OIT)* has been tested for the treatment of food allergy.

allergic diseases: A group of conditions that are all caused by unwanted immune responses that cause inflammation in tissues. They include asthma, atopic dermatitis, allergic rhinitis, food allergy and other specific allergies (such as drug, latex and insect venom allergies).

allergic rhinitis: An allergic disease involving inflammation in the inner lining of the nose; also known as hay fever.

allergy: When your immune system recognises a substance in your environment as harmful and so mounts an immune response to that substance, which can then lead to symptoms of an allergic reaction every time you're re-exposed to that substance.

allergy management plan: An individualised plan for a child with food allergy that includes information on the child's specific allergies, emergency contact details, risk minimisation plan and emergency action plan.

anaphylaxis: A severe IgE mediated allergic reaction affecting the breathing or circulation.

angioedema: Swelling of the skin tissue; during an IgE mediated allergic reaction, the swelling is most frequently seen affecting the face, especially the eyes and lips, but can also be more widespread.

asthma: An allergic disease involving allergic inflammation of the airways.

atopic march: The progression of allergic disorders during childhood. Food allergy and eczema are typically the first allergic conditions to develop and usually present in the first 3 to 12 months of life. Asthma and allergic rhinitis generally have a later onset, at around three to five years of age. Also known as the allergic march.

atopy: An underlying genetic tendency or predisposition to develop unwanted allergic responses to allergens.

clinical trial: An experimental study in human subjects to test the effects of an intervention; in the case of food allergy, a patient is given an intervention that is being tested for its ability to prevent or treat a food allergy. Includes a *randomised controlled trial.*

coeliac disease: A form of wheat intolerance caused by an abnormal immune reaction to enzymes in the intestinal wall (tissue transglutaminase) which is triggered by dietary gluten, found in wheat and other cereal grains, including barley and rye.

colitis: Inflammation of the colon; associated with a *non-IgE mediated food allergy.*

colon: Large intestine.

cross-contact: A small amount of an allergenic food is unintentionally mixed with another food during the cooking process or when the food is being served.

delayed food allergy: *See* non-IgE mediated food allergy and mixed IgE/ non-IgE mediated food allergy.

dermatographism: Where the skin forms a lump if scratched or drawn on.

desensitisation: Where a person can be exposed to a known allergen without reacting to it while on a specific treatment, but once treatment is stopped, that person again reacts to the allergen.

double-blind food challenge: A placebo controlled food challenge test where both the parents and child and the doctor and nurse don't know whether the food or a placebo is being offered to the child.

eczema: An allergic disease involving allergic inflammation of the skin.

emergency action plan: A medical plan that has been completed and signed by the child's doctor that outlines the signs of an IgE mediated allergic reaction, what to do if the child has an allergic reaction, what medications have been prescribed for the child and when to use them.

endoscopy: A test where a *gastroenterologist* looks inside the gut at the lining of the intestine and can take samples of the intestine wall for more detailed examination under the microscope. Endoscopies can help with the diagnosis of *non-IgE mediated food allergy* and *mixed IgE/non-IgE mediated food allergy.*

enteropathy: Inflammation of the small intestine; associated with a *non-IgE mediated food allergy*.

eosinophilic esophagitis (EoE): Inflammation of the esophagus; associated with a *mixed IgE/non-IgE mediated food allergy*. *See also* eosinophils.

eosinophils: Allergy inflammatory cells within the esophagus that occurs with *eosinophilic esophagitis (EoE)*.

food allergy: When the immune system incorrectly interprets food as harmful and the ensuing immune response to that food causes an allergic reaction.

food challenge test: A hospital-based test that involves giving a child the food in question, starting with small amounts and progressively increasing the amount every 15 to 20 minutes, while watching to see if a reaction develops. The food challenge test is positive if a reaction develops and negative if the child completes the challenge and takes a standard serving of the food without reacting.

food elimination and reintroduction challenge: Where a problem food is taken out of the diet for a period of time (usually at least two weeks) and then put back into the diet to check if symptoms reappear.

food hypersensitivity: Any reproducible reaction to food. Food hypersensitivities may be either a *food allergy* or a *food intolerance*.

food intolerance: All reproducible reactions to foods that aren't food allergies. Food intolerances are caused by substances within the food itself that can cause a bad reaction, or problems in the body that make it difficult to digest the food.

food-dependent exercise-induced anaphylaxis: Where a person develops anaphylaxis if that person eats an allergen and exercises within several hours of each other. Known to occur with wheat and shellfish.

food-induced enteropathy: A *non-IgE mediated food allergy* where food proteins cause damage to the lining of the small intestine, resulting in diarrhoea, abdominal pain, bloating and irritability.

food-protein-induced enterocolitis syndrome (FPIES): A *non-IgE mediated food allergy* with inflammation of the small and large intestine. The condition usually presents in the first year of life and is associated with profuse vomiting approximately two to four hours after eating a newly introduced food.

gastroenterologist: Physician specialising in gut conditions.

gastroesophageal reflux: Vomiting and frequent regurgitation; may be associated with a *mixed IgE/non-IgE mediated food allergy* in some cases.

heat labile: Where the structure of the allergen is rapidly changed by heat from cooking.

hives: Itchy lumps that look like mosquito bites.

hygiene hypothesis: The association between improved living conditions and allergies. Researchers now believe that the overall reduction in exposure to microbes has influenced allergic disease rates, and that diverse and abundant microbial exposures in early life play an important role in the development of a healthy immune system that averts allergic responses. Also known as the microbial hypothesis.

IgE antibodies: Responsible for initiating immediate allergic responses; presence of *allergen-specific IgE antibodies* is known as sensitisation. Also known as allergy antibodies.

IgE mediated food allergy: Food allergy where symptoms such as hives, swelling of the face, eyes or mouth, vomiting or anaphylaxis usually occur within minutes of food ingestion, although some symptoms, such as vomiting, diarrhoea or an eczema flare, may occur up to a few hours later. Also known as *immediate food allergy*.

immediate food allergy: *See* IgE mediated food allergy.

lactase: An enzyme that resides in the tips of the villous lining the small intestine and breaks down the milk sugar, lactose.

mandatory statements: Statements that list the most common food allergens — peanut, tree nuts, milk, egg, sesame, fish, shellfish, soy and gluten — as well as products derived from those foods, if used as ingredients in the food. These statements are governed by laws set down by the Australia New Zealand Food Standards code. Customers must be able to identify any potential allergens, including products made from an allergen.

mast cells: Specialised allergy cells that sit in the skin, airways and intestines and that have receptors on their surface that allow IgE antibodies to bind tightly. When an *allergen* binds to the IgE antibodies, the mast cell is activated to release a range of mediators (histamine, leukotrienes and others) that cause the immediate allergic reaction.

mixed IgE/non-IgE mediated food allergy: Food allergy that involves both IgE and non-IgE immune mechanisms. Symptoms are similar to those of *non-IgE mediated food allergy* — usually associated with gut problems, with the most common symptoms being vomiting, diarrhoea, abdominal pain and colic, usually occurring several hours after ingestion of the food. This is a type of delayed food allergy.

non-IgE mediated food allergy: Food allergy that does not involve IgE immune mechanisms. Symptoms are similar to those of *mixed IgE/non-IgE mediated food allergy* — usually associated with gut problems, with the most common symptoms being vomiting, diarrhoea, abdominal pain and colic, usually occurring several hours after ingestion of the food. This is a type of delayed food allergy.

observational study: A gathering of observed data. Includes a *population-based study*.

open food challenge: A food challenge test where both the parents and child and the doctor and nurse know when the food is being offered.

oral allergy syndrome: Where local symptoms in the mouth develop when eating raw fruits and vegetables. This is typically seen in people with pollen allergy, because some allergens in grass and tree pollens are cross-reactive with allergens contained within fruits and vegetables.

oral immunotherapy: Where an allergen compound is taken orally once daily, starting at a low dose and then increasing the dose gradually to reach a higher maintenance dose. The maintenance dose is then continued for varying amounts of time of up to one or two years. This is a research treatment and has not yet been shown to reprogram the immune system to induce tolerance to an allergen. *See also* allergen-specific immunotherapy.

osmotic diarrhoea: Where non-digested lactose takes water with it down the intestinal tract and causes diarrhoea.

peptides: Small protein fragments that don't trigger an immediate allergic reaction during allergen-specific immunotherapy.

population-based study: A study that involves a large random sample of participants from the general population.

prebiotics: Indigestible fibre taken in the diet that can selectively stimulate the growth and/or activity of good bacteria in the gut.

probiotics: Live microbial organisms that benefit the host by improving intestinal microbial balance

proctocolitis: Inflammation of the rectum and colon; causes diarrhoea that can be streaked with blood. This is a *non-IgE mediated food allergy*.

randomised controlled trial: A type of clinical trial where the subjects are randomly assigned to receive the active intervention being tested or a dummy placebo control. This is the best type of clinical trial. Can be *open*, *single-blind* or *double-blind*.

reverse causation: When a lifestyle factor is found to be associated with the outcome (for example, the food allergy) but in the reverse direction. Being at risk of food allergy is the reason someone has chosen a lifestyle factor — the lifestyle factor isn't the cause of the food allergy.

risk minimisation plan: This is part of the individualised *allergy management plan*. Outlines the situations or ways that a child with food allergy could be accidentally exposed to known allergens while at school or child care, and practical strategies to minimise those risks. The plan should also cover who's responsible for implementing these strategies.

sensitised: When a person makes allergy antibodies to an allergen. This may or may not mean that the person is allergic to the allergen; that is, the person may or may not develop an allergic reaction to that allergen when exposed.

single-blind food challenge: A food challenge test where the doctor and nurse know when the food is being offered but the child and parents don't.

skin prick test (SPT): Where a small amount of allergen is introduced into the skin. *See also* wheal.

subcutaneous immunotherapy (SCIT): Where doses of allergen are injected into the fatty tissue in the arm, aiming to reprogram the immune system to develop tolerance to the allergen. *See also* allergen-specific immunotherapy.

sublingual immunotherapy (SLIT): Where an allergen is made up as drops or a dissolvable tablet that's kept under the tongue for two to five minutes and then swallowed or expelled, aiming to reprogram the immune system to develop tolerance to the allergen. *See also* allergen-specific immunotherapy.

T cells: Specialised immune cells that direct immune responses. T helper type 2 cells are responsible for the development of allergic immune responses.

tolerance: A type of immune response to an antigen or allergen where the immune system recognises the antigen or allergen as safe and actively suppresses unwanted responses. Acquisition of tolerance occurs when the immune system in a person with allergy is reprogrammed away from an allergic response towards a tolerance response, and the immune system no longer recognises the allergen as harmful — the person is able to tolerate the allergen without developing an allergic reaction to it.

urticaria: Symptoms of an immediate allergic reaction that look like welts or mosquito bites on the skin. Also known as *hives*.

Voluntary Incidental Trace Allergen Labelling (VITAL): Risk-management tool that requires testing of the food to measure the allergen content and provides a standardised approach for food producers to assess the risk of allergen cross-contact and guidance in assigning appropriate allergen precautionary labelling for their food products. The program is voluntary but is different to other *voluntary statements* that don't require measurement of allergen levels within food.

voluntary statements: These are sometimes listed on food labels by manufacturers to indicate the possibility of cross-contamination with allergen during the production process. Such statements are voluntary and aren't based on any testing or measurement of allergen levels in the food.

wheal: A bump on the skin that can occur during a skin prick test. When the allergen binds to allergen-specific IgE antibodies on the surface of *mast cells*, the mast cells are activated and release a host of immune factors that cause redness and a wheal at the site of the skin test.

Index

FOR DUMMIES®

Health, Fitness & Pregnancy

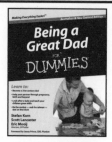

978-0-73037-735-1
$29.95

978-1-74216-972-9
$39.95

978-0-73037-739-9
$39.95

978-1-74216-946-0
$39.95

978-0-73140-760-6
$34.95

978-0-73140-596-1
$34.95

978-0-73037-500-5
$39.95

978-0-73037-664-4
$39.95

978-0p-73037-536-4
$39.95

978-1-74216-984-2
$39.95

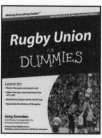

978-1-74031-073-4
$39.95

978-0-73037-660-6
$39.95

 FOR DUMMIES®

Reference

978-1-74216-999-6
$39.95

978-1-74216-982-8
$39.95

978-1-74216-983-5
$45.00

978-0-73140-909-9
$39.95

978-1-74216-945-3
$39.95

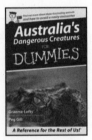

978-0-73140-722-4
$29.95

978-0-73140-784-2
$34.95

978-0-73140-752-1
$34.95

Technology

978-0-47049-743-2
$32.95

978-1-74246-896-9
$39.95

978-1-74216-998-9
$45.00

978-0-47048-998-7
$39.95

FOR DUMMIES®

Business & Investing

978-1-74216-971-2
$39.95

978-1-74216-853-1
$39.95

978-1-74216-853-1
$39.95

978-1-74216-962-0
$19.95

978-0-73037-668-2
$19.95

978-0-73037-556-2
$29.95

978-0-73037-715-3
$29.95

978-0-73037-807-5
$29.95

978-1-73037-695-8
$39.95

978-1-74216-942-2
$39.95

978-1-74246-889-1
$39.95

978-1-74246-848-8
$34.95